NAVIGATING CHAMORU POETRY

Critical Issues in Indigenous Studies

Jeffrey P. Shepherd and Myla Vicenti Carpio
SERIES EDITORS

NAVIGATING CHAMORU POETRY

Indigeneity, Aesthetics, and Decolonization

CRAIG SANTOS PEREZ

THE UNIVERSITY OF
ARIZONA PRESS
TUCSON

The University of Arizona Press
www.uapress.arizona.edu

We respectfully acknowledge the University of Arizona is on the land and territories of Indigenous peoples. Today, Arizona is home to twenty-two federally recognized tribes, with Tucson being home to the O'odham and the Yaqui. Committed to diversity and inclusion, the University strives to build sustainable relationships with sovereign Native Nations and Indigenous communities through education offerings, partnerships, and community service.

ISBN-13: 978-0-8165-4292-5 (hardcover)
ISBN-13: 978-0-8165-3550-7 (paperback)

Cover design by Derek Thornton / Notch Design
Cover art: "Flying Proas of the Ladrone Islands," 1856, in *Ballou's Pictorial Drawing-Room Companion*. Courtesy of the Guam Public Library System.
Typeset by Sara Thaxton in 10/14 Warnock Pro with Semplicita Pro

Publication of this book is made possible in part by the proceeds of a permanent endowment created with the assistance of a Challenge Grant from the National Endowment for the Humanities, a federal agency.

Library of Congress Cataloging-in-Publication Data
Names: Perez, Craig Santos, author.
Title: Navigating CHamoru poetry : indigeneity, aesthetics, and decolonization / Craig Santos Perez.
Other titles: Critical issues in indigenous studies.
Description: Tucson : University of Arizona Press, 2021. | Series: Critical issues in indigenous studies | Includes bibliographical references and index.
Identifiers: LCCN 2021021551 | ISBN 9780816542925 (hardcover) | ISBN 9780816535507 (paperback)
Subjects: LCSH: Chamorro poetry—Guam—History and criticism. | Chamorro (Micronesian people)—Guam—Ethnic identity.
Classification: LCC PL5295.5 .S36 2021 | DDC 808.81/009967—dc23
LC record available at https://lccn.loc.gov/2021021551

Printed in the United States of America
♾ This paper meets the requirements of ANSI/NISO Z39.48-1992 (Permanence of Paper).

CONTENTS

ILLUSTRATIONS

FIGURES

MAPS

PREFACE

From Unincorporated Territory

> Where do we go from here? We are in uncharted waters, or maybe in familiar waters, unable to recognize the signs that show the way. Am I the navigator? Are we moving? Are the islands moving? Have we been following the navigator, so well-guided we don't even know the navigator is here?
>
> With my diminishing eyesight, I try to expand my vision. I have stopped looking for signs and started feeling for signs. The islands are moving, and we are being guided.
>
> —C. T. Perez, "Signs of Being: A Chamorro Spiritual Journey"

I am an Indigenous CHamoru (Chamorro) from the Pacific island of Guåhan (Guam), the southernmost island of the Mariana archipelago (colloquially known as the Marianas), a fifteen-island chain that extends 500 nautical miles in a north-to-south crescent in the region of the northwest Pacific Ocean known as Micronesia.[1] Guåhan lies approximately 6,000 miles west of California and 4,000 miles west of Hawai'i, 1,500 miles east of the Philippines, 1,600 miles south of Japan, and 2,800 miles north of Australia. To find Guåhan on a map, locate 13 degrees north latitude and 144 degrees east longitude. Look closely, because Guåhan is a mere 30 miles long and 4 to 12 miles wide in different parts of the island, comprising an area of 212 square miles. Guåhan also lies at the edge of the Mariana Trench, the deepest known part of the ocean.

My family's clan name is Gollo, and I grew up in the central village of Mongmong. My childhood was a mix of CHamoru customs, Catholic rituals, and American cultural experiences. I attended public and Catholic schools, where I learned to read and write in the English language, and where I was taught U.S. history, politics, culture, and geography. Every Sunday, my family attended Mass at the largest church on Guåhan, the Dulce Nombre de Maria Cathedral Basilica in Hagåtña (Agana). Growing up, I played American baseball, football, and basketball, and I cheered for professional American sports teams, like the Oakland Athletics and Raiders. I watched American television shows and Hollywood movies. I read books by American authors. I ate imported American food, such as Spam and McDonald's. Even though Guåhan lies thousands of miles from the continental United States, American colonialism was an intimately entangled part of our everyday lives.

In 1995, when I was fifteen years old, my family, like many others from Micronesia, migrated to California. I felt unmoored, drifting, and lost as I tried to navigate a new school, city, state, and continent. I remember that during the first day at my new high school, a teacher asked us where we were from. When I said, "Guam," he replied that he had never heard of it and asked me to point it out on the large map of the world that hung on the classroom wall. The map centered the Atlantic Ocean, so the Pacific was split in two and flayed to the margins. I tried to find my homeland where I knew it should be, but it was not there. Guåhan is such a small island that it often does not appear on global maps. I tried to hide my embarrassment by saying, "I am from this invisible island." During the rest of that school year, it became clear to me that most Americans have never even heard of my homeland. They didn't know that Guåhan has been a "territory" of the United States since 1898, and that CHamorus have been U.S. citizens since 1950. I felt invisible. Erased.

I began composing poetry at that time to write myself and my people into existence. Poetry also helped me remember and maintain connections to home and navigate my new surroundings. Those early poems felt cathartic because they created a space to emotionally cope with the traumas of migration and the disconnection of diaspora.

After graduating high school, I attended the University of Redlands in Southern California and gravitated toward the study of literature and creative writing. After completing a BA degree, I decided to pursue a master of fine arts degree in creative writing at the University of San Francisco. During those years, I started seeking out Pacific Islander literature, hoping to find writers like me. However, Guåhan was also hard to find in the sea of Pacific literature. For example, the first major anthologies of Pacific literature do not include any CHamoru writers.[2] To combat this feeling of invisibility, I continued writing poetry.

My poetry centered on memory, family, culture, history, and politics. In 2008, my master's thesis was published as my first collection of poetry, *from unincorporated territory [hacha]*.[3] In the preface to that collection, I mapped the political history of Guåhan and noted how the island is often invisible: "On some maps, Guam doesn't exist; I point to an empty space in the Pacific and say, 'I'm from here.' On some maps, Guam is a small, unnamed island; I say, 'I'm from this unnamed place.' On some maps, Guam is named 'Guam, U.S.A.' I say, 'I'm from a territory of the United States.'"[4] I also discussed how the word *from* has multiple meanings for me besides being a marker of location and origin. Because living in California made me feel fragmented and excerpted, it seemed like a part of me existed somewhere else; thus, I employed the italicized *from* in my work, indicating that every poem is part of a larger whole. Similarly, the title of the book itself includes the *from*, indicating that the collection is part of a larger series that is continuing to unfold. So far, four books in that series have been published.[5] Even though I have now lived away from my home island for more than two decades, and my travels have taken me far beyond the Pacific Ocean and the shores of Guåhan, my poetry has helped me more deeply understand my cultural identity and confidently orient my life with a sense of purpose and direction.

In order to deepen my understanding of Indigenous culture and identity, I pursued a PhD in ethnic studies at the University of California, Berkeley. Completing the course work, the area exams (which focused on Pacific Islander, Native American, and global Indigenous studies), and my dissertation helped me think critically about how colonialism impacted (and continues to impact) Indigenous peoples. During my research, I read every scholarly study of Pacific literature that I could find. CHamoru literature was either not mentioned at all or merely gestured toward.[6] This motivated me to focus my dissertation on CHamoru literature, which has remained an under-studied and underappreciated field (or archipelago) of Pacific, Indigenous, American, and international literature. I am proud to say that this monograph, which grew out of my dissertation after many years of revision and further research, is the first full-length study of contemporary CHamoru literature.

While in graduate school, I also began to think more critically about, and to become involved in, Indigenous rights, decolonization, and sovereignty movements. I joined the Bay Area chapter of Famoksaiyan, a group of diasporic CHamorus who were advocating for decolonization, demilitarization, cultural revitalization, and political self-determination. We created and distributed informational pamphlets and organized events, conferences, and rallies to raise awareness about Guåhan's colonial status and the impact of militarization on our homeland. For me, this activism culminated in 2008, when we traveled to the United Nations headquarters in New York City to testify in front of the Special Committee on Decolonization (Fourth Committee). In my testimony, I highlighted the history of ecological contamination caused by the military presence on Guåhan, and the way in which increased militarization would further harm the environment.[7]

In 2010, I returned to Guåhan for the first time since my family had migrated fifteen years earlier. The Humanities Guåhan (Guam Humanities Council) sponsored my trip as part of their project Community Conversations on the US Military Buildup in Guam. This project created space for residents to discuss the military buildup through "humanities-based conversations." During the trip, I read poetry of mine that addressed militarism and colonialism, engaging with community members and students at Guåhan's public high schools, the Guam Community College, and the University of Guam. One of the most memorable moments came after I shared my work with a high school English class. After my reading, I noticed a student was crying. When I asked her what was wrong, she replied: "I've never seen our culture in a real book before. I just thought we weren't worthy of literature."

I have carried that moment with me since then, as I have continued to write poetry about Guåhan and CHamoru experiences. I deeply believe that my people are worthy of literature, that our literature is worthy of serious scholarship, and that our stories should be taught and studied in classrooms across Guåhan, the Pacific, the United States, and the world. I believe that CHamoru literature is a powerful and creative way to engage with important questions of Indigenous culture, identity, aesthetics, colonialism, militarism, decolonization, history, ecology, and politics. I also believe that CHamoru literature has the power to inspire, empower, educate, humanize, decolonize, and dignify our people as we continue to struggle for our true liberation.

ACKNOWLEDGMENTS

I write these acknowledgments from the island of O'ahu, which has been my home for the past ten years. Mahalo to the 'āina and wai of this sacred place for nourishing me. Mahalo to the Kānaka Maoli for inspiring me with your beauty and resilience. I stand in respect of your ongoing sovereignty, and in solidarity with your movements for demilitarization and decolonization.

The research for this book began when I was a graduate student in the Department of Ethnic Studies at the University of California, Berkeley. I acknowledge the strength and survivance of the Ohlone peoples and the vitality of their unceded homelands. While at Berkeley, I was fortunate to receive support from so many amazing staff and faculty; saina ma'åse' and deep thanks to Francisca Cázares, Evelyn Nakano Glenn, Elaine Kim, Sau-Ling Wong, José David Saldívar, Laura Pérez, and Catherine Ceniza Choy. Saina ma'åse' to my classmates, especially Yomaira Figueroa, John Dougherty, Mattie Harper, Julie Thi Underhill, and Janey Lew. Saina ma'åse' to Margaret Rhee, Tala Khanmalek, and Joanne Rondilla for your encouragement. I was also fortunate to meet other Pacific Islander activists and graduate students at Cal, who inspired me with their fierce commitments. Saina ma'åse' to Migetu Gumataotao Tuncap, Fuifuilupe Niumeitolu, Loa Niumeitolu, and David Ga'oupu Palaita. While living in the Bay Area, I had the honor of being part of the Famoksaiyan crew: saina ma'åse' to Michael Lujan Bevacqua, Victoria-Lola Leon Guerrero, Martha Duenas, Erica Benton, Angela

Carrier, Rima Miles, Jon Blas, Tiffany Naputi Lacsado, Leiana San Agustin Naholowa'a, and Kerri-Ann Borja.

I completed this book while working as a faculty member in the English Department at the University of Hawai'i, Mānoa, as well as an affiliate faculty member with the Center for Pacific Islands Studies and the Indigenous Politics Program. Mahalo to all my colleagues who have welcomed me here and to all my students who have inspired me. It has been an honor to work with and learn from you. Saina ma'åse' to Paul Lyons, Cristina Bacchilega, Georganne Nordstrom, Cynthia Franklin, Laura Lyons, John Rieder, Jeff Carroll, Steve Canham, Glenn Man, Valerie Wayne, Subramanian Shankar, Rodney Morales, Shawna Yang Ryan, Craig Howes, Candace Fujikane, Leora Kava, Kathy Jetnil-Kijiner, Aiko Yamashiro, Lyz Soto, No'u Revilla, Donovan Kūhiō Colleps, Will Nu'utupu Giles, Jamaica Osorio, Norman Thompson, Cavan Scanlan, Leilani Portillo, Anjoli Roy, Kelsey Amos, Amalia Bueno, Keali'i Mackenzie, Joseph Han, Steven Gin, Lynley Shimat Lys, Tina Tofagau, Rachel Reeves, Rajiv Mohabir, Tarcisius Kabutaulaka, Terence Wesley-Smith, Alex Mawyer, Lola Quan Bautista, Julianne Walsh, Jan Rensel, Noelani Goodyear-Ka'ōpua, Noenoe Silva, Vilsoni Hereniko, David Hanlon, Fata Simanu-Klutz, Ty Tengan, Kyle Kajihiro, Kenneth Gofigan Kuper, Melvin Won Pat-Borja, Jesi Lujan Bennett, Vernadette Gonzalez, Christina Gerhardt, Jaimey Hamilton Faris, Laurel Mei-Singh, Maya Saffery, Marie Alohalani Brown, Jon Osorio, Bryan Kuwada, Kim Compoc, Joy Enomoto, and James Perez Viernes.

There are so many scholars, activists, and writers outside of Berkeley and the University of Hawai'i who have inspired and supported me. Saina ma'åse' to Chadwick Allen, Anne Perez Hattori, Peter Onedera, C. T. Perez, Kisha Borja-Quichocho-Calvo, Anghet Hoppe-Cruz, Emelihter Kihleng, Mary Therese Perez Hattori, Tiara Na'puti, Julian Aguon, Lisa Natividad, Alice Te Punga Somerville, Sandy Flores, Clarissa Mendiola, Lehua Taitano, Arielle Taitano Lowe, Baltazar Aguon, Sabina Perez, Bernard Punzalan, Hope Cristobal, Jay Pascua, Anita Hofschneider, Cara Flores-Mays, Carolyn Aflague Arroyo, Alaina Aflague Arroyo, PC Muñoz, Mario Borja, Allison Adelle Hedge Coke, Joy Harjo, Rob Wilson, Paul Sharrad, Michelle Keown, Otto Heim, Richard Hamasaki, Erin Suzuki, Caitlin Yamamoto, John Carlos Rowe, Paul Lai, Hsuan Hsu, Hsinya Huang, Xiaojing Zhou, Bonnie Etherington, Anais Maurer, and Rebecca Hogue.

Saina ma'åse' to the following scholars who supported me with their mentorship, scholarship, and friendship as I struggled to find my way as a diasporic CHamoru and Pacific scholar: Vicente Diaz, Christine Taitano DeLisle, Keith L. Camacho, Robert Underwood, Evelyn Flores, Alfred Flores, Michael Perez, Faye Untalan, Katerina Teaiwa, and Teresia Teaiwa.

Saina ma'åse' to Nicholas Goetzfridt for your annotated bibliographies of Guåhan and the literatures of Oceania, which have been an invaluable resource to me. Saina ma'åse' to the founders, editors, and writers of *Guampedia*, another resource that underpins this book. Saina ma'åse' to Victoria-Lola Leon Guerrero and the University of Guam Press for creating a home for CHamoru texts, several of which I discuss in this monograph. To the CHamoru authors, scholars, activists, and artists whose work I cite in this book: saina ma'åse' for uplifting and empowering our people. Saina ma'åse' to all the scholars and creatives I cite in this book for being the roots and routes of my intellectual and literary genealogy.

This book grew out of my dissertation, and I feel so much gratitude to my dissertation committee for their guidance and feedback. Saina ma'åse' to Hertha D. Sweet Wong, Thomas Biolsi, and Elizabeth DeLoughrey. Special thanks to Liz, for your continued support and engagement over the years.

This book would not exist without my dissertation chair, Beth Piatote. Your course, Native American Literature and Theory, formed the foundation of this project. I am so grateful for your continued and generous mentorship. You are an exemplary model of how to be a Native scholar and creative writer. I would not have completed the doctorate program without your encouragement. I hope I have honored you with this work. Saina ma'åse', Beth.

Thank you to the Ford Foundation, the Lannan Foundation, the Mellon Foundation, and the American Council for Learned Societies for fellowships that sustained me during the research and writing of this book. Thank you to the following editors, who published earlier versions of some of these chapters: Alexandra Campbell and Michael Paye, editors of "World Literature and the Blue Humanities," special issue of *Humanities* (2020); Leila Gómez, editor of "Indigenous Narratives of Territory and Creation: Hemispheric Perspectives," special issue of *English Language Notes* (2020); Otto Heim, Yuan Shu, and Kendall Johnson, editors of *Oceanic Archives, Indigenous Epistemologies, and Transpacific American Studies* (Hong Kong University Press, 2019); Isabel Campos, editor of *Ecopoetics and the Global Landscape: Critical Essays* (Rowman & Littlefield, 2019); Brian Russell Roberts and Michelle Stephens, editors of *Archipelagic American Studies* (Duke University Press, 2017); and James H. Cox and Daniel Heath Justice, editors of *The Oxford Handbook of Indigenous American Literature* (Oxford University Press, 2014).

Saina ma'åse' to Stu Dawrs, senior librarian at the Pacific Collection of the Hamilton Library at the University of Hawai'i at Mānoa, for helping me navigate the archive in which many sources cited in this book are housed. Saina ma'åse' to Candice Steiner, managing editor of *The Contemporary Pacific* at the Center for Pacific Islands Studies, for granting me permission to include the maps. Saina ma'åse' to Florence Taitague, library technician supervisor at the Guam Public Library System Archive Center, for your support and for granting permission to include the illustrations in this book. Saina ma'åse' to Jessica Vergel for your beautiful artwork of the latte stone houses. Saina ma'åse' to C. T. Perez, Kisha Borja-Kicho'cho', Peter Onedera, Anne Perez Hattori, Michael Lujan Bevacqua, Lehua Taitano, Ryan Leon Guerrero, Walla Wai, and Melvin Won Pat-Borja for permission to quote your powerful poems. Saina ma'åse' to the University of Guam Press and Tinfish Press for permission to share cover images of your published books.

Saina ma'åse' to Kristen Buckles, editor-in-chief of the University of Arizona Press, for believing in this book and giving it a home. I am deeply humbled to be part of the Critical Indigenous Studies Series. Saina ma'åse' to the series editors, Jeffrey P. Shepherd and Myla Vicenti Carpio, and to the entire editorial board. Saina ma'åse' to the peer reviewers who offered kind words and critical feedback which helped me craft this book into its final, ocean-ready form. Saina ma'åse' to Matt Gleeson for your careful and thoughtful copyediting. Saina ma'åse' to Elizabeth Wilder, editorial assistant, for guiding me through the process.

Saina ma'åse' to my parents, Helen and Thomas, for nurturing my imagination with books when I was growing up, and for all your sacrifices to support my education. Saina ma'åse' to my siblings, Marla and Brian, for your love. Saina ma'åse' to the tåno' and tasi of my homeland for raising me. Saina ma'åse' to my ancestors, whose blood memories flow through me as I type this. Saina ma'åse' for dreaming our stories into existence. I hope I have made you all proud.

Mahalo to my wife, Brandy Nālani McDougall, for inspiring me with your own brilliant scholarship and radiant poetry. I would not have completed this book without your support, and I am honored that my book will stand beside yours in the catalog. Hu guiaya hao. Mahalo to my daughters, Kaikai and Ku'ulei, for all the stories you will create in the future.

In CHamoru culture, one of our core values is chenchule', which refers to a complex and intimate system of social reciprocity, mutual aid, and relational gift-giving. To me, literature is a form of chenchule', and I am grateful to all the CHamoru storytellers who have gifted us with their words, chants, novels, and poems. In return, this book is my chenchule', which I offer as a gift to you as well, dear reader, with gratitude for all that CHamoru stories have given me.

NAVIGATING CHAMORU POETRY

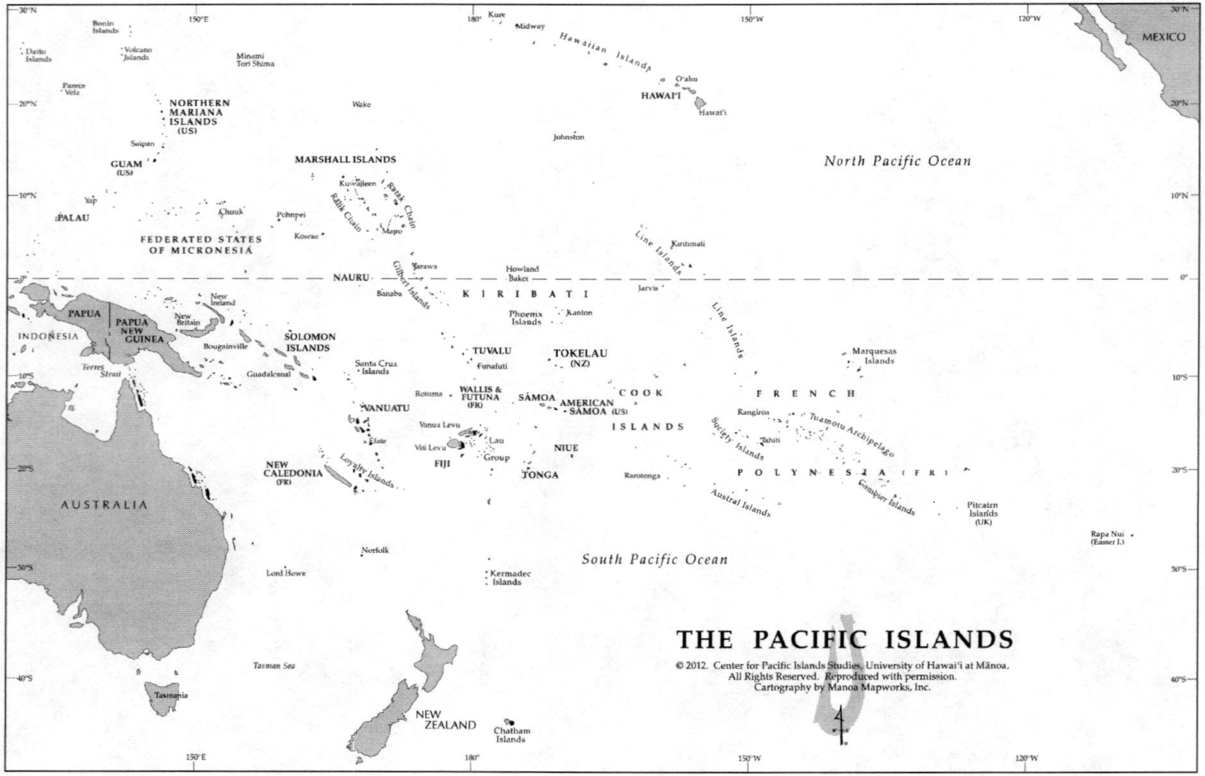

MAP 1 Map of the Pacific islands, 2012. Reproduced by permission of the Center for Pacific Islands Studies, University of Hawaiʻi at Mānoa.

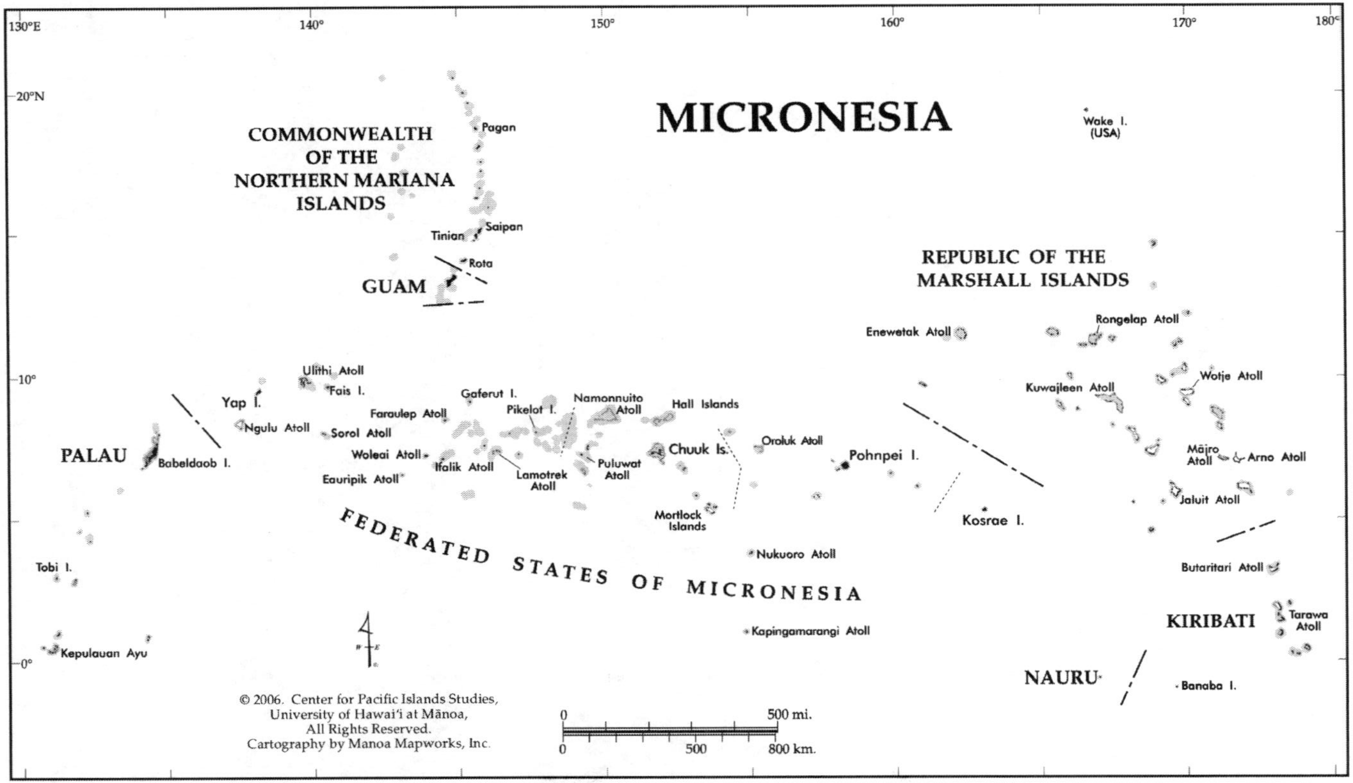

MAP 2 Map of Micronesia, 2006. Reproduced by permission of the Center for Pacific Islands Studies, University of Hawai'i at Mānoa.

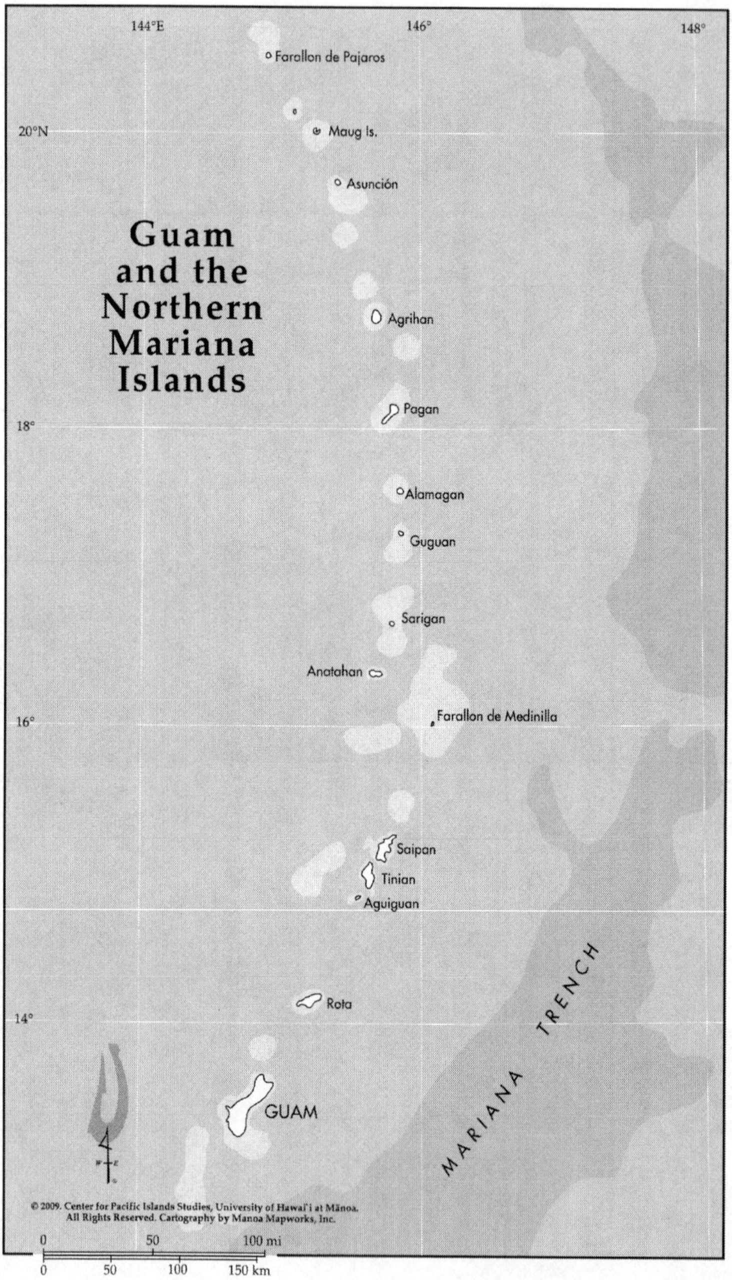

MAP 3 Map of Guam and the Northern Mariana Islands, 2009. Reproduced by permission of the Center for Pacific Islands Studies, University of Hawai'i at Mānoa.

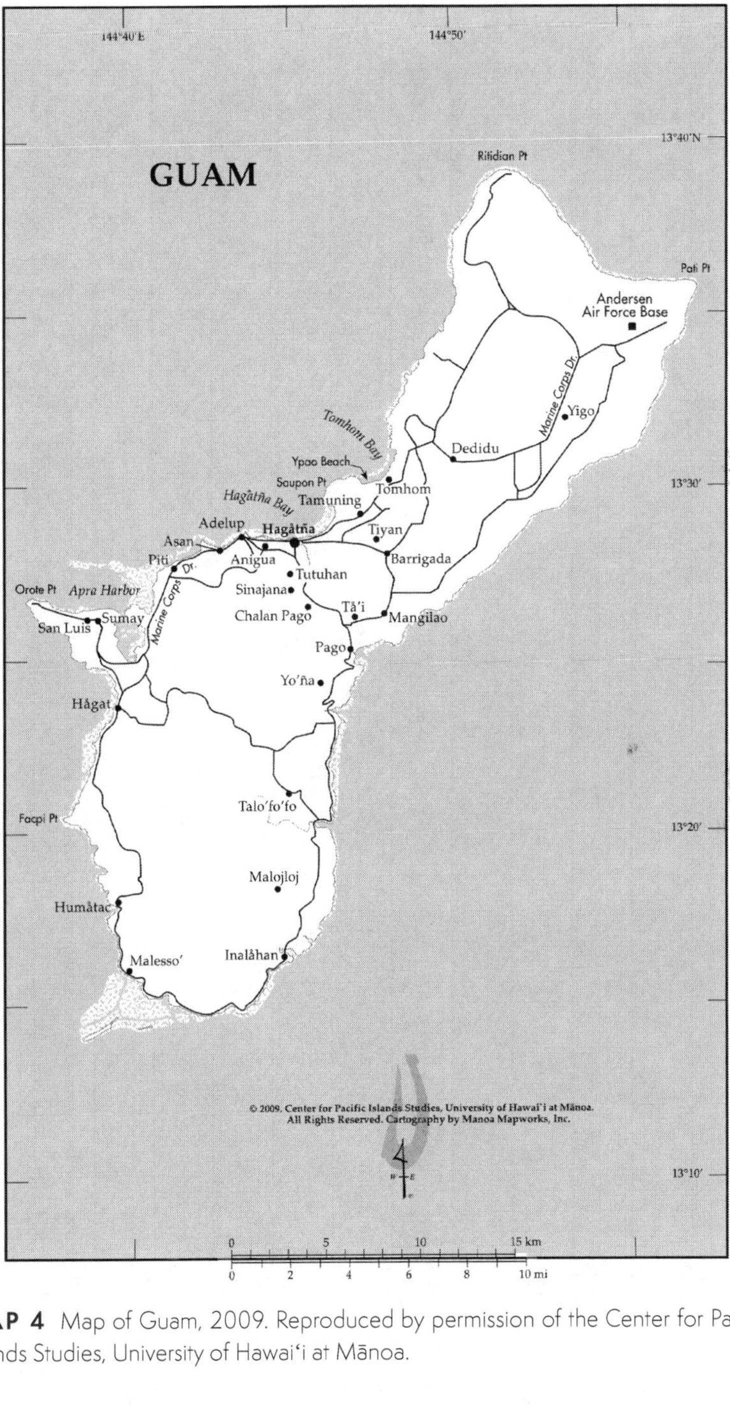

MAP 4 Map of Guam, 2009. Reproduced by permission of the Center for Pacific Islands Studies, University of Hawaiʻi at Mānoa.

INTRODUCTION

On Being ~~Chamorro Guamanian~~ CHamoru

Indigeneity, Aesthetics, and Decolonization

> In looking at the reflection of Chamorro identity
> we find that it is not a smooth, glassy surface we see.
> With all the forces of nature we find that we are looking at reflections,
> as multi-faceted, as full of color, texture and moods, and depths
> and as ever-changing as the ocean's surface.
>
> —C. T. Perez

Plotting the Historical and Political Coordinates of Guåhan

Before embarking on our journey of reading contemporary CHamoru literature, it is important to first orient ourselves within the historical and political coordinates of Guåhan and the Mariana archipelago. The predominant historiographical narrative begins with what has been called the "ancient Guam era," "ancient Chamorro era," or "precolonial era." The story goes: around 2000 BC, the people who would become known as CHamorus sailed in outrigger canoes from the region of Austronesia and settled what would become known as the Mariana archipelago.[1] CHamorus developed clan-based social networks; a matriarchally structured society; a vibrant aesthetic tradition of orature, dance, weaving, and carving; spiritual practices that included ancestor worship and a belief in spirits; and a sustainable communal economy based on fishing and agriculture.[2]

The story then turns to the "Spanish era," which begins in 1521, the year that Ferdinand Magellan made landfall on Guåhan, the first inhabited Pacific island to become known to Europeans.[3] Magellan called the archipelago "Islas de las Velas Latinas" (Islands of Lateen Sails) and "Islas de los Ladrones" (Islands of Thieves). Spain nominally claimed Guåhan in 1564, establishing its first colony in the Pacific. The first cargo of products from Asia was delivered to Mexico that year via the Acapulco-(Guåhan)-Manila trade route. In the following decades, galleons loaded with silver from Mexico (along with soldiers, merchants, missionaries, government officials, mail, and supplies) embarked from Acapulco and reprovisioned off Guåhan before arriving in the Philippines to trade with Chinese merchants. The Spanish Empire mapped "a great circular loop" around the Pacific with Guåhan as "a sure and useful landmark and stopover" on the trans-Pacific trade route[4]—sometimes referred to, in an alternative historiography, as "the matao iron trade."[5] In 1668, Spanish authorities officially colonized the island and shortly thereafter initiated the Christian conquest of the Pacific by establishing a mission on Guåhan supported by a colonial government and military.[6] The Catholic authorities renamed the archipelago "las Islas Marianas" (the Mariana Islands), to honor the queen of Spain, María Ana de Austria, who funded the mission. Many CHamorus resisted the conversion efforts, which led to nearly three decades of active conflict known as the Spanish-Chamorro Wars (1668–95). By the end of the wars, military conquest and foreign diseases had led to massive CHamoru depopulation, and the survivors were subjected to the Spanish ecclesiastical policy of reducción, or the "forced relocation and concentration of the population from rural areas into villages with a garrison and church," to facilitate conversion, acculturation, and taxation.[7]

The Spanish-American War of 1898 ended Spanish control of the Mariana archipelago, thus beginning the "U.S. naval era."[8] After defeat, Spain sold the fourteen Northern Mariana Islands to Germany, and Guåhan became a territory of the United States, along with other former Spanish colonies. The acquisition of these new territories created a controversy within American politics and popular opinion about whether or not they should be incorporated into the nation, and whether full constitutional rights should apply. These questions were taken up by a series of landmark Supreme Court cases, collectively known as the Insular Cases, dating from 1901 to 1922. The court ultimately decided that the rights of the constitution and citizenship did not automatically apply to the new possessions, and would instead be determined by Congress. This decision created a new political category, the "unincorporated territory," which meant that a territory like Guåhan could be a possession of the United States without becoming a fully incorporated part of the nation.[9] From 1898 to 1941, the U.S. Navy administered Guåhan, with a navy captain appointed as governor of Guam, and established schools, hospitals, businesses, and roads as part of its "civilizing" and "militarizing" mission.[10] During this era, Guåhan became a strategic location for U.S. military transports traveling between San Francisco, Hawai'i, and the Philippines.

In 1914, Japan seized the Northern Mariana Islands from Germany, forming the "new Japanese frontier in the equatorial Pacific."[11] In December 1941, Japan bombed and invaded Guåhan and defeated the U.S. forces, uniting the archipelago under Japanese rule, thus inaugurating the "Japanese era." Guåhan was renamed Omiya Jima, or "Great Shrine Island," and Japanese authorities transformed Guåhan into a strategic base for Japan's vision of a "Co-prosperity Sphere of Greater East Asia."[12] This era was marked by traumatic violence and wartime atrocities against the CHamoru people, including land theft, forced labor, rape, beheadings, massacres, death marches, and concentration camps.

On July 21, 1944, the U.S. military began its invasion of and battle for Guåhan, eventually defeating the Japanese forces and reclaiming the island. During the "postwar era," the fourteen Northern Mariana Islands became part of the United Nations Trust Territory of the Pacific Islands, administered by the United States until the 1970s, when their political status changed to the Commonwealth of the Northern Mariana Islands.[13] Guåhan, on the other hand, remained an "unincorporated territory," and its residents became U.S. citizens after the passage of the Organic Act of Guam in 1950, which also established a civilian governor, the government of Guam, the Guam Legislature, and the courts.[14] Throughout the following decades, sometimes referred to as the "Guamanian era," the United States militarily refurbished Guåhan into an "unsinkable U.S. communications and logistics platform, monitoring satellites and missiles, supporting antisubmarine and B-52 bomber operations, and harboring prepositioning supply ships for rapid deployment strike forces."[15] A tourism industry was created in the 1970s, and it would become a major part of the island's economy. Today, Guåhan continues to be an unincorporated territory and one of the most important U.S. military bases in the world.[16]

Guåhan's "strategic" location and topography has made it one of the longest continuously colonized places in the world.[17] Even though Guåhan's strategic value rendered it "far more significant than islands much larger, much less isolated, and much better known,"[18] Guåhan has remained largely invisible (or, at most, a mere footnote) on most global maps and in most world histories.[19]

Plotting the Coordinates of CHamoru Culture

The origin, orthography, and meaning of the name *CHamoru* tells a story about the complexity of CHamoru culture and identity. In previous eras, *Chamorro* was the most common and widely accepted spelling for the Indigenous people and language of the Mariana archipelago. One theory is that the word derives from *Chamori*, a term in the CHamoru language that refers to high-ranking chiefs. Another theory suggests that the name refers to the Spanish word *chamorro*, translated as "he who has his head shorn," which points to the way ancestral CHamorus shaved their heads, leaving only a topknot.[20] In historical archives, several other spellings exist, including *Tsamoru*, *Chamorru*, and *Chamoru*. Following World War II, a new name, *Guamanian*, emerged, which either referred to CHamorus from Guåhan (as opposed to CHamorus from the Northern Mariana Islands, who, if they were from Saipan, for example, were referred to as Saipanese), to any person who lived on Guåhan whether they were CHamoru or not, to "Americanized Chamorros," or to diasporic CHamorus.[21] In 1993, the Chamorro Language Commission held public hearings about a proposal to change *Chamorro* to *Chamoru* because the latter, many argued, reflected an Indigenous orthography and politics.[22] This debate opened the path for others to completely abandon Chamorro *and* Chamoru for another term not suggestive of the Spanish language, such as *I Taotao Tåno'*, a phrase in CHamoru that translates as "the people of the land."[23] The change was not officially adopted, and the commission became inactive for many years. However, it was reestablished in 2016 as Kumision i Fino' CHamoru yan Fina'nå'guen i Historia yan Lina'la' i Taotao Tåno' (Commission on CHamoru Language and the Teaching of the History and Culture of the Indigenous People of Guam). In 2018, the commission decided that the official orthography would be *CHamoru*, now encoded in law. In explaining the capitalization of *CH*, the commission's orthography handbook states: "The letters CH and NG of the CHamoru alphabet will be considered one character and will be capitalized on proper nouns and at the beginning of sentences." The *ch* is a digraph (a pair of characters that represents a single phoneme or distinct sound) and the fourth letter in the CHamoru alphabet (*a, å, b, ch, d . . .*). It is pronounced "tse."[24] The title of this introduction, borrowed from an essay by Robert Underwood entitled "On Being ~~Guamanian Guamese Guamite Guamian~~ Chamorro" (1982), speaks to the complexity and various nomenclatures of CHamoru identity.

Similarly, the name Guåhan has a contested history. On maps and in archival documents, the island has also been referred to as Goaam, Goam, Guan, Guana, Guajan, Guam, and Guahan.[25] Guam was declared the island's official name after it became a territory of the United States, and Guam has been the most common name since. A proposal to officially rename Guam to what many argue is the island's Indigenous name, Guåhan, a word in the CHamoru language that translates as "we have" or "a place that has," sparked controversy and debate. In 2010, the governor of Guam at the time, Felix P. Camacho, proposed to change the official name of Guam to Guåhan via executive order.[26] More recently, an Indigenous name for the archipelago has gained currency: Låguas and Gåni, the former name referring to the southern islands and the latter referring to the northern islands. The fact that *we have* many names—both externally imposed and internally professed—reflects not only a "little war of nomenclature," but also a long history of struggle over defining and representing our islands and CHamoru culture and identity.[27] While I use *CHamoru* and *Guåhan* in this book, when quoting sources that utilize other spellings (such as *Chamorro, Chamoru,* and *Guam*), I remain faithful to their usages to highlight the ongoing debate about naming and representation.

Ancestral CHamoru culture is often described as matrilineal and clan-based, with divisions of labor shared across class and gender to create a balance of power and a system of reciprocity between extended family and village members.[28] CHamorus developed a sustainable subsistence economy based on agriculture and aquaculture. Spiritually, CHamorus believed that ancestral spirits, or taotaomo'na, inhabited the earth alongside the living, and the spirits and the bones of the dead were revered.[29] The main values of CHamoru culture are often noted to be inafa'maolek (interdependence), chenchule' (reciprocity), mamåhlao (shame), and respetu (respect).[30] Indeed, CHamoru culture shared "numerous cultural similarities with other Pacific, especially Micronesian, peoples described at the time: clan-based social networks, economically based on fishing and agriculture, cemented within a kin-structure of female descent principles."[31]

Conceptions of CHamoru culture changed dramatically as a result of Spanish, American, and Japanese colonialism. The Spanish era is characterized as a period of "Hispanicization."[32] Spanish rule disrupted, undermined, and outlawed CHamoru customs, while implementing and enforcing Spanish cultural practices. Catholic missionization, considered the most profound force in shaping CHamoru identity during the Spanish era, forced CHamorus to abandon their gods and religious practices associated with birth, death, and marriage.[33] Additionally, reducción led to the disintegration of land-use practices, traditional clan systems, and social organization.[34] Many CHamorus who survived Spanish conquest, conversion, and disease intermarried with Spanish settlers, creating a mestizo population that would become a "focal point of colonial divisions of society" as well as a central cultural identity in Guåhan during that time.[35]

The idea of Chamoru identity as mestizo or "hybrid" continued into the U.S. naval era. The Americans viewed CHamorus as "Hispanicized Catholics whose indigenous culture and language no longer existed."[36] In 1947, anthropologist Laura Thompson asserted: "The indigenous population of the Marianas continued to diminish until, by the middle of the nineteenth century, no full-blooded natives survived. However, the Chamorros mated with the newcomers and soon after the conquest, a hybrid group began to emerge."[37] Historian Robert F. Rogers echoed the same sentiment: "Pure-blooded Chamorros became a dwindling minority until finally absorbed by the end of the nineteenth century into a hybrid neo-Chamorro mixture."[38] Americans also perceived CHamorus as inferior, lazy children in need of development and civilization.[39] In turn, the American education system acculturated CHamorus by teaching American history and geography, health and hygiene, reading and writing in the English language, industrial and agricultural skills, and even baseball.[40] From 1898 to 1941, the navy attempted to remake CHamorus according to a colonial conception of productive, disciplined, educated, and sanitary Americans.[41]

Even though the "Japanization" of CHamoru culture and identity only lasted three years, it left a lasting impression. Japanese authorities initiated several militarizing and civilizing projects to "eradicate forty years of American symbols, values, and, ultimately, [American] loyalty among the Chamorros."[42] The Japanese viewed CHamorus as "too small in size to be called a race [and] too [culturally] devastated to be called one tribe."[43] Thus, CHamorus were seen as culturally stunted, lazy, and in need of a "mother body" capable of "promoting their growth."[44] The Japanization policy involved education in Japanese language, moral values, music, and exercise. School ceremonies centered on Japanese traditions, history, nationalism, and political power (embodied by the emperor).[45] Beyond education, the Japanization policy included forced agricultural and military labor in order to teach the CHamorus the Japanese spirit of "hard work and devotion."[46] However, it was the wartime atrocities committed by Japanese soldiers that ultimately had the most lasting impact.

Because the return of the American military ended Japanese occupation and violence, CHamorus were more willing to embrace America after the war. Underwood posits that "the [war] experience left a psychological legacy of fear of non-American control and helped generate a relationship of gratitude and debt."[47] Similarly, Vicente Diaz notes that the experience of Japanization boosted the process of Americanization in the postwar period: "The 'Americanization' of the Chamorros . . . received a big boost from the Japanese. The Japanese invasion, and especially Chamorro memories of the brutal occupation, accomplished in less than three years what US Naval officials could not do in almost fifty . . . they fused the Chamorros to their colonial overseer, with religious zeal and cultural prescriptions of gratitude and loyalty."[48] Thus, CHamoru "codes of indigenous indebtedness" ignited feelings of patriotism and loyalty to the United States, feelings that would be bolstered by the pursuit and granting of U.S. citizenship in 1950.[49] The American education system on Guåhan expanded, as did the presence of American culture, with the introduction of American television shows and media in the 1960s and 1970s.[50] Laura Souder described the effect of this new media as having the acculturative power to convince CHamorus that "Guam has become an overseas suburb of Los Angeles County."[51] Scholars have also pointed to how militarization has Americanized CHamoru identity. Not only was the military a major employer of civilian labor after World War II, but CHamorus enlisted in the U.S. armed forces in record numbers in subsequent decades. Today, several of the most successful military recruiters are based on Guåhan, which has one of the highest rates of enlistment per capita out of any state or territory.[52] Underwood described how CHamorus were perceived as wholly Americanized: "The Chamorro people of Guam are frequently described and projected as the most Americanized of all groups of Pacific Islanders associated with the U.S. They have been seen as trying to be more American than Americans and, as a consequence, cannot adequately or accurately even describe their identity and culture."[53]

These historiographical and cultural narratives of demise can be classified as "fatal impact" narratives.[54] This refers to the idea that Pacific Islanders and their cultures were fatally impacted by contact with colonial cultures, and that Pacific Islanders were destined to become assimilated or extinct. Fatal impact theory is based on the conception that Indigenous culture is a static, bounded essence that once existed in a "pure" and "authentic" state before contact but has become degraded and inauthentic because of colonialism, modernity, and globalization. This conception of culture causes an identity crisis. Indeed, Michael Perez argues that the CHamoru identity is "marked by an especially pervasive American cultural hegemony which appears to have generated a disturbing cycle of cultural annihilation and identity crisis."[55] This disturbing cycle involves internalizing the displacement from one's ancestry, the loss of cultural practices and values, the perception of CHamorus as lazy and primitive, and the desire for American culture.[56] Overall, this crisis has created a "social psychological ambivalence" about the authenticity and value of CHamoru culture and identity[57]—so much so that the "acceptance of the American point of reference produced Chamorros who no longer wanted to be Chamorro."[58] In addition to disempowering and disconnecting CHamorus from their Indigenous identity and leaving them lost in a sea of inauthenticity, fatal impact theory also creates a political crisis. As Laurel Monnig highlights, the racialization of CHamorus as mixed, impure, and inauthentic functioned to justify political disenfranchisement, because if CHamorus were not authentically Indigenous, then they did not qualify for Indigenous rights and were not "worthy of self-rule, independence and self determination."[59]

This crisis came to the fore as a contemporary CHamoru decolonization movement emerged, which was deeply influenced by the international decolonization, Indigenous rights, and self-determination movements that emerged during the 1960s, both globally and across the Pacific.[60] The fact that other islands in Micronesia (known as the Trust Territory of the Pacific Islands in the 1960s) were negotiating their political status with the United States also inspired CHamorus to envision themselves in the context of decolonization.[61] Armed with the language, politics, and history of Indigenous rights, several CHamoru rights groups emerged in the 1980s and 1990s that employed Indigenous identity as their major political strategy to advocate for CHamoru language revitalization, land reclamation, decolonization, self-determination, and sovereignty. Some of these groups included the July 7th Committee, the

People's Alliance for Responsive Alternatives (PARA), Para'Pada Y Chamorros, the Organization of People for Indigenous Rights (OPI-R), I Nasion Chamoru (The Chamorro Nation), Guam Landowners Coalition, Ancestral Landowners Coalition, Ritidian Family Association, Fuetsan i Famalao'an Chamoru, and the Commission on Self-Determination.[62] An umbrella organization, the Colonized Chamorro Coalition, formed to foster connections to Native American and Puerto Rican activists who were also challenging U.S. colonialism.[63] Souder discusses this phenomenon: "Guam has witnessed the popularization of the term indigenous in the [1980s]. Responding to the articulation of Chamorro self-determination as an issue of indigenous rights, a growing number of people on Guam now view the political status question in terms of the concept of indigenous rights."[64] The focus on Indigenous political activism not only inspired CHamoru cultural revitalization but also ignited feelings of "justifiable pride in the rebirth of cultural consciousness and the celebration of their heritage. This is part of the Chamorro search for identity and expression as Chamorros."[65]

When CHamorus began to assert their Indigenous identity and rights in the public sphere, critics began questioning the authenticity of these assertions. Monnig notes:

> In comparison to their Pacific Islander neighbors, [Chamorro] colonial mixtures—racial and cultural—inauthenticated their indigenous status. It was perceived that the Yapese, the Pohnpeians, the Palauans, etc., were "real" Pacific Islanders who still had recognizable, unique, and "traditional" cultural traits and phenotypic consistency. Chamorros, on the other hand, practiced too much culture which had roots in the Philippines, Spain, or the US, and their phenotypes were too varied to be consistent with the notion of a "bounded," "truly" indigenous group.[66]

For CHamoru activists and advocates, "proving" Indigeneity became important because "Chamorros must validate their existence 'as an identifiable and distinct cultural group' before they can effectively pursue self-determination. . . . In other words, their peoplehood must be articulated through terms which fit international discourses about what it is to be indigenous."[67] If CHamorus could not *prove* their Indigeneity, then they would be discounted and excluded from international, national, and local avenues for self-determination. As a result, activists and scholars have contested accusations of inauthenticity by invoking the survival and continuity of precolonial CHamoru language, culture, values, and identities despite centuries of cultural colonialism. For example, Elizabeth Diego argues: "Chamorro identity remains distinctly Chamorro as evidenced by the strong presence of unique cultural practices and values that remain viable in contemporary Chamorro life."[68] These markers of CHamoru identity include CHamoru language, values (such as inafa'maolek), and practices (such as weaving, fishing, and farming). In turn, rethinking CHamoru culture involves articulating CHamoru agency and cultural transformation. Carmen Kasperbauer describes this phenomenon as "Chamorrocization":

> We often hear about the "Hispanicization" or "Americanization" of Chamorro culture, but we seldom hear about the "Chamorrocization" of visiting cultures. It is true that the Chamorro culture has been exposed to the influences of the Spanish, American and Japanese cultures for many, many years, but it is not true that the Chamorro culture is just an imitation of these cultures. Many ancient Chamorro customs and traditions still survive. Sometimes they are disguised as Christian practices, and sometimes they have been given a form, but they are still Chamorro in substance.[69]

Despite the discourse of cultural extinction and inauthenticity, CHamorus continue to assert their agency, rearticulate their identities, and engage and negotiate with foreign cultures for their own purposes and interests (even if these negotiations are not always equal in terms of power). CHamoru culture and identity are, therefore, "contested sites on which indigenous identity combined with exogenous identity are created, challenged, and then recreated."[70] The Indigenous rights movement inspired CHamorus to reclaim the continuities of CHamoru culture and to reconceptualize the transformative agency of CHamoru identity. An understanding of CHamorus as a complex Indigenous people formed the foundation of CHamoru resistance and political activism. Connecting to Indigeneity, as Michael Perez argued, has facilitated "cultural renewal, re-articulation, and continuity, but also provide[d] a powerful emotive force of consciousness crucial to political contestation, organization, and mobilization that ultimately propels indigenous resistance and an identity movement."[71]

Inspired by this movement, I offer an alternative reading of contemporary CHamoru culture, history, and identity that counters fatal impact narratives and draws from "articulation theory," Native Pacific cultural studies, and Native American studies.[72] In the pivotal essay "Native Pacific Cultural Studies on the Edge," Vicente Diaz and J. Kēhaulani Kauanui argue that Indigenous Pacific identities are more than a pure, unchanging set of practices and values that were defined in the ancient past and from which any deviation or change marks impurity and inauthenticity. Instead, they view Native Pacific identities as articulated assemblages of meanings, customs, practices, values, subjectivities, and discourses that change in response to historical conditions, political pressures, or colonial force.[73] Crucial to this reconceptualization is James Clifford's "articulation theory," in which he questions "the assumption that indigeneity is essentially about primordial, transhistorical attachments," because such an assumption tends to "bypass the pragmatic, entangled, contemporary forms of indigenous cultural politics."[74] At the same time, Clifford finds it reductive to see Indigenous identity as "the result of a post-sixties, 'postmodern' identity politics . . . functioning as 'invented traditions' [because this perspective] brushes aside long histories of indigenous survival and resistance, transformative links with roots prior to and outside the world system."[75] Understanding identity as an "articulated site of indigeneity" offers a nonreductive conception of cultural transformation wherein "'inner' elements have, historically, been connected with 'exterior' forms, in processes of selective, syncretic transformation."[76] Informed by Diaz, Kauanui, Clifford, and others, I agree that we must understand the complexity of Native identities and cultures as sites of articulation while also highlighting Indigenous survival, continuity, vitality, and agency.

An articulated sense of CHamoru identity is formulated in Diaz's essay "Simply Chamorro: Telling Tales of Demise and Survival in Guam." He offers a counternarrative to fatal impact theory by centering CHamoru cultural survival, adaptation, and articulation: "Guam's history does not have to be understood as the definitive Euro-Americanization of the Chamorro people at the tragic expense of indigenous culture. Nor does Chamorro culture need to be understood in terms of an immutably bounded, neatly contained thing that was once upon a time characterized by essential qualities, pure and untainted."[77] Instead of seeing the changes in CHamoru culture as "signs of cultural demise," Diaz sees these signs as illustrating Indigenous "survival and vitality, indeed, eternal vigilance for future possibilities." Diaz also focuses on the narrativity of CHamoru identity when he emphasizes how "multiple origins and destinations that inhabit Chamorro culture are Chamorro by virtue of their *discursive* claims, that is, by virtue of Chamorro *ways of speaking* as well as unique Chamorro ways of doing things."[78] Paying attention to CHamoru discursive acts allows us to read the "roots and routes of Chamorro cultural survival at various slices of its history, and at various sites—geographical and cultural—of its *expression*."[79] Or, as Mary Therese Cruz succinctly argued: "Chamorus continue to reaffirm their identity through *innovative representations* of their beliefs and realities."[80] CHamoru literature, as I will show throughout this monograph, is one site through which CHamoru identity is expressed, represented, innovated, and articulated.

Plotting the Coordinates of CHamoru Literature

Literature was an integral, everyday part of ancestral CHamoru culture. A Jesuit priest exclaimed in the seventeenth century that CHamorus "admire poetry and believe poets . . . perform wonders."[81] An early nineteenth-century explorer remarked that CHamorus "sing the moment they awake, they sing during the hours of rest, and they fall asleep singing. . . . Their singing may be considered in some measure an emblem of their life."[82] A twentieth-century folklorist noted: "Poetical expression came naturally to the [ancient CHamorus], and songs, chants, and epics set to poetical cadence and (often) to rhyme, were the medium by which a complete, practical, sometimes pragmatic but always honorable, cultural heritage was comprehended and preserved and transmitted—almost as if it had been engraved in tablets of stone."[83] As with other Indigenous Pacific cultures, oral literature was an essential vessel for the intergenerational transmission of CHamoru language, customs, genealogy, knowledge, religion, spirituality, navigation, history, politics, and cultural identity.[84] It is through oral storytelling, as Katherine Aguon remarked, that "the Chamorro learned how to become Chamorro."[85]

In the "Chamorro Literature" entry in *The Pacific Islands: An Encyclopedia* (2000), Keith Lujan Camacho affirmed that the "richest sources of Chamorro literature are to be found in oral traditions, ranging from legends and folk tales to a variety of musical forms." However, he also noted: "To date there are no established Chamorro creative writers."[86] Unfortunately, there are several reasons why a written CHamoru literary tradition does not emerge after the 1960s in the same way that it emerged in other parts of the Pacific.[87] In the editor's comments in a 1996 issue of *Storyboard: A Journal of Pacific Imagery*, a literary journal based at the University of Guam, Jeannine E. Talley commented:

> One does not have to dig too deeply to discover why there is an accumulated body of literature produced by Polynesians and Melanesians, but a dire lack of representative works from Micronesia. Support and encouragement. For at least three decades the University of the South Pacific in Fiji and the University of Papua New Guinea have encouraged the development of indigenous writers in the South Pacific through workshops, special training and emphasis on creative writing and finally by publishing the efforts of a number of writers. Unfortunately there has not been this kind of nurturing of indigenous writers in Micronesia.[88]

Anthropologist Karen L. Nero also attested: "The educational institutions established on Guam and in the former US Trust Territory of the Pacific Islands never supported the arts in a manner comparable to the University of the South Pacific or the University of Papua New Guinea."[89] In 1990, Mark E. Skinner completed a bibliographic study of contemporary Micronesian literature, and he also found that there was a lack of written Pacific literature taught at educational institutions throughout Micronesia. He highlighted how at the University of Guam, only one out of the ten literature courses focused on literature of Guam, Micronesia, and the Pacific (moreover, this class was only offered once every other year); at the Community College of Micronesia in Pohnpei, only one of six literature courses focused on, as it titled itself, Literature of the Sea; and at the Northern Marianas College in Saipan there were only two literature courses, an introductory class and Modern American Literature.[90] The lack of educational exposure to other Pacific Islander literature, the lack of publication venues and creative writing workshops, and the colonial partitioning from other centers of Pacific literary production in Polynesia and Melanesia were all major factors that limited both the formation and the visibility of Micronesian literature in general, and CHamoru literature in particular.

Despite this lack of support and encouragement, several important CHamoru texts were published during the second half of the twentieth century, though many of them are now out of print and only exist in archives (the following survey is not meant to be comprehensive but rather representative of the most cited and visible texts in the canon and archive). One of the earliest examples of contemporary CHamoru poetry is Juan A. Sanchez's epic poem *History's Four Dark Days: An Ode in Honor of the Late John Fitzgerald Kennedy* (1965), which was published in Saipan by the Commonwealth of the Northern Marianas Trust Territory Printing Office. This epic ode (comprising sixty-eight quatrains) is written in CHamoru, and the book includes an English translation by Father Andrew San Agustin. Sanchez expresses his fond feelings for President Kennedy as an ally of the Pacific nations, as well as his sadness over Kennedy's death. In 1973, Clotilde Castro Gould authored three children's texts to teach the CHamoru language: *I Niyok yan i Manha* (*The Ripe Coconuts and the Young Coconuts*), *I Un Punidera yan i Dies Na Babui* (*The Hen and the Ten Pigs*), and *Si Patas Nganga'* (*Patas the Duck*). Gould also created the well-known CHamoru-language comic strip *Juan Malimanga* in 1981, which was published for decades in Guåhan's major daily newspaper, *The Pacific Daily News*.[91] In 1983, Jesus Naputi's historical novella *Nightmare Near the Kiosk* appeared. The book is set at the beginning of the Japanese invasion and revolves around Pedro and Vicente, two CHamoru men who were part of the Insular Guard, an undertrained and poorly armed force of local men recruited by the U.S. Navy in 1941 to defend Guåhan. The story praises the heroism of these young men and critiques the United States for not adequately defending Guam from Japanese military invasion. In 1988, Evelyn Flores published three CHamoru children's books in her Island Cousin series: *Dolphin Day*, *Duendes Hunter*, and *Isa's Avocado Tree*.

One of the most well-known books of CHamoru literature is Chris Perez Howard's *Mariquita: A Tragedy of Guam*, a work that is often classified as a novel, though it is perhaps more accurately described as a fictionalized biography based on the lives of the author's family members, focusing specifically on his mother, Mariquita. The book was first published in 1982 by Guåhan-based publisher PPH and Company, under the title *Mariquita: A Story of Guam*, and republished in 1986 under its current title by the Institute of Pacific Studies at the University of the South Pacific, making the book one of the first contemporary CHamoru literary texts to circulate beyond the Mariana archipelago. The book was out of print for many years until the University of Guam Press republished a revised edition under the title *Mariquita: Revisited* in 2019. Perez Howard was born on Guåhan in 1940 to Maria "Mariquita" Aguon Perez, a CHamoru woman, and Edward Howard, a white American naval officer from Indiana. Mariquita and Edward met and fell in love during the U.S. naval era on Guåhan, but their cross-cultural marriage was violently interrupted in 1941, when the Imperial Army of Japan bombed, invaded, and occupied the island. During the occupation, Edward was sent to Japan as a prisoner of war, and Mariquita was forced to work in the fields and serve a high-ranking Japanese officer. Tragically, Mariquita was murdered toward the end of the occupation, and her body was never found. After the war, Perez Howard and his father moved to Indiana. Thirty-five years later, the author returned to Guåhan to reconnect with his culture and family, as well as to learn about his mother's life and the circumstances of her death. Trained as a journalist, Perez Howard conducted archival research and oral interviews; *Mariquita: A Tragedy of Guam* emerged from his research, which was funded by a grant from the Guam Insular Arts Council. The book begins in 1938 with the story of his parents' courtship and marriage, chronicles the author's birth and early childhood, and ends in 1944 with the last days of Japanese occupation and Mariquita's death. In 2000, Perez Howard wrote a second book about his father's experiences: *Edward: An American Tragedy*.[92]

The most prolific CHamoru writer is Peter R. Onedera, who first started publishing his work (in both CHamoru and English) in the 1980s and is still publishing new work today. Two of his early nonfiction books are *Nå'an Lugåt Siha gi ya Guåhan: Guam Place Names* (1989) and *Fafa'ña'gue yan Hinengge Siha (Ghosts and Superstitious Beliefs)* (1994), and his two autobiographies are *Gi i Tilu Gradu (In the Third Grade)* (2009) and *Wednesday's Child* (2016). He published the novella *Cheffla gi i Manglo (Whistle in the Wind)* (2006) and two poetry collections, *Visions of a Chamoru* (1995) and *Taimanu na Ini* (2018). He has also written nearly (and astonishingly) seventy-five plays, including *Ai Haga-hu!* (a play about "comfort women" on Guåhan during World War II, appearing in 1997), *Nasarinu* (a play about leprosy on Guåhan in the early 1900s, appearing in 1998), and *Chinatsaga (Hardship): Four One-Act Plays* (2004), to name a few.[93]

A new wave of CHamoru literature has emerged since the 1990s that includes poetry, fiction, creative nonfiction, children's books, and comics (some of these books were self-published, and some are now out of print, but others can be purchased via online booksellers or bookstores on Guåhan). These include PC Muñoz's poetry chapbooks *The Daily Balance* (1992), *Half-Truths* (1995), and *Inside Pocket of a Houndstooth Blazer* (2018); Victoria-Lola Leon Guerrero's children's book *Lola's Journey Home* (2004); Baltazar

Aguon's *I Dos Amantes* (2005), an adaptation of a CHamoru legend about two lovers; Julian Aguon's nonfiction books, *Just Left of the Setting Sun* (2006), *The Fire This Time: Essays on Life Under US Occupation* (2006), *What We Bury at Night: Disposable Humanity* (2008), and *The Properties of Perpetual Light* (2021); Tanya Chargualaf Taimanglo's short story collection *Attitude 13: A Daughter of Guam's Collection of Short Stories* (2010) and novel *Secret Shopper* (2013); Steven LeFever's novels *Beautiful Escapade* (2011) and *Mariana Sky* (2016); Stephen Tenorio's novel *An Ocean in a Cup* (2011); M. B. Dallochio's novel *Quixote in Ramadi* (2013) and memoir *Desert Warrior* (2017); Lehua Taitano's poetry collections *A Bell Made of Stones* (2013) and *Inside Me an Island* (2018); Jose M. Torres's nonfiction book *The Massacre at Atåte* (2015); Michael Lujan Bevacqua's children's books *Sumåhi and the Karabao* (2015), *The Adventures of Akli'e'* (2017), and *Hu Guaiya Hao Taiguihi* (2019), and comic books *Makåhna* (2015), *Roque* (2016), and *Ga'pang's Quest* (2020); Paula Quinene's romance novels *Conquered: A WWII Erotic Historical Romance Set in Guam* (2016) and *Stormed: A Contemporary Romance Set in Guam* (2020); Dakota Camacho's collection of lyrics *Na'lå'la'* (2017); former poet laureate of Guåhan Frederick B. Quinene's *An Islander's Voice* (2018); Francisco D. Delgado's flash fiction collection *Adolescence, Secondhand* (2018); and Teresita Lourdes Perez's *CHamoru Legends: A Gathering of Stories*, translated into CHamoru by Maria Ana Tenorio Rivera (2019).

There is also a history of literary journals and anthologies that feature many other talented CHamoru authors who have not yet published book-length works. The journals include *Xanadu*, *Xanadu II*, and *Storyboard*. *Xanadu*, first published in 1966 at the University of Guam, featured work by students and faculty members of CHamoru and non-CHamoru descent. Between 1981 and 1983, the journal was resurrected as *Xanadu II*. *Storyboard: A Journal of Pacific Imagery* has published nineteen issues from its founding in 1991 to 2020. Several anthologies have appeared in recent years: *Chamoru Childhood* (2009); *Pacific Collection: Reading for Civic Reflection* (2011); *Word of Mouth: Pacific Stories from Guam (Sinangan Ginen i Pachot: Estorian Pasifiku Ginen Guåhan)* (2014); *Kinalamten gi Pasifiku: Insights from Oceania* (2017); *Home(is)lands: New Art and Writing from Guåhan and Hawai'i* (2017); *Indigenous Literatures from Micronesia* (2019), and *Pulan Collective: 13 Moons 13 Meals* (2020). In lieu of naming all the writers in these anthologies whom I don't discuss in this monograph, I encourage you to purchase these books and support the publishers.

The University of Guam Press, which has been revitalized under the directorship of Victoria-Lola Leon Guerrero, has recently created a supportive venue for the publication of CHamoru literature.[94] For example, an imprint within the press is Taiguini Books, which is committed to publishing "cultural and indigenous literature for adults and children, with the goal of capturing and preserving the eloquence and depth of the dynamic Micronesian storytelling tradition in written form."[95] Their current catalog includes Peter Onedera's poetry book *Taimanu na Ini* (2018) and several children's books: Dolores Barcinas Santos's *13 Months in Malesso'* (2019); Catherine Payne's *Chepchop Unai* (2016); Dolores Indalecio's *Guaiyayon na Trongkon Mansanita (The Loveable Mansanita Tree)* (2016); Rufina Fejeran Mendiola's *I Malingu na Påtgon (The Lost Child)* (2016); Simone and Dana Bollinger's *Ma Guaiya Yu', si Nåna yan si Tåta (Grandma and Grandpa Love Me)* (2016); and Lance J. Osborn's *Si Pedro yan i Hilet Oru na Ko'ko' (Pedro and the Golden Ko'ko')* (2016).

Beyond the written word, there is also a rich history of theater, playwriting, performance arts, and oral storytelling. As Julius Sotomayor Cena has noted, "Performing theaters on Guam are havens and are great venues through which stories and cultural thoughts are expressed. Although originally a western idea, the people of Guam have adopted theater as a home for Chamorro plays, many of which are unpublished."[96] While there were early plays that were part of community, education, and parish church activities, many were not documented or archived. A few that were include Linda Cruz's *The White Lady on the Bridge of Maina* (1969), Jesus Naputi's *To Build an Island* (1975), and Robert Underwood and Carlos P. Taitano's co-authored *Guahu Taotao Tåno'* (1984). As mentioned earlier, Peter R. Onedera is, by far, the most prolific CHamoru playwright, having written over seventy-five plays (in both CHamoru and English). Nearly half of them have been produced and presented on Guåhan over the past forty years, a majority of which he also directed. Today, plays are often presented at the University of Guam Fine Arts Theater, the Gifted and Talented Education (GATE) Theater, and Southern High School Performing Theater. A recent play that gained island-wide attention was *Pågat* (2014), co-written by Michael Lujan Bevacqua and Victoria-Lola Leon Guerrero. The play featured choreography by Vince Reyes of the cultural dance group Inetnon Gefpå'go, and was directed by Michelle Blas, an associate professor and director of theater at the University of Guam. Blas has directed more than twenty productions at the university, including local and classical plays.[97] In terms of performing arts, two prominent practitioners include Dakota Camacho and Ojeya Cruz Banks. Camacho is a multidisciplinary artist, an educator, the founder of Guma' Matao, and the creator of the albums *All Life Is Sacred* (2013) and *Na'lå'la'* (2017). As an artist, Camacho weaves together chant, hip hop, dance, ritual, ceremonial music, sound design, oral history, installation, and performance. Some of Camacho's multidisciplinary works include *Buried Beneath: Bombs and Latte* (2012), *Guåhu Guåhan* (2015), *Mali'e' / Tåno' Uchan* (2019), and *Etak: An [Un]Traditional Micronesian Navigation Chant* (2021), among others.[98] Another multidisciplinary artist, PC Muñoz, has created experimental performances that combine text, music, art, sound design, film, improvisations, and collaborations. Some of his more literary projects include *Twenty Haiku* (2005), *Light Haiku* (2008), *Half Breed* (2018), *I Remember Her By Name* (2021), and *Black/Pacific* (2021).[99] Performance poet and spoken-word artist Ami Mattison has toured throughout the United States and Canada, sharing her work at art venues, festivals, conferences, schools, and universities. Her three albums of spoken-word poetry include *Strange and Potent Mixture* (2003), *Break the Glass* (2016), and *Speaking of Love* (2017).[100] In 2003, the first storytelling and literary arts group on Guåhan was founded: Ginen i Hila' i Maga' Taotao Association, which translates as "From the Tongues of the Noble People." The group of oral storytellers represented Guåhan at the Festival of Pacific Arts in Palau (2004), American Sāmoa (2008), the Solomon Islands (2012), and Guåhan (2016). Since its founding, Ginen i Hila' has held countless storytelling events throughout the island.[101] In 2017, the Guam Legislature passed a resolution to recognize and commend Ginen i Hila' for its "dedication to perpetuating the Chamorro language and heritage, and for sharing the art of storytelling with the people of Guam and the Pacific region."[102]

This list is neither comprehensive nor exhaustive. While I have tried to gather as many sources of CHamoru literature as I could find over the years, there are many talented CHamoru writers who have not yet published a book or whom I have failed to track. I hope this plotting will simply offer a first mapping of the vibrant and diverse constellation of contemporary CHamoru literature. This is an exciting time because CHamoru and Pacific Islander literature is now taught at the University of Guam, at Guam Community College, and in K–12 classrooms throughout Guåhan and the Northern Marianas. Additionally, there have been many writing workshops, book events, and literary organizations that have all emerged recently, which will give writers the support, encouragement, and publication opportunities that will allow them to continue the current flourishing of CHamoru literature.[103]

Charting the Coordinates of CHamoru Literary Studies

Currently, there are no other published book-length studies of CHamoru literature. There are several published essays by scholars Naoto Sudo, Paul Sharrad, and Valerie Woodward about *Mariquita: A Tragedy of Guam*, as well as an essay on Paula Quinene's romance novels.[104] In 2009, Monique R. Carriveau Storie completed her dissertation on contemporary children's literature set in Guåhan, and in 2010, Sharleen J. Q. Santos-Bamba wrote a dissertation about CHamoru women and literacy in modern Guåhan.[105] In 2016, Caitlin Yuri Yamamoto completed a dissertation about Micronesian literature, with one chapter focused on CHamoru literature.[106] That same year, Michael Lujan Bevacqua and Isa Kelley Bowman co-authored an essay published in a special issue of *Marvels & Tales* that explored the relationship between Indigenous folklore and contemporary activism: "Histories of Wonder, Futures of Wonder: Chamorro Activist Identity, Community, and Leadership in 'The Legend of Gadao' and 'The Women Who Saved Guåhan from a Giant Fish.'"[107] Leiana San Agustin Naholowa'a completed an MA thesis on the theme of mothering in CHamoru narratives in 2018, and Arielle Taitano Lowe completed an MA thesis on mixed-race CHamoru narratives in 2020.[108] I have written several essays on CHamoru poetry,[109] and there is a growing body of scholarship on my own work.[110] The first substantial critical map of contemporary CHamoru literature was Robert Tenorio Torres's MA thesis, "Selected Marianas Folklore, Legend, Literature: A Critical Commentary" (1991), which was eventually published in 2003 and 2004 as three linked essays ("Pre-Contact Marianas Folklore," "Colonial and Conquest Lore of the Marianas," and "Post Colonial and Modern Literature of the Marianas") in the *Micronesian Journal of the Humanities and Social Sciences*.[111]

I consider my work to be in productive and respectful conversation with Torres's study. Torres defines "Marianas literature" as oral and written literature created by natives and nonnatives in or from the Mariana archipelago. He distinguishes between "regional writing" (literature written in English that "assumes an audience familiar with Western literature, but unfamiliar with Pacific themes and forms") and "national local writing" (literature by local writers, written either in English, a mix of English and CHamoru, or primarily CHamoru, about "local themes").[112] While I appreciate Torres's multicultural and archipelagic approach, I am interested in questions of Indigeneity, so I exclusively examine Indigenous Marianas literature, or CHamoru literature, which I define as oral and written aesthetic expressions and narratives composed in CHamoru, in English, or multilingually by authors of CHamoru genealogical descent. Given the natural limits of a monograph and the exponential growth of CHamoru literature over the thirty years since Torres's study, I focus on a selection of CHamoru poets from Guåhan (as well as those who live in various diasporic locations but have genealogical ties to Guåhan), since that is my own personal lineage. I focus on poetry not only because it is the art form I am most passionate about, but also because I believe that the formal elements of poetry invite a robust discussion of CHamoru aesthetics. I define poetry as encompassing written texts, orature, and contemporary "spoken word." While I do not discuss CHamoru fiction, nonfiction, children's books, or comics, I hope other scholars will examine these genres because they deserve their own studies.

Torres categorizes Marianas literature into four periods: precontact (pre-1521), colonial and conquest (1521–1898), postcolonial (1899–1941), and modern (1944–present). I do not employ Torres's historical frame because it is problematic in my opinion. While most historians agree that 1521 marks the beginning of a colonial era, the U.S. possession of Guåhan after 1898 was a *continuation* of colonialism and not a movement toward a postcolonial status. However, I do highlight contemporary CHamoru literature, or what we might call "new CHamoru literature," to echo Torres's formulation of the "New Marianas Literary Tradition."[113] I also situate the term "new" within the movement of "new Pacific literature," which refers to contemporary literature by Indigenous Pacific Islanders that first emerged in the 1960s and 1970s, a period of Pacific cultural revitalization, political decolonization, and national independence movements.[114]

Torres examines a wide-ranging survey of Marianas literature published before 1991. His primary sources for "precolonial" and "colonial-era" literature include four major collections of CHamoru folklore: Eve Grey's *Legends of Micronesia* (1951), the Nieves M. Flores Memorial Library staff's *Legends of Guam* (1971), Mavis Werner Van Peenan's *Chamorro Legends on the Island of Guam* (1974), and the Guam Department of Education's *Legends of Guam*

(1981). These collections sourced oral folktales from pre-nineteenth-century archival documents and twentieth-century anthropological research, as well as from oral interviews with CHamoru elders. Torres's archive of contemporary CHamoru and non-CHamoru literature from the Marianas encompasses novels, poetry collections, and literary magazines, including *Xanadu*; Louise Stout's *Kalou: A Legend of Saipan*; William Peck's *I Speak the Beginning*; Robert Lund's *Hour of Glory*; Chris Perez Howard's *Mariquita: A Tragedy of Guam*; Juan A. Sanchez's *History's Four Dark Days: An Ode in Honor of the Late John Fitzgerald Kennedy*; and John Mazur's *Pacific War, Saipaniana,* and *Typhoons in Paradise*.[115] Torres's bibliography is noncomprehensive due to certain texts being either out of print or unavailable.

Torres analyzes the major motifs, themes, and imagery of CHamoru folklore and legends to conclude that "precolonial" oral stories celebrated CHamoru pride and power, creating "tales out of native mythology to explicate the origins and sources of geographic features, animals, or mysterious occurrences."[116] Yet he also shows how CHamoru folklore changed after Spanish colonialism to depict Christian and Spanish imagery and motifs.[117] When interpreting contemporary CHamoru literature, Torres maps how colonialism shifted CHamoru literature from an oral to a written medium, from the CHamoru to the English language, and from Indigenous forms to Western and European genres, or a hybrid composition of "native traditions and foreign influences."[118] He concludes: "Sadly enough, the native Chamorro writer has become estranged from the precontact literary traditions, Before Time Ancestors, and must forge a new identity within the bounds of these contemporary influences."[119] These dramatic changes lead Torres to question the authenticity of these texts:

> Contemporary Marianas literature reflects the condition of the people today—deterritorialized and estranged from its past. Chamorro, the native tongue, becomes the foreign language; the new society that has emerged out of the ashes of World War II is Western and distant from the traditional Chamorro culture. . . . Today, the literature is no longer intended for continuing the spirit of traditional folklore and oral traditions, but rather more towards a Westernized and Eurocentric, regional perspective.[120]

To Torres, some contemporary CHamoru writers are severed from their native literary heritage, and their works bear the signs of literary acculturation and demise. Similarly, American folklorist Mavis Van Peenan, in *Chamorro Legends on the Island of Guam* (1945), argues that centuries of Spanish colonialism and the ongoing pressures of Americanization have pushed CHamoru literature toward extinction:

> There are many reasons why Guam's folklore will disappear. . . . The family and neighborly groups which previously came together for an evening of storytelling and reminiscing now attend the movies. The young people speak English. They are Christians. The pretty Chamorro girls will find husbands among the thousands of American military men on Guam. Many of these girls will leave their island with their husbands. Many Chamorro boys will join the American Armed Forces and "see the world" and settle in parts far from Guam. The time will come when few remember the stories told of "Our Before Time Ancestors" and the Chamorro legends, uncollected, unwritten, will be forgotten, one by one.[121]

Echoing Van Peenan, W. M. Peck, in *I Speak the Beginning: Anthology of Surviving Poetry of the Northern Mariana Islands*, wrote: "[Chamorro] ancestors no longer speak to their descendants, for the descendants have ceased to listen, and have lost understanding of the once-rich, now partially-obsolete vocabularies, the raunchy idioms, the complex metaphors, the terse (almost short-hand) code expressions that ancestors used to express their poignant, most tender, most robust sentiments."[122] CHamoru literature is, thus, considered to be in "acute danger of extinction."[123] I classify these perspectives as *fatal impact literary theory*. Van Peenan, Peck, and Torres express conceptions of CHamoru literature based on essentialist notions of CHamoru culture, identity, and literature. These notions create an uncrossable divide between the traditional and the modern, positioning CHamoru writers in a severed space of alienation, precarity, hybridity, and endangerment. In turn, CHamoru literature becomes inauthentic and does not fit the classification of a "pure" Indigenous literature.

Throughout this book, I counter the narrative of CHamoru literary demise and instead ground my approach within a genealogy of scholarship on CHamoru aesthetics that has applied a form of articulation theory to CHamoru dance, music, and literature. Judy Flores, in "Art and Identity in the Mariana Islands: The Reconstruction of 'Ancient' Chamorro Dance," draws from her experience as the folk arts coordinator for the Guam Arts

Council in 1986.[124] In order to follow the guidelines of the Folk Arts Division of the National Endowment for the Arts (NEA), Flores needed to "identify, encourage, document and showcase the traditional folk arts of Guam."[125] At the time, the most prevalent and visible form of CHamoru art was a movement of CHamoru dance that emerged in 1984, led by Frank Rabon and his group, the Taotao Tåno' Dancers. Flores faced a dilemma because these dances had not been passed down since precolonial times, CHamoru dances having long been replaced by Spanish and American dances. Instead, these dances were created by Rabon based on "only educated guesses at what the ancient dances might have been."[126] As a child on Guåhan, Rabon grew up learning the Spanish waltz and the cha-cha. When he attended college in Washington State, he joined a Polynesian student group and learned their dances, eventually becoming a professional Polynesian dancer in Hawai'i and Guåhan in the 1970s. In 1984, Rabon established the Taotao Tåno' Dancers on Guåhan and began to choreograph Hawaiian hula dances set to CHamoru music. Rabon was inspired to re-create ancestral CHamoru dances when he learned more about them through archival sources. To Flores, Rabon's dances are CHamoru not because they have been passed down uninterrupted from precolonial times, but because they creatively represent "Chamorro beliefs that have persisted through colonial transformations and local appropriations."[127] As such, these new CHamoru dances rearticulate CHamoru identity through "a very emotive form of consciousness raising within the community."[128]

Similar to Flores, historian Michael Clement Jr., in his dissertation "Kustumbre, Modernity and Resistance: The Subaltern Narrative in Chamorro Language Music," maps how CHamoru music changed from the Spanish era to the end of World War II. He observes that most CHamoru songs are composed in Western styles (such as country and western or rock and roll), and some are translations, adaptations, or rearrangements of popular American songs.[129] Since CHamoru music does not "necessarily conform to modern expectations of what indigenous music should sound like," one could interpret CHamoru music as an impure, inauthentic, and degraded practice.[130] However, Clement Jr. argues that CHamoru music is instead a site of CHamoru survival, vitality, and resilience. To illustrate, he points to how CHamoru songs became a "vehicle for the perpetuation of the Chamorro language." Moreover, these songs "told stories about past and contemporary life from Chamorro perspectives, countering the homogenizing effect of English language media, education and entertainment options that dominated Guam's public sphere."[131] The practice of adapting and borrowing foreign musical styles "demonstrates the ways Chamorros helped define the colonial encounter, selecting which foreign influences they found useful or enjoyable."[132] Beyond being a sign of CHamoru agency in the face of aesthetic colonialism, Clement Jr. asserts that CHamoru songs were also "intuitively understood as resistance to Spanish/American/Japanese cultural hegemony."[133] Lastly, Clement Jr. argues that CHamoru-language songs have "roots that are traceable to the pre-colonial era [through] apparent continuities in musical sensibilities, particularly in humor, competitiveness, extemporaneity, and word phrasing."[134] As I will discuss more fully in chapter 4, other scholars have examined the rearticulation of the CHamoru oral tradition known as kåntan chamorrita in contemporary literary practices.

Monique R. Carriveau Storie makes a parallel argument in her dissertation "All Fifty Kathousand Cousins: Chamorro Teachers Responding to Contemporary Children's Literature Set in Guam," in which she defines Chamorro cultural authenticity "as a complex matrix of cultural images, a community's value system and personal experiences."[135] She theorizes that texts accrue cultural authenticity through the presence of CHamoru language, themes, values, customs, beliefs, physical details, characterization, historical figures, and local geographies.[136] These elements of CHamoru culture (what other scholars have termed "markers of authenticity," "cultural identifiers," and "summarizing symbols") can be interpreted as signaling the continuity of CHamoru identity.[137] In her analysis of several contemporary CHamoru children's books, Storie suggests that the presence of these signs evidences CHamoru identity and vitality. CHamoru literary authenticity, then, is "not just about recognizing an accurate image but rather is about understanding how cultural elements and cultural values are melded into authentic or true meanings through the written word or by an artistic rendering."[138]

Aligned with these scholars, I conceptualize contemporary CHamoru literature as *assemblages* of meanings, subjectivities, and discourses that change in response to historical conditions, political pressures, or colonial force, but still maintain a connection to ancestral CHamoru customs, practices, aesthetics, and values. Reading CHamoru literature as a site of articulation and struggle honors the complexity of CHamoru culture and aesthetics while also highlighting Indigenous survival, continuity, vitality, and agency.

Plotting the Coordinates of a Pacific Literary Methodology

Throughout this book, I develop a Pacific literary methodology that I term *wayreading*, which involves conceptualizing CHamoru cultural identity and literature as complex articulations rather than static entities; centering CHamoru literary creations within Indigenous intellectual, historical, cultural, and political contexts; examining contemporary CHamoru literature through the lens of customary CHamoru oral, visual, and performing arts; and foregrounding the role that CHamoru literature plays in imagining and enacting decolonization.

The concept of wayreading is inspired by the theory and praxis of Pacific *wayfinding*, navigation, and canoe traditions. In "Voyaging for Anti-colonial Recovery: Austronesian Seafaring, Archipelagic Rethinking, and the Remapping of Indigeneity," Diaz describes the Micronesian wayfinding technique of etak, or "moving islands," as a method that calculates distance and position by "triangulating the speed of the islands of departure and destination with that of a third reference island. This is accomplished, furthermore, by plotting these islands' courses in the celestial sky, which in effect serves as a veritable map for the world below."[139] The islands are understood as *moving* along star courses. Diaz explains another important technique, pookof, which refers to knowing the creatures indigenous to specific islands and their travel habits.[140] For example, if you see a bird native to a certain island, then you know that island is nearby; thus, islands *expand* and *contract*.[141] Additionally, wayfinders *read* marine and atmospheric signs to aid in navigation, such as cloud formations and wind patterns, star formations and sun positions, wave currents and ocean efflorescence.[142] Amid this movement, the canoe feels still and unmoving, with the wayfinder "at the center of a circle of sea and sky, trusting mind and senses within a cognitive structure to read and interpret nature's signs along the way as the means for maintaining continuous orientation over vast oceanic distance to remote, intended island destinations."[143] As is evident, Pacific wayfinding is an important and culturally grounded form not only of travel and mobility, but also of mapping, literacy, reading, and interpretation.

Moreover, Diaz suggests that navigation is a critical framework through which to envision and interpret the mobile complexities of Native Pacific cultures and identities. As he writes: "The conceptual takeaway from etak/moving islands as a technology to measure time/space is that indigenous subjectivity can similarly be understood as a technology if not a measure of time/space."[144] To translate the above into navigational terms, we can say, figuratively, that Indigenous identities and cultures are not static, unchanging islands; instead, Native cultures *move* the way islands move. We can go further to say that the pookof of these moving islands/identities represents the assemblages of cultural signs and markers that we might associate with a given Indigenous population. Pacific wayfinding, then, is a "deep, substantive and compelling vantage point with which to map and move what are after all the mobile coordinates of indigenous cultural and political consciousness."[145] Additionally, critical wayfinding is a compelling framework through which to conceptualize Pacific narratives, discourses, and literatures. Narrativity relates to wayfinding because navigational techniques rely on narratives. For example, before voyagers left their island of origin, they learned and memorized the etak and pookof of their journey through navigational chants, stories, and "song maps."[146] Oftentimes, these narrativized "mnemonic map[s] for travel" were inherited across generations.[147] Diaz speaks to the importance of narratives when he argues that Native identities are "fundamentally discursive and narratological" because Native subjectivities are shaped by the narratives and discourses of race, class, gender, sexuality, and more. In other words, Indigeneity equals "time/space/self/narrative."[148]

Given the epistemological and cultural richness of Pacific wayfinding, it is no surprise that scholars have often used the metaphor of navigation to describe the interpretation of the spatial, historical, and geographic complexity of Pacific literature.[149] As Elizabeth DeLoughrey points out, the oceangoing vessel has become a crucial theme, concept, and "master trope for Pacific literary production," and a "crucial bodily metaphor of a people's connection to their genealogy, history, and sovereignty."[150] The first novels, poetry collections, literary journals, and anthologies written and edited by Indigenous Pacific Islanders were indeed conceptualized as symbolic canoes expressing a "transoceanic imaginary," establishing "maritime narrative legacies," and carrying their stories "towards a new Oceania."[151]

While rooted in the tradition of Pacific wayfinding, I also situate the practice of wayreading within the traditions of *indigenizing* literary methodologies. Linda Tuhiwai Smith defines "indigenizing" as the centering of our critical or creative practices within Indigenous ecologies, images, languages, themes, metaphors, stories, identities, histories, cultural practices, values, traditions, aesthetics, and epistemologies.[152] Scholars have *indigenized* Pacific literary theory by centering the cultural, linguistic, historical, social, and political themes and contexts of Pacific writing, which also involves foregrounding the continuing impact of colonialism and the struggle for cultural revitalization and political decolonization.[153] Moreover, I route wayreading through Native American literary studies and its rich legacy of indigenizing literary theory by centering interpretive practices within Native American epistemologies.[154]

Another important aspect of indigenizing literary theory is to prioritize the analysis of contemporary Indigenous literature through the lens of customary Indigenous aesthetics. Many Pacific literary scholars have searched for and theorized multiple "literary antecedents" of contemporary Pacific literature.[155] For example, Peggy Fairbairn-Dunlop affirms that the major antecedent of Sāmoan written literature is the Sāmoan oral storytelling tradition known as fāgogo.[156] Hawaiian scholar ku'ualoha ho'omanawanui details how aesthetic elements in contemporary Hawaiian poetry (such as dualistic pairings, repetition, chant, rhyme schemes, connectors, closing lines, and other mnemonic devices) are drawn from customary Hawaiian orature.[157] Epeli Hau'ofa puts it most poetically when he figures contemporary Pacific literature as "silent story-telling," and the act of reading as "listen[ing] to stories told silently by invisible tellers."[158] In addition to orality, several scholars have considered Pacific visual and material arts as viable antecedents. Examples include tattooing, lei (flower garlands), spiral art, pottery, weaving, petroglyphy, carving, canoe design, architecture, fashion, and cartography.[159] Indigenous performance arts and dance (such as Hawaiian hula) have also been read as narrative arts.[160] Albert Wendt notes that even though Pacific writers have experimented with realist, modernist, and postmodernist modes, at the heart of these experiments are "the indigenous ingredients: the techniques of oral storytelling and other oral traditions; art, dance and music."[161] Beyond the Pacific, many Native American scholars have theorized contemporary Native American literature through tribalcentric aesthetics.[162] The most influential scholar for me has been Chadwick Allen, especially in his work *Trans-Indigenous: Methodologies for Global Native Literary Studies*. He examines how Indigenous visual aesthetics and material technologies (such as earthworks, navigation, pictographs, weaving, and carving) function not only as a text's "primary theme" but also as a "primary logic for its elaborate formal structures and multiple structural patterns."[163]

Lastly, wayreading involves being attentive to how Indigenous literature contributes to decolonization, self-determination, and sovereignty movements. Wendt describes how Pacific literature was an important part of the Pacific decolonization movements in the 1960s and 1970s because literature created space to "[indigenize] and [enrich] the language of the colonisers and [use] it to declare our independence and uniqueness; to analyze colonialism itself and its effects upon us; [and] to free ourselves of the mythologies created about us in colonial literature."[164] Pacific literature articulates stories of "marvelous endurance, survival and dynamic adaptation, despite enormous suffering under colonialism."[165] The relationship between decolonization and literature is a prevalent topic in both Pacific and Native American literary studies. Scholars have illustrated how Indigenous literature contributes to decolonization by serving the interests of community, supporting the sovereignty and formation of Native nations, and reflecting the social, political, and cultural realities, struggles, and resistances of Native peoples.[166] Many Indigenous authors have also been engaged in protest, activism, civic engagement, legislation, direct action, political organizing, and movement building.

Overall, the interpretive methodology of wayreading navigates the complex articulations of CHamoru culture, identity, and aesthetics by mapping and locating the moving signs of Indigenous presence, such as CHamoru language, values, customs, beliefs, histories, and arts. Wayreading reveals the continuity, resistance, and vitality of CHamoru culture, identity, and aesthetics. In each chapter of this book, I wayread different examples of contemporary CHamoru poetry that explore important subjects related to CHamoru culture and identity. I will show how the primary themes articulate CHamoru cultural symbols and identities, as well as how the primary narrative structures and forms articulate customary CHamoru aesthetics, technologies, and ecologies. Ultimately, this book asserts that new CHamoru literature has been—and continues to be—a crucial vessel for expressing the continuities and resilience of CHamoru identities, as well as the vital possibilities of CHamoru decolonial futures. I hope wayreading will become a productive contribution within Pacific, Indigenous, Native American, American, and world literature studies, and that this monograph will introduce local, national, and international readers and scholars to contemporary CHamoru poetry and poetics.

Plotting the Chapters

In chapter 1, "Taotao Tåno': Sacred Land, Banyan Tree Aesthetics, and CHamoru Ecopoetics," our destination texts will be "Signs of Being: A Chamorro Spiritual Journey" (1997), by C. T. Perez, and "I Kareran i Palåbran Måmi: The Journey of Our Words" (2010), co-authored by Kisha Borja-Kicho'cho' and Anghet Hoppe-Cruz. This chapter will make landfall by grounding us in the importance of i tåno' (the land) as a symbol of CHamoru identity, belonging, and genealogy. Then we will examine the CHamoru creation story as an "eco-theology," or an articulation of ecological ethics. After this, we will familiarize ourselves with CHamoru spiritual beliefs about connections to the land as ancestor, kinship network, and site of co-belonging and mutual care. We will then learn the tragic history of ecological imperialism that has devastated the environments of Guåhan and alienated CHamorus from the land through plantationism, urbanization, militarization, and tourism. In turn, we will explore the inspiring history of CHamoru reclamation of ancestral lands and the struggle over Indigenous land rights. I will then wayread various poems from the aforementioned manuscripts to show how the primary themes of these texts articulate a women-centered CHamoru ecopoetics in order to restore Indigenous stories about the sacredness of the land and inspire ecological healing and connection. In the case of both texts, I will illustrate how their formal structures embody a CHamoru "earth aesthetics" of the trongkon nunu, or banyan tree, a revered symbol in CHamoru culture.

After surveying the land, we will turn our attention to CHamoru houses and the relationship between Indigenous architecture and CHamoru identity. In chapter 2, "The CHamoru House of Story: Guma' Åcho' Latte and Na(rra)tive Architecture in the Poetry of Peter R. Onedera," we will explore the origins and ruins of customary CHamoru housing architecture, known as guma' åcho' latte (also referred to as guma' latte), or latte stone house, and acquaint ourselves with its forms, functions, and values. We will then study the blueprints of "architectural colonialism," detailing how colonial forces changed Indigenous dwelling spaces and consequently disrupted CHamoru housing practices and familial ties. I will then wayread poetry from two of Onedera's poetry collections, *Visions of a Chamoru* (1995) and *Taimanu na Ini* (2018), in relation to the primary theme of housing and latte stones. Since guma' åcho' latte was a space of storytelling, customs, rituals, family, and genealogy, I will end by developing the concept of "Na(rra)tive architecture" to connect the aesthetics, form, and function of CHamoru architecture to the craft, structure, and purpose of Onedera's poetry.

Our next destination will take us away from the lands and houses of Guåhan, beyond the reef, and into the vast expanse and far-flung locations of the CHamoru diaspora. In chapter 3, "The Flying Proa: Outrigger Aesthetics, Migration, and Diasporic Indigeneity in Lehua Taitano's *A Bell Made of Stones*," we will navigate the cultural currents of Pacific voyaging traditions, the colonial history of restricting Indigenous mobilities, and the decolonial revitalization of seafaring practices and customs in Guåhan and the Pacific. We will also consider the figure of the canoe and the idea of seafaring as powerful symbols of CHamoru migration and diasporic cultural identity. I will wayread Taitano's book to show how poetry helps CHamorus navigate the traumas of migration and remain connected to home. In terms of poetic form, I will argue that Taitano's visual experimentation with typography and space embodies outrigger design and navigational techniques. In the end, we will catch a glimpse of the distant horizons and farthest stars of the CHamoru experience, something especially important to recognize within CHamoru cultural studies, since the CHamoru diasporic population continues to grow and now outnumbers its on-island kin.

We will then turn our canoes back toward the northwestern Pacific, catch the trade winds, and return to Guåhan. Chapter 4, "Singing Forward and Backward: Kåntan Chamorrita, CHamoru Intertextuality, and Spoken-Word Poetry," addresses the most well-known form of CHamoru orature: kåntan chamorrita, a call-and-response, extemporaneous, communal oral poetry. We will discuss the form and function of kåntan chamorrita and review how literary scholars have theorized orality in relation to written Indigenous literatures. I will wayread the interwoven aesthetics of the kåntan chamorrita as embodied in the intertextual references between two CHamoru poets from different generations, Michael Lujan Bevacqua and Anne Perez Hattori. Furthermore, I will argue that the kåntan chamorrita is rearticulated in the recent emergence of CHamoru spoken-word poetry and the proliferation of slam poetry competitions on Guåhan. Overall, I propose that new CHamoru written and spoken-word poetry rearticulates the communal situations and aesthetic forms of the kåntan chamorrita tradition. At the end of this chapter, we will listen to CHamoru poets weaving their voices together in new, exciting forms—singing backward to the ancestors and forward to future generations.

Our journey will conclude with a final gathering, a farewell, and the promise of new beginnings. The conclusion, "Prutehi yan Difendi: CHamoru Literature as Decolonial Activism," will wayread CHamoru literature as an important act of decolonizing representations of CHamoru history, culture, and identity as well as an activist tool in the CHamoru decolonization, demilitarization, and sovereignty movements. We will meet three CHamoru poets from different generations—Fredrick Quinene, Bernadita Camacho-Dungca, and Melvin Won Pat-Borja—and bear witness to how their poetry has been employed in political spaces to question and challenge Guåhan's colonial status, to advocate for the protection of the land, and to revitalize CHamoru culture.

Maria Yatar once described the passage of CHamoru lives as parallel to the shape of a canoe: "The journey commences with a star falling from the sky to signify a birth and is represented by the slightly turned-up bow of a canoe. The journey continues throughout life, much like the narrow hull of a canoe. Finally, the journey concludes upon the death of an individual when one's spirit travels upward along the turned-up stern of a canoe and returns as a star that is recovered into the sky."[167] Similarly, we will passage through this book as in a canoe, wayreading the moving stars, currents, islands, and texts of CHamoru literature. Even though we will inevitably reach the end of our journey together, we will always be able to look into a CHamoru text, read the words, and find our way home.

CHAPTER 1

Taotao Tåno'

Sacred Land, Banyan Tree Aesthetics, and CHamoru Ecopoetics

> Scientists have shown that Chamorros have lived in Guam for more than 4,000 years, sharing a unique and special relationship with the land and sea. Chamorros are commonly referred to as "taotao tano," which literally means "people of the land"; it is also a way of indicating that a person is native to these islands. Land is the soul of Chamorro culture; it, together with the sea, gives life to the Chamorro. . . . Therefore, the issue of land persists as an essential component to the survival of the Chamorro people especially in the face of persistent exploitation of land.
>
> —Michael Phillips, "Land"

Introduction

In the beginning, Fu'una and her brother Puntan decided to sacrifice their lives to create Guåhan and give birth to the CHamoru people.[1] Fu'una took apart Puntan's body and transformed his back into the land, his chest into the sky, and his eyebrows into rainbows. She changed one of his eyes into the sun, and the other into the moon. Fu'una then sacrificed her own life so that the sun would shine, the land would blossom, and the waters would flow. Her body became Laso Fu'a (Fu'a Rock), which is located in Fouha Bay in Humåtak, a village in southern Guåhan.[2] CHamoru people were birthed from Fu'a Rock and its surrounding sands.

The CHamoru creation story (and its variations) has been passed down for thousands of years and "constitutes one of the most important oral histories of the Chamorro people."[3] The name Fu'una translates as "first," and the name Puntan translates as "coconut tree sapling."[4] Fu'una and Puntan are considered the earliest CHamoru ancestors, "who through blood and genealogy are bound to all Chamorros."[5] To honor them, CHamorus annually pilgrimaged to Laso Fu'a, made offerings, and sought blessings for their seeds, crops, and fishing implements to ensure successful harvests and catches. The CHamoru creation story and the practices associated with the pilgrimage are often noted as evidence of pre-Christian spirituality and ancestor worship. For this chapter, I interpret the story through the lens of "eco-theology," which is the study of the "ethical and ecological implications of reading, interpreting, and transmitting foundational stories."[6]

One ethical and ecological implication of the CHamoru creation story is the belief that kinship, gender equality, and land customs are interwoven. The relationship between Puntan and Fu'una shows that the sibling relationship is paramount, and that CHamoru siblings relied on each other to "protect family property, raise the children of the family, and generate assets to keep the family well-endowed."[7] Thus, men and women were respected as contributing members of a society in which gender roles were equitably balanced.[8] In CHamoru culture, families controlled land tenure and usage rights, and both men and women had different obligations to sustainably care for the land and its resources. However, land was inherited through the women's lineage, reflecting the overall matrilineal aspects of CHamoru society.[9]

Because land was created from the bodies of Puntan and Fu'una, CHamorus view land as an ancestor; thus land, genealogy, and spirituality are interconnected. CHamorus often refer to themselves as *taotao tåno'*, or "people of the land," and several villages on Guåhan refer to body parts, such as Barrigada (flank), Tiyan (stomach), Hagåtña (blood), and Mongmong (the sound of a heartbeat). In CHamoru epistemology, the spirits of the dead, referred to as *taotaomo'na* (literally translated as the "people of before"), continue to dwell on and in the land and are revered by the living.[10] The taotaomo'na had the power to protect or harm people, and they often guarded areas of land.[11] When CHamorus died, they were often buried in the earth beneath the family home so that their spirits could continue to support and protect the family. In times of crisis, CHamorus would call on the taotaomo'na for aid.[12] As is evident, land is a key site, symbol, and marker of CHamoru identity. Land is, as Michael Phillips puts it in the opening epigraph, the soul of CHamoru culture.

One especially prevalent space where the taotaomo'na are believed to dwell is near i trongkon nunu, or the banyan tree. The banyan species that is indigenous to Guåhan begins as an epiphyte that grows from seeds dropped by birds onto other trees, then sends down "aerial roots" that embrace and ultimately envelop the host tree. The branches will send down threadlike

FIGURE 1 Banyan tree, 2020. Photograph by Brandy Nālani McDougall.

hanging roots that intertwine and fuse as they reach for the ground. They enter the soil and will eventually become thick supporting props, forming a compound trunk. A single tree can, over time, come to resemble a grove. CHamorus consider the banyan tree sacred.[13]

Another ethical and ecological implication of the CHamoru creation story is the belief in reciprocity and mutual care between nature and human beings. If the land is your ancestor and the dwelling place of ancestral spirits, then the land must be treated with respect and reverence. When entering

FIGURE 2 Banyan tree aerial roots, 2020. Photograph by Brandy Nālani McDougall.

certain lands guarded by taotaomo'na, CHamorus would first ask petmisu, or permission, to enter (failure to follow protocol could result in sickness or misfortune).[14] The taotaomo'na were invoked and prayed to when planting and fishing. They were also offered drinks and a part of the catch or harvest. In CHamoru epistemology, "all that is, all that exists, is a testament to the cooperation between the ancestral spirits of Chamorros and those currently living."[15] This belief in interconnection is further embodied in the most important CHamoru cultural value, inafa'maolek, or the "interdependence between nature, man and woman, and relatives."[16] This idea of interdependence is a crucial element of the CHamoru worldview that is embodied in the CHamoru creation story.[17]

In this chapter, I *wayread* contemporary CHamoru women writers who highlight the articulations of CHamoru culture, identity, and aesthetics through the representations of land, banyan trees, and the creation story. Even though I have discussed wayfinding in terms of a maritime practice, wayfinding can operate on land because it also signifies the process of navigating space (interior and exterior, built and natural environments) through the observation and interpretation of signs.[18] Furthermore, we can think about wayfinding as something that is able to navigate the "tidalectics," to use Kamau Brathwaite's brilliant phrase, of the complex entanglements of land and sea.[19]

The poets I discuss in this chapter are C. T. Perez, Kisha Borja-Kicho'cho', and Anghet Hoppe-Cruz, three respected and accomplished CHamoru writers from different generations who have been published in national and international journals and anthologies.[20] By wayreading their work, I will show how they craft a CHamoru ecopoetics to invoke the Puntan and Fu'una creation story, to reconnect to i taotaomo'na, to reestablish the central place and power of CHamoru women, and to rearticulate a CHamoru ecological consciousness. I root my analysis within the scholarship of Pacific, postcolonial, trans-Pacific, and Indigenous ecopoetics to demonstrate how literature that focuses on the environment is an important site for articulating Indigenous identity. I also situate this literature within the context of Spanish, American, and Japanese "ecological imperialism" on Guåhan to historicize how colonial agriculture, militarism, urbanism, and tourism have displaced spiritual beliefs about the land, changed traditional land tenure systems, removed CHamorus from the land, and contaminated the land.[21] Beyond analyzing the primary ecological themes of the literature discussed, I also explore how ecology is embodied in the primary structural and formal elements of these texts. Specifically, I will illustrate how narrative forms embody the "earth aesthetics" of a banyan tree. The phrase *earth aesthetics* is inspired by Édouard Glissant's idea of an "aesthetics of the earth," which refers to appreciating beauty even in environments ravaged by colonialism and degradation.[22] I use "earth aesthetics" to more simply refer to the aesthetic designs of nature. For example, the earth aesthetics of a banyan tree refers to its formal elements of woven, aerial roots. In the end, I affirm that the writings of Perez, Borja-Kicho'cho', and Hoppe-Cruz articulate a CHamoru identity and ecopoetics grounded in an environmental vision of mutual care, co-belonging, and healing.

Plotting CHamoru Ecopoetics

Before navigating the literary texts, allow me to first plot the routes and roots of CHamoru ecopoetics through the genealogies of Indigenous, Native American, postcolonial, trans-Pacific, and Pacific ecopoetics. Many Indigenous traditions maintain that the earth is an ancestor, all life is interconnected and sacred, and human beings should act according to the values of multispecies reciprocity, environmental sustainability, and mutual care.[23] Scholars of Native American and Native Pacific literary studies have highlighted how the primary themes in Native texts express the idea of the interconnection and interrelatedness of humans and nature, the centrality of land and water in the conception of Indigenous genealogy, identity, and community, and the importance of knowing the Indigenous histories of a place. Moreover, they show how Native writers employ ecological images, metaphors, and symbols to critique colonial and Western views of nature as an empty, separate object that exists for men to control and profit from.[24]

Literature as a critique of colonial views of nature is a key point in Graham Huggan and Helen Tiffin's *Postcolonial Ecocriticism* (2010) and the critical anthology *Postcolonial Ecologies: Literature and the Environment*, edited by Elizabeth DeLoughrey and George B. Handley (2011). The introduction of the latter book develops a postcolonial frame for the study of literature, nature, environmentalism, and ecological thought—broadly referred to as ecocriticism. In a postcolonial context, postcolonial ecocriticism reckons with the devastations of ecological imperialism such as the displacement of Indigenous peoples from ancestral lands, the establishment of plantation, industrial, and chemical agriculture, the development of tourism and urbanism, the contamination caused by militarism and nuclearism, rapid deforestation and desertification, the extraction of natural resources and Indigenous remains, and species extinction and endangerment. In addition, these scholars foreground how "precolonial epistemologies of place . . . survive and are transformed and translated through narrative."[25] These transformed and transformative stories articulate land as a "primary site of postcolonial recuperation, sustainability, and dignity," reinforcing the idea that the ecopoetic imagination is "vital to liberating land from the restrictions of colonialism and . . . from neocolonial forms of globalization."[26]

The "trans-Pacific" and Pacific turns in ecocriticism complement the Indigenous and postcolonial turns in the field. Rob Wilson, in "Oceania as Peril and Promise: Towards Theorizing a Worlded Vision of Trans-Pacific

Ecopoetics," highlights how the perils of ecological degradation demand a new, politically and culturally committed ecological worldview: "Oceania means not only having a sense of history and cultivating a set of attitudes and beliefs, it means cultivating a sense of belonging to the earth and ocean as a bioregional horizon of care."[27] He describes this movement as articulating "a vision of altered transnational belonging, ecological confederation, and trans-racial solidarity."[28] Literature is crucial to nurturing this worldview because "stories, images, art, dance, and legend give a deeper sense of Pacific belonging; long-woven networks of interconnected reciprocity prove crucial to this formation, as islands and oceans are connected, linked, and would counter the late-capitalist world from before, within, and after it."[29] The Pacific ecopoetic region of care is extended in Hsinya Huang's "Toward Transpacific Ecopoetics: Three Indigenous Texts" to include a "multispecies ecopoetics rooted in the indigenous stories and myths of the Pacific."[30] Within an imperial ecological framework, animals exist to benefit human beings; however, the "indigenous imagination in the transpacific context breaks down the division between human and nonhuman."[31] Through literature, Pacific writers aim to articulate the region as "a site of cobelonging and cohistory across species boundaries and racial/ethnic and cultural borders."[32] Several other scholars have shown how Pacific literature articulates Pacific ecological knowledge, practices, and struggles.[33]

Inspired by this scholarship, I contend that CHamoru ecopoetics articulates a CHamoru ecological identity and worldview that re-members the CHamoru creation story, reconnects CHamorus to the land and its sacredness, honors CHamoru ancestors and taotaomo'na, protests against further environmental degradation, and insists that land (along with literary representations of land) is a site of healing, belonging, and decolonization.

"Signs of Being: A Chamorro Spiritual Journey"

C. T. Perez is the author of "Signs of Being: A Chamorro Spiritual Journey" (1997), an unpublished, creative MA thesis that she completed in 1997 as part of her graduate work at the Center for Pacific Islands Studies at the University of Hawai'i, Mānoa.[34] Perez would return to Guåhan and become one of the most well-known CHamoru poets, even appearing on television reciting her poems—a testament to the power and influence of her writing. "Signs of Being" is a ninety-one-page manuscript composed mainly of poetry, with a few selections of short prose nonfiction. The manuscript is divided into five thematic chapters, or what Perez terms "passages": "Hinasso (Reflection)," "Finakmata (Awakening)," "I Fina'pos (Familiar Surroundings)," "Lala'chok (Taking Root)," and "I Senedda (Finding Voice)." Each poem or prose story is followed by endnotes, which include translations and references, and a prose commentary providing the author's own insight about her work.

Perez describes this multigenre, multilingual collection as a "documentary in the form of creative writing, on the politics of cultural identity and historical memory in the process of decolonization of the Chamorro mind and senses" ("Signs," ix). Through CHamoru literature, Perez aims to "encourage new approaches to Chamorro cultural history [because current] discussion[s] of Chamorro cultural identity primarily [focus] on the static approach to understanding culture" (viii). Here Perez critiques colonial cultural ideologies and speaks to the idea that literature is an important site for articulating contemporary CHamoru cultural identity. While Perez's thesis explores a broad range of themes, I examine the entries that focus on the environment. Through a close reading of the themes and forms of her work, I argue that she critiques the legacy of ecological imperialism on Guåhan and reclaims a CHamoru eco-theology and environmental ethics through which to symbolically heal the people and the land. Lastly, I will suggest that the interwoven form of the manuscript embodies a CHamoru earth aesthetics based on the form of a banyan tree.

The first poem we will turn to is "Kafe Mulinu," from the chapter "Finakmata (Awakening)." The title translates as "Ground Coffee," and the first two stanzas, which I quote in full below, capture the speaker drinking the caffeinated beverage in her home:

> Taste bitter.
> Taste sweet.
> We sit
> sipping
> coddling cups
> of brown liquid
> and yawn in awakening
> for the hour is late.

As we drink in
the brew,
our feet hesitate to rest
on what they know
too well
to be
concrete poured thick
over compacted wetlands.

Venetian-blinded windows
encase us in
conditioned air
conditioned minds
and keep us from seeing
keep us from feeling
the surrounding sesonyan.

("*Signs*," 17)

The poem takes place in the speaker's concrete home, which symbolizes development and a separation from the land. Perez draws a parallel between air-conditioned homes and the colonial conditioning of the mind, as well as the "Venetian-blinded windows" and the inability to see the surrounding "sesonyan," or wetlands, which have been compacted and "poured thick" with concrete. In the next two stanzas, the speaker invokes the taotaomo'na, the ancestral spirits that dwell within the environment:

Taotaomo'na,
our beloved ancestors
wail.
Cries from the past
whirl in the present
are hurled at our presence
but only blow at us
like a whisper.

Our eyes perk
our heads tilt

as if to listen.
We are roused to remember
Their pain is our legacy.

("*Signs,*" *17*)

To understand the pain of the speaker's "beloved ancestors," and before we move forward in the poem, it is important to understand the traumatic depths and histories of ecological imperialism in Guåhan. During Spanish colonialism, not only were CHamorus displaced from the land, but the land itself was transformed. Packed-earth roads and limestone bridges were built to connect the mission villages, and European-style farms were established. Land was cleared and razed to cultivate foreign crops such as coffee (a prominent symbol in the poem), corn, tobacco, cacao, and sweet potatoes, and to improve grazing conditions for introduced livestock such as cattle and horses. After severe depopulation due to warfare and disease, the surviving CHamoru population was given land allotments, referred to as a lancho, or ranch, to grow crops for the priests, the garrison, and the foreign population, and to resupply the Spanish galleons. As Cynthia Ross Wiecko notes in "Jesuit Missionaries as Agents of Empire: The Spanish-Chamorro War and Ecological Effects of Conversion on Guam, 1668–1769":

> The natural environment sustained profound changes as introduced species exchanged from around Spain's global empire created an equally global imperial ecology. . . . Indeed, Guam's indigenous species and ancient introductions interwove with species from the Indian subcontinent, Southeast Asia, the Philippines, China, Africa, and the Americas to create a pan-tropical ecology. Thus, indigenous ironwood trees came to stand alongside introduced *tangantangan* trees from Nueva España. Philippine carabao might rest under the shade of a flame tree (*Delonix regia*) from Madagascar.[35]

Overall, Spanish religious and ecological imperialism subverted traditional land tenure systems and transformed the environment into a global, imperial plantation.

When the United States took possession of Guåhan in 1898, the Spanish "Crown lands" (nearly a third of the island) were ceded to the U.S. government. In 1899, the United States abolished the Spanish real-estate tax system, which was based on how much revenue one earned from one's property, and instituted a land tax system based on the size and type of land one owned. This new tax system forced the CHamorus who owned ranches into a difficult choice:

> either register their properties accurately and lose them because they could not pay the taxes, or not register their lands and lose them because they could not pay the taxes, or not register their lands and lose them because they were not properly registered. Many Chamorros who owned parcels in the villages as well as farmlands in rural areas had to decide which lots to save. When the naval government began finding "mistakes" in the declaration of the lot sizes, it began registering the lands as government property. Some of these declarations of "Crown" land took place over 35 years after the US took possession of Guam from Spain.[36]

This new policy slowly alienated many CHamorus from their land through foreclosure for delinquent taxes. In addition to appropriating more land, the U.S. naval government began construction throughout the island, creating drainage systems, new government buildings, a water distillation plant, water storage plants, outhouses, a telephone station, a military commissary, a post exchange, hospitals, and roads.[37] Moreover, the U.S. naval administration focused on building a colonial agricultural industry on Guåhan, which, as Elyssa J. Santos has shown in her thesis "'Practicing Economy': Chamorro Agency and U.S. Colonial Agricultural Projects, 1898–1941," worked to "inscribe notions of American patriotism and loyalty onto Chamorro bodies and instill into them western economic values and practices."[38] Even though the U.S. Navy was able to accomplish several development projects, lack of funding, high freight and labor costs, and cheap imported foods from Asia hampered more extensive development.[39]

From 1941 to 1944, the Japanese authorities also focused on increasing agricultural production and military fortification. The Japanese agricultural program conducted "deforestation, soil preparation, irrigation, and a 'back to the land' campaign."[40] One of the most urgent priorities was the production of rice. Ignoring private land titles, the Japanese authorities appropriated land to create rice paddies; more than a dozen rice farms were established throughout the island.[41] Individual CHamoru families were assigned small farms in order to cultivate food; however, the food was allotted first to the military, then to Japanese civilians, and lastly to CHamorus.[42] As the war progressed, agricultural labor was made compulsory for CHamorus, to support the Japanese war effort. In just three short years, Japan managed to utterly reshape Guåhan through colonial agriculture and industrialization.

During the three-week battle between the United States and Japan, the bombing and fighting devastated the environment of Guåhan, destroying many farms and homes. After the war, land that had been taken by the Japanese military became U.S. military farms and eventually fell under the jurisdiction of the U.S. Department of Agriculture. Two typhoons (in 1962 and 1963) destroyed nearly 90 percent of the island's buildings. The passage of the Guam Rehabilitation Act of 1963 by Congress allocated federal funds to mass-produce prefabricated concrete-and-rebar houses, built by the Kaiser Company, which "transplanted United States suburbia to Guam."[43] In the 1980s, hollow-block cement housing (also known as "hollow block concrete masonry units," or CMUs) was introduced, with amenities such as sewage disposal, air conditioning, and indoor kitchens.[44] As a result of this development, Guåhan would become the most developed and urbanized island in all of Micronesia.[45]

This centuries-long history of land dispossession, colonial agriculture, and suburban and urban development has not only alienated CHamorus from the land but also turned the voices and pain of i taotaomo'na into mere whispers under the suffocating weight of concrete, the hum of the air conditioner, and the next "numbing sip" of coffee. Despite all this, the speaker in Perez's poem can't ignore her ancestors' cries any longer, and the poem turns into a CHamoru linguistic landscape. The translation is included by Perez in the commentary of the poem, and I quote both here:

> Ai, mohon yanggen siña ta hungok,
>   yanggen siña ta nginge,
>   yanggen siña ta li'e.
>
> Mohon yanggen siña ta siente
> na ti apman esta i ora,
> siempre ti man manmatåtåchong hit . . .
>
> (If only we could hear,
> we could smell,
> we could see,

If only we could feel
That the hour is late,
we probably wouldn't be sitting . . .)[46]

("Signs," 18)

The repetition of "mohon" (to express desire, hope, or a wish), "yanggen" (if), and "ta" (we) creates a chant-like structure throughout the stanzas. In the passage, the speaker suggests that if only we could hear (hungok), smell (nginge), see (li'e), and feel (siente) our ancestors near, embedded in the environment, then we wouldn't be sitting around drinking coffee. The author's use of CHamoru language, when evoking the "sesonyan," perhaps speaks to the connection between Indigenous language and ecological biodiversity.[47] Furthermore, the fact that the CHamoru verses are not italicized—the usual convention to mark non-English language—suggests that these lines rise above a whisper and are typographically equal to the English language. The poem ends with the suggestion that if we do not reconnect with the land, then we will be left "thirsting, / heaving / groundless . . . tasting / bitterwithsweet" ("Signs," 18).

Another devastating force that has impacted the land is the development of a tourism industry on Guåhan. Perez addresses this theme directly in her poem "View of Tumon Bay," from the section "I Fina'pos (Familiar Surroundings)." The title ironically alludes to a tourist postcard, and the poem begins:

Big hotels
skew the view,
and as if what we've got
ain't enough
the gov. wants
to build
MORE! MORE! MORE!

I thought selling yourself
was illegal
in this great
Ter-ri-to-ry.

("Signs," 42)

Tumon is a village located on the northwest coast of Guåhan. Once a rich agricultural and fishing area, the land and beaches of Tumon were taken by the U.S. military and used for "R and R" ("rest and rejuvenation" or "rest and recreation," a term the military uses to refer to free time or vacation) before and after World War II. Rather than being returned to the original CHamoru landowners, these lands were transferred to the government of Guam, which then leased the land to private businesses to build hotels and resorts. A mass tourism industry began to develop in Guåhan after the U.S. Navy repealed the naval security clearance policy that restricted travel into and out of Guåhan in 1962. Guåhan was poised to become the "next American tourist island in the sun [after Hawai'i]."[48] Pan American Airlines had begun its operations in Guåhan in 1935, the Guam Visitors Bureau was established by the government in 1952, and the Guam International Air Terminal was established in 1966. Foreign investment from the United States and Japan, as well as thousands of foreign workers, spurred the development of hotels, restaurants, and other tourism-related businesses. By 1971, the Cliff Hotel, the Fujita Tumon Beach, the Continental Travelodge, the Hilton Hotel, and the Guam Dai Ichi Hotel had been constructed in Tumon.[49] And by 1985, the tourism industry generated two hundred million dollars annually. In 1988, almost 600,000 tourists visited; in 1995, over 1.5 million visitors arrived. Another wave of development flooded Tumon in 1997 with the construction of Planet Hollywood, Hard Rock Café, and the Westin Resort. The poem alludes to two governors ("gov.") of Guam, Joseph Ada (1987–94) and Carl Gutierrez (1995–2002), who aimed to increase the number of annual tourists to the island. Perez humorously critiques them for promoting "cultural activities for the purpose of selling Guam to tourists," as Keith Camacho once put it, echoing Haunani-Kay Trask's critique of tourism as "an insidious form of cultural prostitution."[50]

The speaker of the poem then responds to the governor not with stereotypical Native hospitality, but with Native resistance:

> Let ME
> tell you
> something,
> I don't feel much like waving,
> I DO NOT
> Welcome
> All
> Visitors
> Enthusiastically.
>
> *("Signs," 42)*

Despite the fact that the tourism industry is the major economic driving force in Guåhan, some see it as a form of neocolonialism. In "Enframing i Taotao Tano': Colonialism, Militarism, and Tourism in Twentieth Century Guam," Camacho shows how "many tourism industries in the Pacific privilege place over peoples, emphasizing the supposed unchanging European characterization of island beaches and weather as paradisiacal while portraying Pacific peoples as homogenous tokens of tourist exploitation."[51] Camacho locates the beginning of Guåhan's tourism industry in 1521, when Magellan first made landfall on the island and CHamorus began trading with European visitors. Camacho traces the modern tourism industry to the "American enframing of Guam as touristic" prior to 1898 through travel writing by whalers, missionaries, anthropologists, governors, and other visitors to the island. In addition, Camacho illustrates how the U.S. military contributed to the touristic endeavor by framing the land as feminized, virgin, and paradisiacal and the CHamoru people as essentially hospitable and happy. The intersecting system of militarism and tourism, or "militourism," has led to land dispossession, environmental pollution, commodification of culture, overpopulation, and overdevelopment.[52] The acrostic that ends the passage quoted just above, "Welcome / All / Visitors / Enthusiastically" (WAVE), refers to a 1995 promotional slogan created by the Guam Visitor Industry Education Council, which encouraged residents to wave at tourists. Part of the program included creating WAVE clubs in several of Guåhan's public elementary, middle, and high schools. Movie theaters in Guåhan also played thirty-second WAVE advertisements featuring people smiling and waving at tourists.[53] The speaker of the poem, having established a tone of anger and disgust, continues:

> You WAVE.
> My hands are
> too busy
> fanning away the stench
> of tourist industrial waste
> and praying
> for that
>   threatened silence
> "if there were
> no tourism"
> on Guam.

It's getting
so it's hard
to find a fish
anywhere
but a hotel dinner plate
these days.

("*Signs*," 43)

The speaker does not support the tourism industry because it also pollutes the land. Sewage, chemically treated waste, and grease from hotel toilets, gardens, and kitchens flow into Tumon Bay.[54] Reef removal, mechanized sand sweeping, and soil erosion have all negatively affected the ecology of Tumon.[55] Tumon was once a rich fishing area for manahak, or young rabbit-fish, but the fish are disappearing because the noise from jet skiers, kayakers, and swimmers scares them from their natural habitat.[56] When the poem's speaker prays for silence, she is ironically responding to an advertisement by the Guam Visitors Bureau that aimed to silence the critics of the tourism industry by threatening that there would be a "silence of cash registers" and loss of jobs if the industry failed.

The speaker then calls upon the government to diversify the local economy so that Guam is not entirely dependent on the environmentally and culturally destructive tourism industry: "Tourism, / the ONLY industry? / Now that's / a hard fish / to swallow" ("Signs," 43). The speaker's humorous, searing sarcasm brings the poem to a dramatic close:

Maybe it's time to call
the legendary big fish
to come and chomp
Tumon
back to the sea,
but you'd probably
just find a way
to sell that,
too.

("*Signs*," 44)

In a well-known CHamoru legend, a giant fish began eating the middle of Guåhan, and the people knew that if they didn't stop the fish the whole island would be devoured. A group of young women wove their long hair into a net and sang beautiful songs to lure the fish to the surface. When the fish emerged, they cast their net and saved the island.[57] While her ancestors were terrified of this monstrous fish, Perez ironically suggests that CHamorus should call on it to return and devour the tourism industry, which has become the figurative monster that is now destroying the island. Throughout this poem, Perez's short lines, enjambments, and capital letters create an urgent, angry rhythm that chomps, so to speak, at the white space of the page, as if the speaker herself is biting away at the legitimacy and desirability of tourism.

With all of the changes that have occurred throughout the island's history, Perez hopes to wake up and reconnect to the land. Another poem, "Strange Surroundings," speaks to this theme and appropriately appears in the chapter "Finakmata (Awakening)." This poem describes how the speaker's island home has become so unfamiliar that she feels "lost in a wilderness / not of my making" ("Signs," 21). In the commentary to this poem, Perez writes that Guåhan has become "developed beyond recognition" and laments the fact that people are no longer "able to walk through villages, family ranches, beaches and jungle areas to find respite in familiar verdant surroundings and the free harvest of betelnut and *pupulu* (pepper leaves chewed with betelnut), fruit, fish, game, wood, flowers, and leaves" (23). Guåhan's hålom tåno, or deep jungle, is no longer a space for "retreat and rejuvenation"—perhaps a linguistic play on and juxtaposition against militarized "rest and recreation." Because of this, the speaker yearns to be pulled from the "brackish waste" of urban development and return to "the finest wet air / of our deepest hålom tåno, / our deepest jungle, / to find the graces of / the Ones Who Walked Before" (21). To the speaker, the "healing powers" can only be found in Guåhan's deepest jungles, guarded by the "Ones Who Walked Before," the taotaomo'na, "the keepers of the land" (21). As in "Kafe Mulinu," Perez invokes the linguistic ecology of the CHamoru language ("hålom tåno") to lead the reader toward a recognition of CHamoru ancestors, who are everywhere present and constitutive of the environment itself. Thus, Perez once again suggests that a connection to more-than-human nature and the ancestors is necessary to heal and restore the abundance of our hålom tåno and the ecological ethics of communal sharing, or inafa'maolek.

This reconnection to the land is further emphasized in the preface of "Signs of Being," in which Perez retells the CHamoru creation story: "From legends we know that the Chamorro people claim their origins from the islands themselves. The story is told of the first two beings, Puntan and Fu'una. It was from her brother's body that the sister, Fu'una, made the sky, and all that we find in nature" ("Signs," iv). Perez further illustrates the importance of connecting to our ancestors in the title essay, "Signs of Being—A Chamorro Spiritual Journey," which also appears in the chapter "Finakmata (Awakening)." She writes:

> It is not in words spoken that we have been taught, but rather in the silent teachings of our *Saina*. What we learn is to open ourselves to the "collective memory" of our People who came before us and help us to move ahead—*I Taotaomo'na*. They show us how to remain in spiritual love and connectedness with each other and our homelands. ("Signs," 24)

Saina translates as "elder" or "parent" and refers to both recent and distant ancestors, including i taotaomo'na. By opening ourselves to "collective memory," or the oral stories and literary genealogies of our ancestors, CHamorus will learn how to once again love and care for each other and the land.

Another crucial aspect of Perez's CHamoru eco-theology is the importance of honoring the power of women and the matrilineal customs of ancestral CHamoru culture, customs that were suppressed by Christian conquest and patriarchal Spanish, Japanese, and American rule. In the preface to "Signs of Being," Perez explains that during her childhood she was called Hagan Ita, which translates as "daughter" or "blood" of Ita, her mother's name ("Signs," vii). As CHamoru language scholar Kenneth Gofigan Kuper has explained, *håga'* means "blood" and *håga* means "daughter":

> This beautifully reflects the matrilineal nature of Chamorro society where land and heritage are given and traced through your mother, and where women have the ultimate respect. Your daughter would be your blood because she continues your lineage and produces those who will care for your land. It is through her that life is perpetuated and it is through her that our people continue to exist.[58]

The theme of CHamoru womanhood is further developed in the poem "Sky Cathedral," which appears in the chapter "Lala'chok (Taking Root)." In the poem, the speaker describes the relationship between herself and the spirit of her deceased grandmother:

Nåna lives
in jewelled nights,
stars
like candles
lit
in a sky cathedral.

("Signs," 61)

By figuring the stars as jewels and the sky as a cathedral, Perez refigures the earth as a sacred space, as opposed to a Catholic cathedral with its candles and gold. Nåna, which can be translated as "mother" or "grandmother," dwells in the "dancing light" of "gualåffon" (the full moon), and, as the poem progresses, she visits the speaker, sings to her, and strokes her hair with "moonbeam fingers" (61). The speaker can even feel Nåna's hair as it drapes her in the past. The recognition of seeing her Nåna living within nature allows the speaker to see herself within the genealogy that connects humans to the environment:

I am Nåna's daughter
born of earth and sky
scented breath
of salted breeze
surrounding seas
receive my soul
as Nåna takes
my hand
to pray.

("Signs," 62)

In the commentary to this poem, Perez describes how the sharing of prayer "endears and connects generations within a family to each other" (64). Commonly, this prayer is expressed through the Catholic rosary; however, throughout the manuscript Perez instead prays to i saina, i taotaomo'na, Puntan and Fu'una, and the earth itself. "Sky Cathedral," then, is not only "an expression of a grandmother's love and a granddaughter's inheritance of a legacy of Chamorro spiritual vitality"; it is also "about connecting generations by their continued respect and love of ancestors as they manifest themselves in nature" (64).[59]

In addition to articulating a CHamoru ecopoetics through the primary themes of her work, I argue, Perez articulates ecological consciousness through the structural form of "Signs of Being." The manuscript contains five prose essays interspersed approximately fifteen to twenty pages apart, both opening and closing with one. Between each prose essay are poems with accompanying pages of "notes" and "commentaries." Visually, the prose essays are dense pages of text, while the left-justified lyric poems resemble roots reaching down the page. I suggest that this form reflects the earth aesthetics of i trongkon nunu. The prose essays symbolically represent a textual tree trunk, while the poems symbolically represent the auxiliary (or aerial) roots. Since the poems, notes, and commentaries are connected, they weave and fuse into braided units. Because it mimics the structure of i trongkon nunu, we experience the manuscript itself as a dwelling space for the ancestors and a space for the speaker to honor and speak to ancestral spirits.

Throughout "Signs of Being," Perez laments and protests the ongoing ecological imperialism caused by development, tourism, and missionization. She shows how these colonial forces have paved over and polluted the land, as well as displaced and disconnected CHamorus from the land and the spirits that dwell there. However, Perez also insists that literature is a site of reconnection, reimagination, and revitalization because it creates a space for us to remember the sesonyan and hålom tåno, to listen the voices of i saina and i taotaomo'na, to retell the CHamoru creation story of Puntan and Fu'una (the ancient root of all CHamoru literature), and to reclaim the power of CHamoru women. Wayreading the form of Perez's manuscript as an embodiment of the earth aesthetics of i trongkon nunu further illustrates how literature creates a symbolic space in which to articulate a CHamoru ecological identity. "Signs of Being" teaches us that by honoring, respecting, and caring for more-than-human nature, we can also wake up, reroot ourselves in the sacredness of the land, and heal our wounds.

"I Kareran i Palåbran Måmi—The Journey of Our Words"

Thirteen years after Perez submitted "Signs of Being: A Chamorro Spiritual Journey" for her MA degree at the Center for Pacific Islands Studies, two CHamoru women from Guåhan, Kisha Borja-Kicho'cho' and Anghet

Hoppe-Cruz, submitted a collaborative, creative MA thesis to the same program. Their manuscript, titled "I Kareran i Palåbran Måmi—The Journey of Our Words" (2010), echoes Perez's manuscript because its title focuses on the theme of the journey and because it includes both poetry and prose.[60] Borja-Kicho'cho' and Hoppe-Cruz were born and raised on Guåhan. Hoppe-Cruz migrated to Hawai'i in 1997, while Borja-Kicho'cho' migrated in 2004. In Hawai'i, they came to terms with the devastations of colonialism in the Pacific and the pain of being separated from their home island and culture. Their journeys intertwined in 2008, when they met in a graduate class, Learning Oceania, a required course in their degree program. They then decided to collaboratively write their creative MA project and include a community-engaged component. Aligned with other Indigenous methodologies, the authors aimed to "decolonize western curricula and the field of Pacific Islands Studies by choosing the communal over the individual and honoring our oral histories/storytelling through using poetry as a means to heal, to feel empowered, to be resilient, to 'write' the wrongs" ("Kareran," 3).[61] Through their collaboration, Borja-Kicho'cho' and Hoppe-Cruz became more than daughters of Guåhan; they became "sisters" (3).

The overall structure of "I Kareran i Palåbran Måmi" also embodies the earth aesthetics of i trongkon nunu. The manuscript comprises five chapters, several of which are collaboratively written. The authors composed chapter 1 together so that their voices interweave as they articulate the purpose and overall mission of the work. Chapter 2, which features two essays by Borja-Kicho'cho', and chapter 3, which features two essays by Hoppe-Cruz, weave together to form the major critical component. Chapter 4 contains two sections called "Reflections," in which the authors take turns reflecting on their collaboration and community-engaged events. Chapter 5 is made up entirely of poetry; however, instead of dividing the chapter into two sections (one section for Borja-Kicho'cho' and one for Hoppe-Cruz), the authors' poems alternate in groups of one to four poems. Significantly, the poems themselves do not include the authors' names, emphasizing communal making.[62] The overall effect of these formal choices is to create a complex woven pattern, similar to the aerial roots and compound trunks of the banyan tree, in which the voices of the authors intertwine, fuse, and journey from Hawai'i toward their home island of Guåhan. Just by wayreading the interwoven table of contents, we see a sign that "I Kareran i Palåbran Måmi" is articulated as a dwelling space of ecological ethos, ancestral Indigenous voices, and decolonial resistance.

Throughout the manuscript, Borja-Kicho'cho' and Hoppe-Cruz expose the devastating impacts of militarism on Guåhan. Both authors center their protests on the ongoing plans for a military buildup on the island. In 2006, the United States and Japan announced a major "realignment" of U.S. military forces and operations in the Asia-Pacific region, which would include one of the largest military buildups and relocations in U.S. history. This "mega-buildup" would include the construction of facilities to house and support the transfer of 8,600 marines and their 9,000 dependents from Okinawa to Guam, as well as 7,000 transient navy personnel, 600–1000 army personnel, and 20,000 foreign workers.[63] Additionally, the buildup would establish an air and missile defense task force, a live firing range complex, and the creation of a deep-draft wharf in Apra Harbor for nuclear-powered aircraft carriers. As the "westernmost sovereign territory of the United States," Guåhan allows the military to conduct operations with maximum "freedom of action."[64] Hoppe-Cruz warns: "As the day draws near for the buildup, land continues to be cleared, and paved over, pipes fitted, lines drawn, and more signs going up that say: NO TRESPASSING—FEDERAL PROPERTY" ("Kareran," 65). Borja-Kicho'cho' points to how the military buildup would result in effects ranging from "land condemnations, the displacement of our people, unhealthy and unsustainable water and other natural resource issues, to threats on our culture, environment, and social lifestyle" (36).

In the poem "To the Peoples of Nations Under US Occupation," Borja-Kicho'cho' specifically addresses the theme of militarism. The poem opens:

I come from a land,

a small island,
lined with fences
where my people
are used to looking
at the lands of our ancestors
through holes.

("Kareran," 166)

The militarism of Guåhan has a long history, dating back to the Spanish era. Between 1671 and 1835, the Spanish built fourteen fortifications of various types and sizes, including stockades, half-enclosed parapets, and open batteries.[65] After 1898, the United States also militarized its new territory, establishing its own bases and installations. During the Japanese occupation, the authorities initiated mining and logging efforts to generate lumber for military construction, firewood, and charcoal. Forced CHamoru labor was used to construct several airfields, munitions storage depots, pillboxes, real and dummy cannons, man-made caves, and tank traps.[66] After the reoccupation of Guåhan by the United States, the Department of Defense aimed to develop the island into a more substantial military base, second only to Pearl Harbor in Hawai'i. In the postwar years, the U.S. military took nearly 50 percent of Guåhan's landmass (about 75,000 acres) through purchase, lease, or condemnation (most of which was coercive and extralegal) to build bases. Today, the U.S. military occupies about 30 percent of Guåhan's landmass, making the island one of the most militarized places in the world.

One of the most prominent signifiers of this militarization is the ubiquitous presence of barbed-wire fences that demarcate military land and civilian land. Moreover, the fences represent all the land that was taken from the CHamoru people. As Borja-Kicho'cho' states in the opening of her poem, CHamorus are used to looking through fences at the lands of our ancestors. The poem continues:

> I come from a people,
>
> a small people,
> lined with wrinkles
> deeply entrenched canyons
> displayed on their faces,
> each red vein in their bloodshot eyes
> leading to a time
> of death
> struggle
>
> War.
>
> *("Kareran," 166)*

The decades-long U.S. military presence has caused severe environmental devastation, which has led to major health disparities among CHamorus. Eighty contaminated military dump sites currently exist on the island. The now-civilian Ordot landfill (a former military dump site) contains seventeen toxic chemicals. The same seventeen pollutants are also found in the landfills located over the island's aquifer at Andersen Air Force Base. In the 1970s, the military used the waters around Guåhan as a decontamination site during its nuclear testing in the Pacific, which resulted in massive radiation and strontium 90 exposure. During the Vietnam War, Agent Orange and Agent Purple, which were used as defoliants, were stored on Guåhan in drums. Military dumping and nuclear testing also contaminated the Pacific with PCBs and radiation, polluting Guåhan's largest barrier reef system and poisoning fish and fishing grounds. In parallel, CHamorus disproportionately suffer high incidences of various kinds of cancer and neurodegenerative diseases.[67] Despite all these damages, "To the Peoples of Nations Under US Occupation" continues to insist that Guåhan and the CHamoru people are strong and resilient. The speaker hopes that Guåhan will one day be free and no longer "confined / by guns, fences, and national security" ("Kareran," 166). The poem ends with a powerful statement of resistance when the speaker states that if we ever forget why we are struggling against militarism, "there will be / 'No Trespassing' signs / to remind us" (177).

In addition to militarism, Borja-Kicho'cho' also addresses how the tourism industry has polluted the land in her poem "Walking Through Tomhom," echoing Perez's poem "View of Tumon Bay" (Tomhom is the Indigenous name for Tumon). The poem opens with a nightmarish vision of ecological devastation:

> I had a dream last night.
> I was walking through the jungle,
> and as I passed each tree,
> they collapsed right beside me.
> The ground was dug up,
> the naked raw earth exposed.
>
> How could this happen—
>   to our tåno'
>   to our mañaina
>   to our manggåfa
>   to us?
>
>   The big strong håyon nunu
>   the taotao mo'na hid in
>   were no more.
>
> *("Kareran," 139)*

This seemingly apocalyptic vision reflects the reality of tourist development on Guåhan. To build the hotels, roads, and restaurants of Tomhom, CHamoru families were removed from the land and the jungle was bulldozed and cleared. Even the sacred banyan trees were removed. The speaker asks: How could this happen to our land, our ancestors (mañaina), our family (manggåfa)? This list shows that there is a genealogical connection between CHamorus and the land; as such, any harm done to the land harms us too. The speaker's pain is so deep that she screams, cries, and falls:

> I fell to the ground,
> my palms touching
>   the unfamiliar earth,
> my eyes searching
>   for the old håyon nunu,
> my ears open
>   to the calling of our mañaina.
>
> I didn't know this earth.
> I couldn't see the trees.
> But
> in the distance,
> I could hear:
>
> "Munga ma'åñao, hagå-hu.
> Munga ma'åñao.
> Ningai'an na in dingu hao."
>
> "It's okay, our daughter.
> It's okay.
> We will never leave you."
>
> *("Kareran," 139)*

Like Perez, Borja-Kicho'cho' finds herself in unfamiliar surroundings. In order to awaken from this nightmare, she has to use all her senses to feel and listen for the signs of her ancestors. Through this interaction, she is reminded that CHamorus are "i manaotao tåno' yan tåsi, the people of the land and ocean, our people, us" (8).

Now let us turn to three poems by Anghet Hoppe-Cruz that focus on militarism, environmental injustice, and gender. The first, entitled "BRAVO for Heart and Soul," addresses the impact and legacy of nuclear testing in the Marshall Islands (an archipelago near Guåhan in the Micronesia region). Between 1946 and 1958, the United States detonated sixty-seven nuclear weapons in the Marshall Islands, destroying entire islands, creating massive craters in the lagoons, irradiating the lands, waters, and bodies of the Marshallese people, and displacing the people from their islands.[68] Hoppe-Cruz's poem, whose title refers to Castle Bravo, the name of one of the nuclear tests, uses the analogy of rape to describe the violent acts of nuclearism:

> BRAVO is equivalent to
> 1000
> Hiroshima
> BOMBS BOMBS BOMBS
> 1000
> Big Fat Dicks
> Penetrating Mother Earth
> . . . .
> Tainting Life
> Contaminating her Daughter's Womb
> . . . .
> **Disfigured Disheartened Injustice**
> **BRAVO**
> **the equivalent of 1000 Hiroshima**
> **BOMBS**
> **BOMBSBOMBS**
> **B**
> **O**
> **M**
> **B**
> **S**

("Kareran," 142–43)

The nuclear bombs detonated in the Marshall Islands were far more powerful than the nuclear bomb that ravaged Hiroshima. Hoppe-Cruz compares the bombs to "Big Fat Dicks" raping "Mother Earth," tainting, or irradiating, the ecosystem, and disfiguring the womb—a reference to the horrific fact that Marshallese women who were exposed to the radiation would miscarry disfigured fetuses (sometimes described as "jelly babies"). The poem ends in the center of the page as the typeface emboldens and visually embodies the phallic mushroom-cloud shape of a nuclear detonation. By making these connections, Hoppe-Cruz draws our attention to the relationship between militarism, environmental injustice, and gendered violence.

Hoppe-Cruz continues to elucidate this theme in the poem "Security's Whore." The poem begins: "'i'm writing in captivity' / a daughter of colonialism / and / security's whore" ("Kareran," 178). These lines reference Hawaiian poet and scholar Haunani-Kay Trask, who authored the book *From a Native Daughter: Colonialism and Sovereignty in Hawai'i* and the article "Writing in Captivity: Poetry in a Time of Decolonization."[69] Throughout her work, Trask critiques both the military-industrial complex and the tourism industry, and she has articulated the relationship between militarism, tourism, environmental contamination, and violence against the bodies of women. Hoppe-Cruz's poem describes how the islands of Guåhan and Hawai'i are treated as whores to the military's national "security," their health and the bodies of their people simply used for military purposes. The poem ends with the powerful line "my children will reap the fruits of sacrifice" ("Kareran," 179). The use of the word "sacrifice" is pointed, as it alludes to how soldiers and citizens are asked to "sacrifice" themselves for the security needs of the nation, as well as to how Pacific islands and Native islanders have become "sacrifice zones" for the U.S. military. Moreover, this statement could allude to the fact that sexual violence against women increases in places that are militarized, especially places near military bases. Both Guåhan and Hawai'i, along with other places that host U.S. military bases, such as Okinawa, South Korea, and the Philippines, have experienced high rates of rape and sexual assault perpetuated by soldiers against local women.[70] In response, women have organized and formed groups advocating for demilitarization, decolonization, and environmental justice in order to create "genuine security," since the claim that U.S. militarism gives people and islands "security" is clearly false when it comes to the security of women's bodies and the environment, which are intertwined. For example, in 2007, a group of women on Guåhan formed Fuetsan Famalao'an (which translates as "Strength of Women") to address the impacts of the proposed military buildup. In 2008, members from the group met with members of Okinawan Women Act Against Military and

Violence who visited Guåhan. As a result, women from Fuetsan Famalao'an joined the International Women's Network for Genuine Security, a trans-Pacific feminist network founded in Okinawa in 1997.[71] This network aims to "redefine security, especially for women, children, and the environment." Its members "envision a world of genuine security based on justice, respect for others across national boundaries, and economic planning based on local people's needs." They strive to "build and sustain a network of women to promote, model, and protect genuine security in the face of militarism" and to create "societies free of militarism, violence, and all forms of sexual exploitation . . . and to ensure the safety, well-being, and long-term sustainability of all our communities."[72] As Sylvia Frain highlights in "Women's Resistance in the Marianas Archipelago: A US Colonial Homefront and Militarized Frontline," CHamoru women question the notion of "militarized security," "protection," and "the masculinist ideal of national security," and oppose the further militarization of the Marianas and the gendered violence that comes along with it.[73] Hoppe-Cruz's poems embody transnational and trans-Pacific solidarity through the lens of gendered violence and demilitarization, as well as through the mission of creating "genuine security" for women, children, and the environment. We can even think of this kind of solidarity through poetry as another exemplification of banyan tree aesthetics, in the sense that Hoppe-Cruz weaves together the aerial roots of women from different islands.

The final poem by Hoppe-Cruz that I will discuss is titled "My Name Is Truth," and it makes a connection between militarized gendered violence and other kinds of domestic and intimate partner violence (Hoppe-Cruz has also worked in the field of domestic violence advocacy). This poem is longer than the others: three pages in total, composed in a mix of long sentences that form their own stanzas with shorter phrases, some of which are enjambed. The first page of the poem shares various stories of domestic abuse, and the first of these stories reads:

> My Name is Silence
> I once saved Mommy's life when I was 6
> I simply refused to leave her side as
> Daddy
> held a gun to her head.
>
> *("Kareran," 200)*

The survivors of these abuse stories are not revealed by name, so they could be anyone, and these lines show how abuse can detonate into shrapnel of trauma. After a few other stories of abuse are shared, the poem makes this profound statement:

> My name is Silence
> I am a Man.
> I am a Woman.
> I once was a Child.
> Look around; Open your eyes to the many Names of Silence
> That take Form.
>
> *("Kareran," 201)*

The poem insists that domestic abuse can happen to anyone; however, those who experience violence often do not speak up to share their stories—they become "Silence." Despite this understandable silence, Hoppe-Cruz invites us to confront this abuse through poetry because poetry is how silences "take Form" and become story. The poem then makes a connection between domestic abuse and militarized violence:

> Slit after slit numbing the fact that the devil, loving uncle to all, sleeps with her, loving her the most at night.
> Mother Earth bombed, Kwajalein, her descendants bear the fruit of
> deformed injustice
> . . . .
> The dumping of US nuclear waste off the Wai'anae Coast, the ocean our playground.
>
> *("Kareran," 201)*

In these lines, Hoppe-Cruz juxtaposes various kinds of violence, even weaving in language from her other poem about nuclear testing in the Marshall Islands and her poem about Hawai'i, where the Wai'anae Coast is located. After all these horrific stories of abuse, the speaker proclaims:

> My name WAS silence.
> It is now Truth, and
> I tell stories.

Truths that I once denied.
Truths that were buried from me, for my protection.
For Uncle Sam
. . . .
Truths that once spoken
can no longer be
IGNORED.
Concretized, I tell stories to heal.

("Kareran," 202)

Here the speaker shows that once a story is told, it is no longer named Silence but instead becomes Truth. These truths about domestic and militarized gendered violence have formerly been denied, but once they are spoken into stories, they can no longer be ignored. As Camarin Meno and Nicole Allen highlight in "Exploring Community Narratives of Violence Against Women Among Domestic Violence Responders in Guam," there is growing concern about violence and sexual assault against CHamoru women, and there needs to be a closer analysis of culture and colonialism in order to improve community and professional responses to this violence.[74] With that in mind, we can understand Hoppe-Cruz's poem as insisting on the importance of storytelling in order to empower, heal, and offer hope to women and survivors.

Throughout "I Kareran i Palåbran Måmi," Borja-Kicho'cho' and Hoppe-Cruz highlight the vital role of CHamoru women, daughters, mothers, and sisters in the resistance against militarized and colonial gendered violence, and also in the articulation of a matrilineal CHamoru eco-consciousness. Borja-Kicho'cho's poem "Nu i Che'lu-hu Palao'an" articulates this theme beautifully. The poem begins:

Like the two lovers,
the sisters tied their hair
and together
they jumped off
Puntan Dos Amantes
into the tåsi,
cleansing themselves
of all

the pain,
mistrust,
hurtful words,
awkward moments
of silence.

In this ocean,
the ocean of their Mother,
they immerse themselves
regaining strength,

Loving each other all over again.

("Kareran," 162)

This poem alludes to, and rearticulates, a well-known CHamoru folktale known as "Puntan Dos Amåntes," or "Two Lover's Point." There are several variations of this story. One involves two CHamorus who fall in love, but their love is unacceptable and forbidden because they are from different social classes within CHamoru society.[75] They are banished from their villages and, instead of living in exile while being pursued by their relatives, they tie their hair together, jump from a high cliff, and drown together in the ocean. Another version of the story emerged during the Spanish era. The story goes: The parents of a wealthy Spanish-CHamoru mestizo family aim to arrange a marriage between their daughter and a Spanish captain. However, the daughter does not want to marry the captain, so she flees her home. While away from home, she meets a young CHamoru man from a modest family, and they fall in love. Her father, the captain, and a group of Spanish soldiers pursue the lovers until they trap them at the edge of a cliff. The two lovers decide to tie their hair together in a single knot and jump off the cliff into the ocean, never to be seen again.[76] Borja-Kicho'cho' and Hoppe-Cruz rearticulate this folktale as a story about two sisters faced with the trauma and pain of the subject matter they write about, and perhaps also about the difficulties of the process of completing a collaborative thesis. The ocean, which gives them strength and healing, is cast as a mother figure, further emphasizing the importance of understanding the relationship between gender and nature. Instead of drowning like the figures in the folktale, the sisters, with their hair still connected, rise "like dolphins / and jump / into the air of their Mother" ("Kareran," 162). While in the ocean, they hear the "såyan tasi of their father" say: "It's time to go back. / Nånan Tåno' is calling for you" (162). The "såyan tasi" (vessel of the sea) is a canoe, which is figured here as the voice of their father telling the sisters to come back because Nånan Tåno', or Mother Earth, is calling them. When the sisters return to the land, their hair is untied and they press their bodies to the sand to listen to Nånan Tåno', whose words end the poem:

> "Fanmanaguaiya.
> Fana'asi'e'.
> Yan hassuyi mo'nana,
> na en fanafa'maolek."
>
> "Love each other.
> Forgive each other.
> And always remember,
> to take care
> of each other."
>
> *("Kareran," 163)*

Nånan Tåno' teaches the poet-sisters the importance not only of mutual care, but also the deep history of CHamoru women in their role as "culture-bearer, culture preservationist, and agent of change."[77]

Throughout the manuscript, Borja-Kicho'cho' and Hoppe-Cruz honor many other Pacific women authors who have contributed to sovereignty and literary movements.[78] Their work embodies what Laura Souder, in "Unveiling Herstory: Chamorro Women in Historical Perspective," called "the ultimate power of women as the source of life and controller of their environment."[79] Alongside Souder, who wrote *Daughters of the Island—Contemporary Chamorro Women Organizers on Guam* (1992), other CHamoru scholars have discussed the importance of CHamoru women, culture, and identity. For example, Sharleen Santos-Bamba explores the identity of Chamorro women as bearers of Chamorro culture, land, and language in her dissertation, "The Literate Lives of Chamorro Women in Modern Guam."[80] Even though CHamoru women have often been envisioned as rooted bodies that represent a blood connection to the land, scholar Christine Taitano DeLisle explores the complexities of CHamoru feminisms, mobilities, and subjectivities in her extensive research.[81] Leiana San Agustin Naholowa'a examines the theme of mothering and develops the concept of "Chamorro feminist indigeneity" in her thesis "Beyond Matrifocality: A Literary Analysis of Mothering in Chamorro Narratives of Guam," which also centers the power of women in CHamoru culture.[82] These scholars, like Borja-Kicho'cho' and Hoppe-Cruz, all affirm the importance of women as the source of CHamoru life, wisdom, empowerment, eco-consciousness, and resistance.

Another powerful aspect of Borja-Kicho'cho' and Hoppe-Cruz's project, and a reflection of inafa'maolek, is their collaboration on a series of community-engaged poetry events conducted between 2009 and 2010, during which they read their poems and facilitated talk-story sessions about the issues in their work. Chapter 4 of "I Kareran i Palåbran Måmi" consists of each author's reflections on the events. Similar to the form of the manuscript, both poets take turns speaking during the readings, "like the ebb and flow of waves" ("Kareran," 85). The poetry readings created spaces for "Chamoru women to speak; instill empowerment in our people; [and] share the Chamoru ways of thinking and doing things" (86). After the performances, the audiences were broken into groups and encouraged to share their thoughts. As the authors note, "This created links for those who attended [and] allowed us to do exactly what we often become too busy for us to do: talk and listen to each other" (97). According to the authors, the poems and the talk-story sessions aided "the processes of raising awareness, decolonizing, and healing, looking at each other and communicating how we truly feel about who we are, where we come from, and the devastating atrocities that our Chamoru people, indigenous peoples in general, have been forced to suffer and live through" (115). In this way, Borja-Kicho'cho' and Hoppe-Cruz were able to weave themselves into the audience and weave individual audience members together. The interwoven quality of this collaboration and public engagement once again embodies the earth aesthetics of the banyan tree.

The final poem of "I Kareran i Palåbran Måmi" is titled "Continuing Our Journey." Since an individual author is not listed for this poem, I assume the poem is collaboratively written—a powerfully symbolic way to end this poetic interweaving. The poem is filled with many island and ocean images, including seashells, sands, and waves. Within the journey of the poem, Fu'una and Puntan are evoked to help guide the poets through a storm. Ending this collaborative project by referencing the collaborative CHamoru creation story is a poignant way to weave the end of the journey into a new beginning.

Today, Borja-Kicho'cho' is a doctoral candidate in the Department of Political Science (with a specialization in Indigenous politics) at the University of Hawai'i at Mānoa, and she is an instructor at the University of Guam. Hoppe-Cruz currently resides in the Waianae Coast of O'ahu, and she is a program counselor for a local nonprofit, the Institute for Native Peace Education and Culture, as well as an instructor at Leeward Community College. Despite the distance between them, they continue to weave together their work through a focus on Indigeneity, education, and community.

Even though ecological imperialism—through the processes of plantationism, militarism, tourism, and urbanism—has expropriated and contaminated the land to the point where even sacred banyan trees and the dwelling spaces of the taotaomo'na have been removed, Borja-Kicho'cho' and Hoppe-Cruz show that literature can be a space to rearticulate and reclaim a woman-centered CHamoru ecological identity. Wayreading the primary themes of their work highlights the importance of reconnecting to the land and to the ancestors that continue to dwell in it. Furthermore, wayreading the form of the manuscript—the structural interweaving of voices—reveals that it reflects the banyan tree's interweaving of aerial roots and formation of compound trunks. This form suggests that the manuscript itself is a symbolic banyan tree, a space from which its authors and readers can listen to, reconnect with, and learn from CHamoru ancestral spirits. This communal space offers the possibility of healing, not only for the land but for the taotao tåno' as well.

Conclusion

Throughout the history of ecological imperialism in Guåhan, CHamorus have continued to protest their displacement from the land, the expropriation of land for military, tourist, and urban development, and the contamination of the land. At the same time, many CHamoru writers and artists have created works that represent the sacredness of the land and critique ecological imperialism. In the context of Guåhan, we can conceptualize these efforts to protect, preserve, and revitalize the fragile environment as "ecological decolonization."

During the last seventy-five years, the struggle over land and land rights has been a central component of the contemporary CHamoru decolonization movement. As scholar Anne Perez Hattori notes in "Guardians of Our

Soil: Indigenous Responses to Post–World War II Military Land Appropriation on Guam," CHamorus resisted the military taking of land after the war.[83] Similarly, scholar Michael Perez, in "Contested Sites: Pacific Resistance in Guam to U.S. Empire," maps how the legal and political activism that emerged in the 1970s focused on the return of land occupied by the federal government and the military to the original landowners and other landless CHamorus. In the 1980s and 1990s, activists also focused on the desecration of ancient CHamoru burial grounds due to tourism and urban development.[84] Several CHamoru rights groups emerged, including I Nasion Chamorro and Organization of People for Indigenous Rights (OPI-R), that framed the struggle over land within the context of Indigenous rights. The activism of the period successfully advocated for the creation of the Chamorro Land Trust Act and the establishment of the Chamorro Land Trust Commission to implement the act. Even though the commission has issued deeds to more than 2,500 acres of land, thousands of CHamorus have remained on the waiting list for decades. In 1994, the Guam Excess Lands Act was passed, and the Guam Ancestral Lands Commission was later established to facilitate the transfer of unused federal property to the government of Guam; as of 2011, only 3,000 acres have been transferred.[85] These historic and modest gains in the struggle over land speak to this fact:

> The role native ownership of land plays in the preservation of Chamorro culture and social stability cannot be underestimated. Land is the only significant asset of the Chamorro people and it is the basis of family organization. It traditionally passes from generation to generation, creating family identity and contributing to the economic well-being of family members.[86]

Despite the fact that there is still much work to be done to return land to CHamorus and to protect the land, the ecological decolonization movement has taken vital steps.[87]

Alongside the political and legal activism centered on land reclamation, there exists a parallel movement to renarrate CHamoru land as sacred space and not simply as an idle asset for tourist or urban development or a strategic base for military training and operations. For example, during protests against the ongoing military buildup on Guåhan, several new activist groups emerged—namely, We Are Guåhan and Our Islands are Sacred—that emphasized the sacredness of land. One of the proposals for the military buildup was to transform an area of Guåhan known as Pågat, the site of an ancestral CHamoru village which houses many ancient artifacts and remains, into a live firing range complex, thus restricting access to Pågat. In a letter written by a coalition of University of Guam faculty and addressed to the Department of Defense, scholars highlighted the religious significance of Pågat:

> [The taotaomo'na] dwelling places can be found everywhere in Guam . . . but are known to have an especially strong presence in Pågat. . . . As a place of religious significance, Chamorros treat Pågat with great respect, and our generation's responsibility is to protect and nurture the site so that it is treated with the respect paid to the world's great cathedrals and temples.[88]

Additionally, many activists highlighted the fact that Pågat was home to several endangered species, particularly the Mariana eight-spot butterfly, and a possible future home for endangered bird species of Guåhan that currently survive in captivity.[89] One ongoing and irreversible effect of ecological imperialism in Guåhan has been the extinction and endangerment of more than two dozen native and endemic species of birds, mammals, reptiles, mollusks, and plants. This species loss has been caused by habitat destruction, environmental pollution, and the introduction of invasive species. After World War II, brown tree snakes arrived on Guåhan as stowaways on a U.S. military ship or aircraft. Having no natural predators, the snakes quickly multiplied and colonized the entire island. In just a few decades, thousands of native birds were killed, and most species either became entirely extinct or, in a few cases, were taken into captivity and are now bred in U.S. zoos.[90] The loss of birds in Guåhan is also reverberating through the island's ecology; without birds to spread and germinate seeds, many native trees may go extinct, and the tropical forests may experience desertification.[91]

The group Our Islands Are Sacred spearheaded a campaign that involved demonstrations during a Department of Defense public meeting, as well as at rallies in Hawai'i and the continental United States. One of their actions was to have participants create protest signs about why the islands are sacred to them, and then to post these photos online using the hashtag #OurIslandsAreSacred (which can be considered a literary act as well).[92] By articulating land as a sacred dwelling place of CHamoru spirits, contemporary CHamorus are articulating an ecological identity that is tied to genealogy and spirituality. Furthermore, this narrative strategy has also become a powerful political strategy to resist the idea that land is simply a base for militarism.

A poignant cultural revitalization project known as Lukao Fuha, meaning "a procession to Fuha," also emerged from the CHamoru ecological decolonization movement. Before Spanish colonization, CHamorus pilgrimaged to Fu'a Rock in Humåtak to honor Fu'una and Puntan. They made offerings and asked Fu'una to bless their seeds, fishing implements, and harvests. Because of religious colonialism, this tradition was suppressed and had not been exercised for centuries. However, on February 1, 2014, Our Islands Are Sacred and another CHamoru cultural group, Hinasso, revived this ancient eco-spiritual practice. According to the ancestral thirteen-month CHamoru calendar, the first day of February marks the CHamoru new year. As CHamoru genealogist Bernard Punzalan has written, the Lukao Fuha celebrated not only the new year but also "the birth of life emanating from the stories of Fo'na (Fu'una) yan Pontan (Puntan)."[93] The CHamoru creation story, having survived centuries of narrative repression, has once again birthed a CHamoru identity that is reconnected to the taotaomo'na and the sacredness of the land.

The creative writing of C. T. Perez, Anghet Hoppe-Cruz, and Kisha Borja-Kicho'cho' is part of this larger decolonial movement to articulate and reclaim an ecologically ethical CHamoru identity. Their work is exemplary of a CHamoru ecopoetics that aims to remember eco-theological stories, rearticulate CHamoru connection to the land, evoke the spirits of ancestors, and offer healing for the land and the taotao tåno'. As Borja-Kicho'cho' affirms: "Guåhu taotao Guam. I hagå'-hu ginen i tano' ini. I manggafå-ku ginen i tano' ini. I hale'-hu ginen i tano' ini. I am from Guam. My blood is from this land. My family is from this land. My roots are in this land" ("Kareran," 55). By wayreading their powerful works, we highlight the articulation of CHamoru ecological identity in the primary themes of their creative writing as well as the formal structures of their texts. Wayreading also reveals how the three authors employ a structural weaving that reflects the banyan tree's aerial roots and the resultant compound trunks. The authors are thus rerooting CHamoru ecological beliefs and visions onto the page, so that the page becomes a symbolic space where the voices of the ancestors can continue to dwell, and where future CHamorus and readers can commune and interweave with their voices.

CHAPTER 2

The CHamoru House of Story

Guma' Åcho' Latte and Na(rra)tive Architecture in the Poetry of Peter R. Onedera

> But what people erected above the earth those imposing masses, more than thirty feet high, well carved, regular, without sculpture nor any sign which fixes or which gives a clue, even of the probable epoch of their mysterious foundation? What has become of the architects?
>
> —Jacques Arago

Introduction

While the previous chapter wayread the symbolism of land in CHamoru literature, this chapter turns our attention to the symbolism of houses, and to the relationship between CHamoru poetry, housing architecture, cultural identity, and aesthetics. First I will introduce the origins, methods, functions, values, and aesthetics of the customary CHamoru housing structure known as guma' latte. Relatedly, I will detail the history of "architectural colonialism" on Guåhan, charting how colonial forces changed Indigenous dwelling spaces and consequently disrupted CHamoru housing practices and familial ties. I will then examine two poems from Peter R. Onedera's *Visions of a Chamoru* (1995) and *Taimanu na Ini* (2018) that relate to the theme of housing. I will show how Onedera's work embodies the form of the latte stone, which served as the foundation of CHamoru houses. Throughout, I will argue that his work can be theorized as an architectural space that rearticulates guma' latte housing design—or what I term "Na(rra)tive architecture"—to create a narrative home for CHamoru cultural identity.

Guma' Latte: CHamoru Housing Architecture

A customary CHamoru housing structure is known as guma' latte. *Latte* refers to the åcho' (stone) megaliths that formed the foundation of the guma'

FIGURE 3 Latte stone houses. Illustration by Jessica Vergel, 2020.

(house). An individual latte is composed of a haligi (vertical pillar) and a tasa (bowl-shaped capstone). The haligi ranges in height from three to nine feet and is wide at the base and narrow toward the top. The tasa sits atop the haligi with the help of a cavity or groove in the bottom of it. A large completed latte could weigh more than thirty tons. While smaller pillars and capstones were created from naturally pillar-shaped stones and inverted brain coral from the reef, larger pillars and capstones were carved from quarried limestone. To transport these massive stones, workers likely pulled them with rope, litters, and bipod levers. At the construction site, the haligi was placed in a large hole and packed with smaller stones. The tasa was likely pushed up an earth ramp to the top of the haligi.[1] Completed latte structures were arranged in parallel rows of at least four evenly spaced pairs, framing a rectangular space.[2] Even though most latte sets were built in coastal and inland areas, usually parallel to the shore or river, a small number were built perpendicular to the water. Once the latte stones were aligned, timbers and coconut-fiber rope were used to create a floor and an A-frame dwelling structure, with open doorways and windows, atop the latte stone foundation (see figure 3). The roof was thatched with woven palm leaves, pandanus, or sword grass. Besides houses, the architecture of the raised guma' latte was also utilized to construct schools, canoe houses, food sheds, and ceremonial spaces. Archaeologists date the beginning of latte stone construction and architecture to around 900 AD.[3]

Guma' latte architecture offered several practical benefits. The latte stones resisted rot, termites, and beetles; discouraged crabs and vermin searching for food; absorbed earthquake shocks and resisted typhoon winds; protected against flooding; allowed air to circulate; and provided a tactical defensive position. Artifacts recovered from the areas beneath the floors of these raised houses suggest that these areas were used as a cooking space (stone tools, stone mortars and pestles, ovens and cooking areas, storage and cooking vessels, shell and stone scrapers) and a work space (shells, fishhooks, hammer stones, shell adzes, stone drills, coral files, bone awls, and fishing implements).[4] Besides creating a raised, protected dwelling space and a work space, the guma' latte also provided a burial ground beneath the house. Archaeologists have found bones, jewelry, and even canoes buried between the latte and on each side of the house.[5] The use of local materials such as limestone, timber, and coconut leaves and fiber ensured that everyone had access to building materials. Furthermore, the shared labor of constructing the house strengthened kinship networks. Because thatched roofs do not hold up during typhoons, the frequent rebuilding and repairing became "collaborative, not individual endeavors . . . and a variety of kin [were] likely to assist. In addition, everyone [had] equal access to this type of assistance without needing any cash income."[6] Thatched houses also provided considerable social interaction because of their open design: "Cooking, eating, and visiting, for example, are not regular indoor activities; houses serve primarily as places to sleep and to store clothes and other personal items. Much of daily life occurs outside the houses themselves . . . the open structures ensure that these activities are quite public and visible."[7] Overall, guma' latte architecture created a practical space for eating, socializing, sleeping, and communing.

Beyond practicality, guma' latte architecture, materials, and construction methods housed symbolic meaning. Similar to other Indigenous dwelling spaces, guma' latte "demonstrate[s] local responses to natural environmental conditions, and incorporates design features supportive of cultural values and practices."[8] The spirits of the dead who were beneath the guma' latte could be "called upon by their descendants and relatives for a number of purposes. Primary among these functions was the assurance of good fortune to households."[9] By creating this burial space in which the dead could protect the living, guma' latte architecture "symbolized a sacred space for the Chamorros who buried the dead between the stones as part of that construct of space made sacred."[10] Thus, guma' latte is grounded in genealogy and in "the ancient Chamorros' concept of *aniti* (spirit), and a sense of origin, life and passing to the next life within—theoretically—the protection of the *latte*."[11] Additionally, the use of local materials reflects an ecological ethics of sustainability and a "fundamental connection of spirit and nature."[12] Since Indigenous settlement patterns are often symbolic,[13] we can interpret the proximity of guma' latte to a water source both as practical and as symbolic of a deep connection to and reverence for water as the source of life. Because thatched houses had to be constantly rebuilt after storms, they "represent self-sufficiency . . . and reciprocity, both within and between households."[14] The use of stone suggests a connection to the CHamoru creation story, in which our ancestral mother, Fu'una, transformed herself into a stone and birthed the CHamoru people, thus connecting the symbolism of the land as dwelling space for i taotaomo'na (ancestral spirits) to the symbolism of the house as dwelling space for i taotao tåno' (the living people of the land). Overall, guma' latte architectural design and construction reflected both practical concerns and the deeper symbolism of CHamoru identity, values, and customs.

Na(rra)tive Housing in the Poetry of Peter R. Onedera

Peter R. Onedera was born on Guåhan in 1953 and raised in the village of Sinahånña (Sinajana). He studied at the University of Guam and earned an MA in Micronesian studies. His thesis, which focused on CHamoru theater, was the first to be written entirely in the CHamoru language. He has published poetry, fiction, nonfiction, and plays.[15] He directed several of the plays for performance at the University of Guam Fine Arts Theater and other community theaters and schools throughout Guåhan.[16] His work explores themes of tradition, social issues, cultural identity, history, politics, and CHamoru experiences (some of his works are based on interviews with CHamoru manåmko', or elders). Besides being an author, Onedera was a CHamoru language professor at the University of Guam for many years. He founded the annual CHamoru language competition at the university, which brings together students of all ages from across the Marianas for a day of performance and competition—an important event to promote and honor

FIGURE 4 "Ancient Ruins of Columns Seen on the Island of Tinian," illustration by Jacques Arago for Louis de Freycinet's *Voyage autour du monde*, 1824. Courtesy of the Guam Public Library System.

CHamoru language. He has also served as the director of the Chamorro Language Commission, which developed a standardized orthography and dictionary, as well as creating language policies. In 2011, he was involved in establishing both the Chamorro Studies minor program at the University of Guam and the Chamorro Language Documents Reference Room at the university's Richard F. Taitano Micronesian Area Research Center, and he served as an advisor for *Guampedia*, an online encyclopedia. In 2003, he was one of the founding members and president of the first Guåhan storytelling and literary arts group, the Ginen i Hila' i Maga' Taotao Association—From the Tongues of the Noble People, which represents Guåhan at the Festival of Pacific Arts and hosts storytelling events on Guåhan every year.[17] In 2015, he was given the prestigious title of "Master Storyteller," or, in CHamoru, "Sainan Minenhalom Sinangan Ginen i Hila," by the Guam Council on the Arts and Humanities Agency.[18]

Onedera's impressive oeuvre deserves a book-length study of its own; but for the scope of this chapter, I will limit my analysis to his poetry from *Visions of a Chamoru* (1995) and *Taimanu na Ini* (2018). Specifically, I will discuss two poems that most directly relate to the theme of this chapter: guma' latte. First, *Visions of a Chamoru* is a twenty-four-page collection that is now out of print, though I accessed it in the archives of the Hawaiian and Pacific Collections at the Hamilton Library of the University of Hawai'i at Mānoa. *Visions of a Chamoru* contains twenty-four poems in English, CHamoru, and pidgin (also referred to as "Guam dialect of English," "Guam's Colloquial Chamorro English [GCCE]," "Chamurized English," and, humorously, "English the Chamorro way").[19] Most of the poems are centered on the page, though a few are left-justified. While the poems are not composed in a rhythmic pattern, many of them are in patterned stanzas (such as couplets, tercets, and quatrains) and many have rhymed end-word patterns (both the English poems and the CHamoru poems contain rhyme). The themes include cultural identity, childhood, language, nostalgia, colonialism, acculturation, militarism, the environment, and decolonization.

The cover of *Visions of a Chamoru* is worth discussing here because it speaks directly to the theme of guma' latte (see figure 5). It is composed of the title arranged vertically on the left side and a single black, abstract shape resembling both a latte stone and a face on the right side of the cover. On the tasa is a red, eye-shaped oval, and near the bottom of the haligi is a red shape that resembles lips. This collage-style artwork is signed "Onedera '95." All of

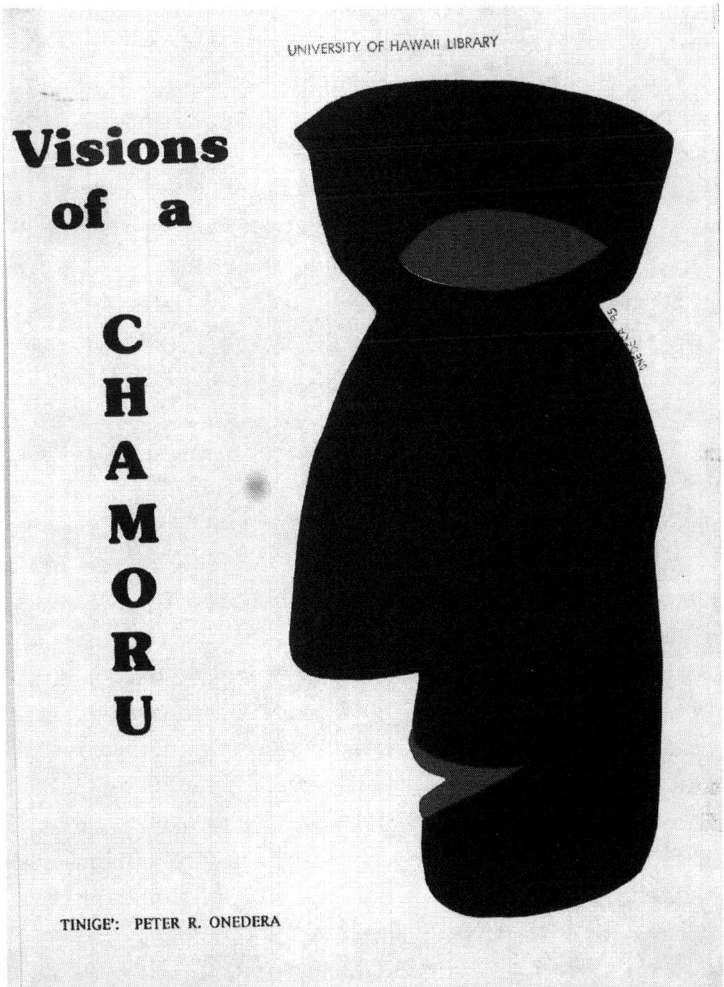

FIGURE 5 *Visions of a Chamoru* book cover, 1995. Courtesy of Peter Onedera.

the above is set against a white background. The typography of the title itself is meaningful, as it is clearly shaped into a single latte stone, with "Visions / of a" representing the capstone and "CHAMORU" representing the pillar. Visually, the word "visions" is parallel to the red eye shape in the image, and the word "CHAMORU" parallels the pillar. It appears almost as if the words might have emerged from the lips of the latte stone itself. Taken as a whole, the cover suggests that we can envision the CHamoru experience through the foundational architecture of the guma' latte and through the eyes of all that the latte stone represents culturally, and that we can hear about the CHamoru experience through the voices of our ancestors. The fact that it is only a single latte stone, though, and not a completed house, also gestures toward loss and trauma.

The poem that most directly addresses the theme of latte stones and housing is the eighth one in the collection, "I Walked Down Every Street." While the poem is not dated, nor does it name the streets the speaker is traversing, the nostalgic tone suggests that the speaker might have returned to his childhood village of Sinahånña after many years away. Sinahånña is a small village in central Guåhan, perched along a hilltop above the capital village of Hagåtña. The origin of the name comes from the word *chinåhan-ña*, which means "his or her cooking ground," referring to the process of harvesting and cooking wild yams that grew abundantly in the area and were cooked in earthen ovens dug into the ground. The village existed before the arrival of Spanish missionaries in 1668, and it was considered the domain of Hineti, a CHamoru who supported the missionaries, was baptized don Ignacio de Hineti, and even joined the Spaniards during the CHamoru-Spanish wars to fight against other CHamorus for control over Hagåtña. He eventually became a sergeant major in the Spanish military. Sinahånña remained an agricultural village specializing in growing coffee during the Spanish colonial era, and many residents who lived in Hagåtña moved to Sinahånña after the destruction of the island during World War II, when the U.S. military built temporary housing there. In 1962, a supertyphoon destroyed many structures, which led to an "urban renewal" of the village.[20] Onedera's poem likely takes place later, perhaps in the 1980s or early 1990s.

The poem begins: "One day, I began an odyssey that took me somewhere // First, there was that house where Familiarity lived. / But no one was there, they left for a better life."[21] The fact that the speaker describes the place as "somewhere" shows that he does not recognize the streets anymore, perhaps due to the passing of time and to changes caused by urban development. This is further embodied in the personification of "Familiarity," who either left the village for another, or perhaps moved off-island entirely. The next stanza reads: "Next, to its left, I came upon a park and in that park / stood a lone figure, its name was latte and it was alone. / Why, I ask, why must it be so?" To answer this question, we must take our own walk across the longer history of housing changes that occurred during the Spanish and

American colonial eras, a phenomenon that we can refer to as "architectural colonialism." Archaeologists date the end of the so-called latte period to the year 1521, which marks the beginning of Spanish imperialism. During that time, the Spanish burned CHamoru houses and pushed over or removed the latte stone foundations. Furthermore, they destroyed approximately 180 CHamoru settlements and forcefully relocated the CHamoru population into a few large parish villages. Indeed, part of the colonial process of "converting and 'civilizing' islanders involved extensive changes to settlement patterns, houses, and households."[22]

In addition to changing housing patterns, the Spanish introduced several new kinds of colonial structures (including wood-pole-and-thatch homes, churches, and military forts) and new construction methods (including de sillería and mampostería). Common houses within the new parishes were made from rectangular wood poles and thatched roofs with a slightly raised floor, bonded with wooden pins and metal nails.[23] De sillería (dressed cut stone) buildings consisted of imported tile flooring, terra-cotta roofing, wooden doors, and windows with metal bars.[24] Mampostería (stone and mortar) buildings were composed of stone rubble walls mortared together upon a bed of compacted stones, sand, and dirt, after which the interior and exterior walls were plastered.[25] These houses were sometimes referred to as *budega* if they had storage cellars. Mampostería homes usually had heavy wooden doors, shuttered windows, second-story balconies, and exterior stairways that connected the yard to the terrace and the house to the kitchen. These new structures, construction methods, and materials displaced guma' latte and its Indigenous values. For example, the ability to purchase imported materials, and to pay the labor costs of those who had experience with these new building methods, was often beyond the reach of many CHamoru families. Because the new construction methods were more durable than thatched housing, there was less need for communities to come together to repair or rebuild the houses. The result of these changes is similar to what Juliana Flinn observed about housing changes in other parts of the Pacific: "the new houses [became] visible symbols of incipient differentiation and declining importance of reciprocal kin relations."[26] Beyond the changes in affordability, access, and labor, colonial housing structures also replaced openness with privacy. Colonial houses had "several rooms, with interior walls so that nuclear families have separate areas within the structure . . . consistent with missionary emphasis on the conjugal couple and

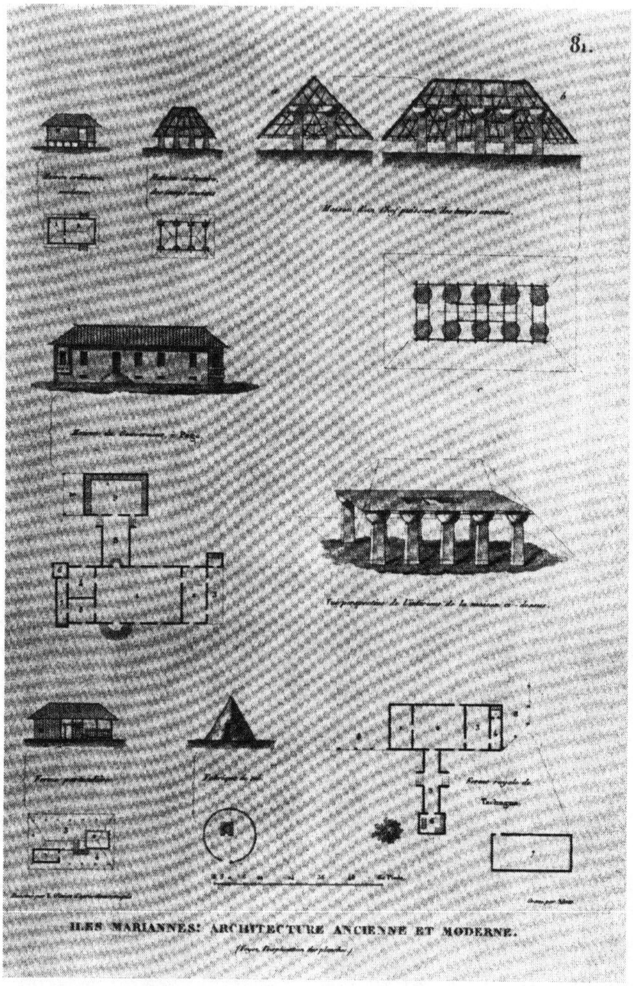

FIGURE 6 "Mariana Islands: Ancient and Modern Architecture," illustration by E. Oliver, from Louis de Freycinet's *Voyage autour du monde*, 1824. Courtesy of the Guam Public Library System.

nuclear family."[27] Even the locks on doors and bars on windows were "visible signs of increasing privatization."[28] As I will show later in this chapter, these new housing structures attempted to enclose what was once an open-space design in CHamoru housing architecture.

The Spanish also introduced religious and military buildings. A parish settlement was guarded by a garrison and arrayed around a church. The

Dulce Nombre de Maria Church in Hagåtña, for example, was built in 1709 using the de sillería method. Stones from the reef, as well as loose stones from inland (including fallen latte stones), were collected and cut with a chisel and hammer. A trowel was used to place mortar between the stones. The foundation consisted of coral rock bonded with mortared joints. The interior of the church was decorated in lavish Spanish custom, with silver and gilded lamps and wooden saint statues. The church was cruciform in design, which means it had the shape of a cross. The Spanish military also built fourteen fortifications (mainly open batteries that could fire cannons through embrasures) between 1671 and 1835, using the mampostería style. Because of Spanish architectural colonialism, guma' latte were no longer the dominant housing structures on the island, as many of the stones were either repurposed into Spanish-style dwellings or else forgotten and overgrown in the jungles outside parish boundaries. The architecture of the church and the fortifications correlates with a narrative of colonial power, control, and surveillance, which in turn embodies the narrative of colonial occupation and Indigenous loss.

After the war of 1898, the United States Navy became the new colonial landlord of Guåhan. The navy imported cheap and durable tin, which replaced the coconut-thatched roofs of the wood-pole houses and the Spanish tiles of the stone-and-mortar structures.[29] The navy also conducted house inspections. Across the Indigenous world, colonial governments often "established housing regulations for public welfare purposes, especially health and sanitation, but promoted other changes, such as clustered settlement, for administrative convenience."[30] This was true in Guåhan during both the Spanish era and the American naval era. Dramatic American architectural changes took place after World War II. Eighty percent of all homes on the island were destroyed during the war; after the war, the U.S. military bulldozed many remaining houses in order to construct military bases and airfields.[31] In a little over a year, the navy built more than one thousand wood-and-tin homes throughout Guåhan to house the newly houseless CHamoru population. During this time, another colonial structure was introduced: the cheap, lightweight, and prefabricated Quonset hut, manufactured by the George A. Fuller construction company.[32] Easy to construct and transport, thousands of these semicircular corrugated-steel structures (an average size of sixteen by thirty-six feet, with an eight-foot radius) were built on Guåhan and used as homes, schools, hospitals, and military facilities.[33] These new homes were not well suited to the island because they retained heat and because heavy rains corroded the steel. Despite this, the Quonset huts and the wood and tin houses became the most common houses built on Guåhan until the 1960s.

As I mentioned in the previous chapter, new types of housing structures were introduced in the 1960s and 1980s, including the pillbox-shaped "Kaiser prefab homes," and the "hollow block concrete masonry units" (CMUs). Wendt once described how these types of houses were made from "dead materials" that represent "the spiritual, creative, and emotional emptiness of modern man."[34] He warned that the "change from traditional dwelling to box-shaped monstrosity is gathering momentum: the mushrooming of this bewildering soulless desert of shacks and boxes is erupting across Oceania."[35]

Over the past three hundred years, architectural colonialism has evicted CHamorus from guma' latte and moved them into colonial dwellings. The loss of guma' latte and the process of urbanization affected not only the geography of the island but also the integrity of the family. According to Faye Untalan Muñoz, "the assignment of families to nuclear-type homes changed familial land residences and separated extended families, and eventually weakened the family structure."[36] From local woods to rock and mortar, imported steel, and concrete blocks; from thatched coconut leaves to imported tile and tin; from open windows to steel bars and aluminum jalousies; from communal construction to imported prefab and foreign labor; from open living arrangements and outdoor cooking areas to pillboxes and indoor kitchens, the story of architectural colonialism on Guåhan is a story of further and further alienation from the foundations and values of CHamoru latte stone housing.

During the decades of postwar reconstruction of the island, many latte were vandalized, neglected, or otherwise disturbed by urban, suburban, tourist, and military development. As colonial architecture scholar Setha Low notes:

> Political implications lie at the root of all aesthetic sensibilities, and certainly the design of an urban space reflects the political agency of the state. In this sense, architecture and urban design contribute to the dominance of one group over others and function as mechanisms for coding their reciprocal relationships at the level of the surveillance and control of bodily movement. Physical space is ordered by and reflects the power structures to which the community is subordinated; the community may contest this subordination

> through local interpretation and use of space. Examining the origins and use of spatial forms provides insight into the discourse of power relations.[37]

Clearly, the architecture on Guåhan makes visible the colonial changes that occurred over the past five hundred years. The buildings testify to the power of the church, the military, and the state in the control and surveillance of the CHamoru population. Or, as Jan Rensel argues in *Home in the Islands: Housing and Social Change in the Pacific*: "Tales of imperialism and resistance, identity and resilience, transformation and persistence . . . are [dramatized] and recorded in changes in housing over time."[38]

Since this long history haunts the opening of Onedera's "I Walked Down Every Street," allow me to requote the first stanzas:

> One day, I began an odyssey that took me somewhere
>
> First, there was that house where Familiarity lived.
> But no one was there, they left for a better life.
>
> Next, to its left, I came upon a park and in that park
> stood a lone figure, its name was latte and it was alone.
> Why, I ask, why must it be so?
>
> *("I Walked")*

Because of housing colonialism and the destruction of the guma' latte tradition, contemporary CHamorus usually only encounter latte as either ruins in the jungle or disembodied artifacts in public parks. Thus, the latte also represent feelings of loss, trauma, and absence because they comprise the "ultimate link with a distant past for which the [CHamoru] soul will always harbor deep nostalgic longings."[39] The lone latte stone in Onedera's poem embodies the colonial devastation of CHamoru culture and the longing for reconnection with the past. Moreover, the alliteration of *l* words (*lived, left, life, left, lone, latte*) echoes this sense of loss.

The poem continues as the speaker passes children in the park who are playing American games and wearing American jewelry (hula hoops and "dangling earrings"). He wonders about the acculturation of island youth and asks: "What have they become and what do they want to be?" Farther down the street, the speaker sees that "the house where my friend / Afa'maolek once lived had a sign on its door. / It said Konnichiwa and Arigato. I miss my friend so very much" ("I Walked"). In CHamoru, the name Afa'maolek means to collaborate, form a group, help, and cooperate. It comes from the word *inafa'maolek*, which is the most important CHamoru value of interdependence, interconnection, mutual aid, and social reciprocity. Perhaps the loss of the speaker's friend represents the loss of CHamoru cultural values that he sees in the children at the park and in the lone (and lonely) latte stone.

Given the fact that Japanese words now adorn the door, it is important to map the migration of Japanese people to Guåhan. The first Japanese arrived in 1868: about forty farmworkers who came at the request of the Spanish governor, possibly "the first group of Japanese migrant workers sent abroad as an organized labor force."[40] A Japanese trade boom in the Pacific commenced in the 1890s as several Japanese companies operated copra plantations on Guåhan. By 1910, the Japanese population had grown to over a hundred. Many Japanese workers settled in Guåhan beyond their contracts, married CHamoru women, and started independent businesses. Japanese immigration halted in 1924, with the passage of restrictive U.S. immigration policies; relatedly, the Japanese Society of Guam formed in 1928 to combat anti-Japanese racism as tensions grew between the United States and Japan. By 1941, there were around 200 Japanese and Japanese-CHamorus living in Guåhan. According to the 2010 census, the Japanese population numbered 2,400, or about 1.5 percent of the total population.

The relations between Japanese and CHamoru people changed during the Japanese occupation of World War II. Japanese residents who lived in prewar Guåhan were conscripted to work for the occupation forces. CHamorus were forced to "[bow] to Japanese officials, just so they could move on with their daily lives and familial obligations. Chamorro parents also discouraged their daughters from developing relations with Japanese soldiers and sailors. . . . From the level of individual interaction to that of the family, Chamorros distanced themselves from the Japanese and their policies whenever they could."[41] CHamoru men were conscripted to construct military defense structures, and CHamoru women were forced into food production activities for the Kaikuntai, an agricultural unit whose goal was to feed the Japanese military, as well as into sexual slavery as "comfort women." By June 1944, there were some 19,000 Japanese soldiers in Guåhan, compared to a CHamoru population of 20,000. As the U.S. military neared its invasion of Guåhan, Japanese behavior "degenerated into a kind of destructive nihilism."[42] Approximately 500 CHamorus were killed because of Japanese atrocities, and thousands of others were tortured, raped, and assaulted.[43] Because of the wartime experience, "profound feelings of distrust and hate came to characterize most relationships between Chamorros and Japanese in Guam," and many CHamorus rejected public affiliation with Japanese and CHamoru-Japanese families.[44] After the war, some members of these families were imprisoned, insulted, and abused on the suspicion that they had aided the Japanese occupation, and other Japanese nationals and CHamoru collaborators who worked for Japan were tried by the United States in war crimes tribunals.[45] Many of these families opted to replace their Japanese surnames with CHamoru surnames to avoid anti-Japanese sentiment.[46]

These feelings stayed with the CHamorus who survived the occupation and the war, were passed down to postwar CHamoru generations, and shaped how CHamorus perceived the next wave of Japanese presence: the Japanese tourist. The rise of Guåhan's tourism industry is sometimes described as a "second invasion"—the first being the military invasion of Japanese soldiers who arrived upon the shores of Tumon Bay. There are other palimpsests: The Guam International Airport was originally an airstrip for the Japanese during World War II, built by forced CHamoru labor. A major road in Tumon is Marine Corps Drive, named in honor of the U.S. Marines who invaded in 1944. These spaces not only "serve as past reminders of war" and "contemporary symbols of tourism" but also show how militourism's infrastructure "literally paved the way for the second invasion of the Japanese in the 1960s."[47] As one CHamoru elder commented about the presence of Japanese tourists, in light of her experience during the occupation: "When I think of those times, I hate the Japanese. . . . I know people say we need a strong economy, but I don't care. We did just fine before they came and we don't need them now. . . . I do forgive the Japanese for what they did, but I will never forget."[48] As a result of these unforgettable memories, some CHamorus viewed the Japanese as "a homogenous group of militarist murderers and rapists."[49] Even the Japanese government attempted to reshape views of the Japanese into a peaceful people: "The emerging peace movement in Japan and the gradual proliferation of 'bone-collecting' missions and peace memorials all contributed to producing representations of the Japanese as peaceful, proud, and prosperous people."[50]

From 1960 to 1967, Japanese tour groups arrived on Guåhan and combed through the jungle for Japanese remains; after they collected the bones, they performed religious and memorial ceremonies.

Even though this is not mentioned in the poem, Onedera himself descends from a CHamoru-Japanese family. He was, at one point, the acting president of the Guam Nikkei Association, which first began in 2007 and was officially established as a nonprofit organization in 2012. The association conducts classes, performances, and events, as well as travel to Japan, to perpetuate the culture of those with Japanese ancesty born on Guåhan, and to "educate the community about the impact and contribution of first generation Japanese and their descendants on the social economic fabric of Guam and to inculcate Japanese culture, art, traditions and history to succeeding generations of Japanese-Chamorro-Guamanians."[51] Given both the historical and political context of Japanese presence on Guåhan, as well as Onedera's own genealogical background, we can interpret the sign in Japanese language on the door as perhaps also alluding to this complex, entangled history of Japanese and CHamoru relations, experiences, and cultural identities. We can also interpret it as an invitation to the speaker himself to connect more fully to his Japanese heritage, something he did many years after this poem was published through his involvement in the Guam Nikkei Association.

In the next stanza, the speaker passes by a store owned by "Tan Ånghela," where he used to "wheedle pixie / sticks, rocky road, and Bireley's from her" ("I Walked"). However, he points out: "Now there is a difference to it, she no longer owned it." The new owner, the speaker shares, lives in a big house next to the store: "It was nice, elegant, and there were four nice cars in its garage." The memory of a locally owned, beloved "mom-and-pop" store juxtaposed against the wealth of a new owner highlights the urbanization of Guåhan and the gentrification of village life. The poem ends with the speaker finally reaching what I assume was once his childhood home:

> And then, next door, thereupon I came,
> It was a shack or so it seemed because the tin roof, shabby curtains and
> spam was wafting out the open front door.
> It was my house, right on the street where
> my odyssey ended.
>
> *("I Walked")*

The speaker, at first, does not recognize his old house, just as he does not recognize the neighborhood and streets of his youth. The first thing he notices about the house is the poverty of the dwelling, especially in contrast to the wealthy home next door. The "shack" is characterized by its cheap materials and the scent of Spam, a common canned meat product consumed in Guåhan that, in some contexts, signifies poverty.[52] Onedera ends his poem without further comment, and we are left standing there to dwell amid the transformations that have occurred in the speaker's village, which reflect the historical and colonial transformations of Guåhan.

As Rensel highlights, housing dynamically functions as "shelter, container, status symbol, home; it may provide a basis of belonging, represent membership or dominance by an encompassing macro-society, or assert cultural uniqueness or resurgence."[53] She also notes how changes in housing are "inextricably tied to changes in the social relationships that housing embodies and represents and from which it emerges. Further, housing, in its physical forms, uses, and meanings, is impacted by and responds to changes in global political economy. Houses can be seen as a nexus where sociocultural, economic, and political forces interact."[54] Indeed, we can imagine the speaker standing in front of his old house like the lone figure of the latte in the park, contemplating the dramatic changes that occurred on Guåhan between his birth in 1953 and the publication of this book in 1995. The poem is, indeed, an odyssey, not only down every street but also down the shifting paths of history and culture, in order to find his way home.

Onedera returns to the figure of the latte in his most recent poetry collection, *Taimanu na Ini* (2018). This collection contains fifty-six poems, totaling around ninety-four pages, entirely in the CHamoru language. The title translates as "How is this?" Onedera stated in an interview that the book "answers generational questions such as: 'How is a CHamoru supposed to exist and survive in this ever-changing world of challenges?' And 'Is this what we perceive things to be in our lifetime as CHamorus?'"[55] The book explores themes of culture, identity, history, politics, family, the environment, and language.

I will examine one poem titled "O Åcho' Latte," which speaks directly to the theme of this chapter. While the poems in the book are written wholly in CHamoru, I will also be discussing Onedera's English translation of the poem, provided to me through personal communication and featured here publicly for the first time. Since the translation does not appear in the book, I quote it in full as formatted by Onedera:

O ÅCHO' LATTE

O ROCK OF STRENGTH

Tumachu i åcho' latte gi me'nan i matå-hu.
The rock of strength stood before my eyes.

Ha na'bongbong kurason-hu sa' guaha fino'-ña.
My heart beat furiously because he said something profound.

Mampos linekkå'-ña, mampos fineddå'-ña.
He has towered so tall, and yet so wide.

I haligi sumapotte desde fondo asta hulo'.
Its supportive post has held it strong since way below to up so far.

Tåddong gi papa' odda' yan takhilo' ti hu li'e'.
Deep below the earth and high up above I could not see.

O åcho' latte, håfa malago'-mu nu guåhu?
O rock of strength, what is it that you bid from me?

O åcho' latte, håfa na un sungon todu i hinanao-hu?
O rock of strength, why have you withstood the struggles along my way?

Kao magåhet na noskuåntos siklo tumohge-mu?
Your eternal centuries spoke the truth where you have stood?

Håyi kumonne' hao mågi yan håfa malago'-mu nu guåhu?
Who brought you here and what do you bid from me?

Ti un oppe i ginagao-hu sa' metgot-ña i fuetså-mu.
You may not answer my query because your enduring strength forbids it so.

Lao munga yu' sumotta gi manmamaila' na tiempo.
But don't forsake me throughout the coming of time.

Sa' siempre tåya' kurason-hu para todu i fegge'-hu.
Because I will have no soul despite the steps I take.

Mantieni i direcho, mantieni i espiritu.
Do what is right, do what the spirits say.

O åcho' latte, O åcho' latte
O rock of strength, O rock of strength

Ma funas hao gi i hinasso.
You may be erased from the minds of everyone.

Ma funas hao gi i lina'la'.
You may be erased from life by everyone.

Ma funas hao entre pumalu.
You may be gone from everything there is.

Lao gaige ha' hihot-mu para guåhu ni' i kurason-mu.
But you will forever be near to me through your heart.[56]

Onedera translates "åcho' latte" as "rock of strength," foregrounding the latte as a symbol of strength and referring both to its solid materiality and to its function as the foundation of CHamoru housing. The poem opens with a scene similar to the one in which the speaker faces a lone latte in the park in "I Walked Down Every Street," written nearly twenty-five years earlier. However, this time the speaker stops to engage with the latte stone. In this poem, the latte stone comes alive (reminiscent of the latte figure on the cover of *Visions of a Chamoru*, who has a mouth and eyes), stands before the speaker, and says something profound, though what was said is not shared in the poem. The speaker goes on to praise the strength of the åcho' latte, which becomes mythic in that its haligi extends "tåddong gi papa' odda' yan takhilo' ti hu li'e'" (deep below the earth and high up above I could not see). The poem turns into a series of questions, as if the speaker is asking an ancestor for truth and wisdom. The final question is especially compelling: "Håyi kumonne' hao mågi yan håfa malago'-mu nu guåhu?" (Who brought you here and what do you bid from me?). The speaker is seeking to know the history of his CHamoru ancestors, the history of colonialism, and the purpose of his life. The latte stone remains silent, and the speaker interprets this as strength: "Ti un oppe i ginagao-hu sa' metgot-ña i fuetså-mu" (You may not answer my query because your enduring strength forbids it so). The use of the word "ginagao," which translates as "query," is interesting because it alludes to "quarry," and to the act of quarrying stone to build a latte stone house. This could also allude to quarrying or querying the self for answers. A few lines later, it seems that an answer to the speaker's query is given, though the origin of the voice is ambiguous: "Mantieni i direcho, mantieni i espiritu" (Do what is right, do what the spirits say). Is this the latte speaking, or is it the poet discovering this answer for himself? Either way, it provides the speaker with "direcho," the *right direction*. The poem ends with the speaker praising the latte stone, "O åcho' latte, O åcho' latte," and then acknowledging that even if the latte stones continue to be erased from the land and from CHamoru culture and everyday life, the åcho' latte will always be "hihot-mu para guåhu ni' i kurason-mu" (near to me through your heart). While the poem does not specifically mention houses, the lone latte in the poem provides shelter to the speaker, a symbolic form of housing that gives the speaker strength to withstand struggle and to quarry/query in search of cultural connection, purpose, and wisdom.

Na(rra)tive Architecture and Poetic Form

For the remainder of this chapter, I will develop the concept of "Na(rra)tive architecture" to address the intersection between the aesthetics, form, and function of Native architecture and the craft, structure, and purpose of Indigenous narratives and stories. This concept has been inspired by studies of Māori writer Patricia Grace's novel *Potiki*, which houses the story of the Tamihana family, who struggle to protect their marae (gathering space) and wharenui (meeting house) from tourist developers in Aotearoa (New Zealand).[57] In Māori culture, the marae is the most important architectural space, consisting of a wharenui, or main meeting house, a building for dining, and the land itself. The marae is "the community gathering place where the customs, protocols, and rituals of Māori life are most fully expressed."[58] Besides being an important center for Māori custom, the wharenui also embodies Māori whakapapa, or genealogy, because it is built in the shape of a body and includes carved figures of poupou, or ancestors. In *Potiki*, tourism industry developers threaten to interrupt the Tamihana way of life when they offer the family money to build a road through their land, which would destroy the marae and wharenui. After the family refuses their offers, the developers terrorize the family by flooding the cemetery, damaging the family gardens, and even burning down the wharenui. Instead of giving in to the developers, the family rebuilds the wharenui and holds on to their land. The scholarship on *Potiki* examines these architectural and storytelling spaces for their thematic and symbolic content, as well as for how these spaces structure the form of the novel itself. As several scholars point out, the wharenui is not only a central setting, symbol, and text within *Potiki*, but also the "central metaphor for narrativization"—a "house of story," so to speak.[59] In an interview, Grace explains that the narrative shape of *Potiki* is patterned after Māori whaikōrero, or speech making. She claims she did this to "give circular shape suitable to the storytelling content of the book and to reflect the way that talk moves in a circular fashion inside the meeting house."[60] In *Potiki* itself, Grace explicitly makes the connection between house and text: "[The] main book was the wharenui which is itself a story, a history, a gallery, a study, a design structure and a taonga. And we are part of that book along with family past and family yet to come."[61] The text performs this kind of storytelling. For example, the prologue of *Potiki* focuses on the carver of the wharenui, and each subsequent chapter is told from the different perspectives of various family members and generations. As Elizabeth DeLoughrey reveals, the construction of the novel through the architectural form and aesthetics of the wharenui gives *Potiki* an Indigenized "spiral" narrative and temporal structure.[62] This idea of the wharenui as a Māori "house of story" is further emphasized when the Tamihana family rebuilds the wharenui and fills the space with their voices: "And the stories continued well into the night, moving from one person to the next about the house until the circle had been fully turned."[63] Overall, the scholarship on *Potiki* lays the foundation for way-reading the relationship between Indigenous cultures, customary housing architecture, architectural colonialism, and Pacific literature.[64]

Similarly, the latte house was a space of storytelling and the teaching of orature in CHamoru culture. Here I argue that Onedera rearticulates latte housing architecture through various formal elements in *Visions of a Chamoru* and *Taimanu na Ini*. Entering these collections, then, becomes akin to walking into a latte stone house, or a "CHamoru house of story." In *Visions of a Chamoru*, Onedera embodies multiple voices by including poems composed in different languages (CHamoru, English, and pidgin). As explained at the beginning of this essay, the latte stone has a two-part structure (the capstone and the pillar). This architectural structure, I suggest, is reflected in the two-part narrative structure of *Visions of a Chamoru,* which Onedera specifically captures in the alternating arrangement of poems: for example, the first poem is in English, the second in CHamoru, the third in English, the fourth in CHamoru, and so forth. This creates the sensation of a bilingual latte formation that houses the stories of CHamorus. *Taimanu na Ini* is quite different because the book is written entirely in CHamoru. However, the presence of the individual poem "O Åcho' Latte," which is situated in the middle section of the book, grounds the book as a CHamoru house of story. The shape of the poem is a single stanza, with the first half of the lines resembling a capstone while the lines toward the end (or bottom) of the poem resemble the pillar. Even the translation that the author shared with me, which is centered on the page, concretely resembles a latte stone, bringing the reader into CHamoru Na(rra)tive housing architecture. Of course, you cannot build a CHamoru house with a lone latte, but, as Onedera shows, a single, surviving latte can give us the wisdom, strength, and inspiration to rebuild the CHamoru house of story even after centuries of colonial ruination and erasure.

Conclusion

Latte stones and the guma' latte are prevalent symbols throughout CHamoru literature. We can find two other powerful examples in work by C. T. Perez and Kisha Borja-Kicho'cho', which I will briefly discuss as a gesture to interweave this chapter with the previous one. In "I Kareran i Palåbran Måmi—The Journey of Our Words," Borja-Kicho'cho' includes a poem titled "Nåna," which is dedicated to "famalao'an Chamoru," or CHamoru women. The poem compares the shape of the tåsa and haligi of the latte stone to the shape of a "healthy" CHamoru woman's "full-figured hips" and "powerful arms" ("Kareran," 129; figure 7). Like Onedera, Borja-Kicho'cho' highlights how the latte stone represents strength, persistence, and endurance; but in Borja-Kicho'cho's poem the latte stone specifically symbolizes the strength, persistence, and endurance of CHamoru women. Just as the latte stone is a connection to the past that inspires CHamorus to stay connected and rooted to culture, the latte stone and, by extension, CHamoru women, also inspire her to "live my

Like the tåsa and haligi of the ancient Chamoru latte stone
so, too, does your body maintain the shape
of the healthy Chamoru woman.
With those full-figured hips
features delivered
through natural birth for generations
and with those powerful arms
reaching for the past calling on our mañaina
you have remained strong throughout the years
continuously inspire me to live my culture
allow me to grow into a young Chamoru woman myself.
Through you I have witnessed the persistence
and endurance of my ancestors who never failed in constructing a latte.
I gima` taotao mo`na the house of the ancient people.
Hågu i acho` latte-ku. You are my latte stone.

FIGURE 7 "Nåna," by Kisha Borja-Kicho'cho', 2010. Reprinted courtesy of Kisha Borja-Kicho'cho'.

culture" and "grow into a young Chamoru woman." As one can see from the image of the poem, it is shaped like a latte stone, with the capstone resembling arms and the pillar resembling hips. The word "birth" also appears in the middle of the shape, suggesting that the center of the poem is its womb. The position of the final line—"Hågu i acho' latte-ku. You are my latte stone"—roots the poem firmly to the page, just as CHamoru women root the speaker to the land and to "i gima taotao mo'na / the house of the ancient people."

In the title essay of her thesis, "Signs of Being: A Chamorro Spiritual Journey," C. T. Perez describes her transformative journey with her friend Lina to As Nieves, a latte quarry site in the northern island of Luta (Rota). She sets the scene: "Some pillars lay above ground, cracked perhaps in the effort to move them. Other pillars and capstones still lay embedded in the ground that bore them" ("Signs," 25). When the speaker and her friend kneel by an unfinished tasa, Lina speaks to the ancestral spirits: "*Guella yan Guello, hafa na ti un na'fonhayan I che'cho-miyu?* What happened to make you leave your work? Did you have to fight? Did you get sick? Were you killed as you tried to finish your work?" (26). Both characters feel the power of their ancestors as they walk through the site: "The spirit of the People who came before is in us and surrounds us. It is in the call of the wind, and the breath of our kiss. It permeates our psyche and fortifies our will to survive" (26). As they commune with the ancestors and listen for answers to their questions, the speaker realizes: "The fallen Latte is the sign. It is from within the row of Latte that we feel our strength. It is the severed capstone that gives us Their message, 'Ti monhayon I che'cho'.' We will not rest until the Latte is whole" (26).

Archaeologists have found nearly three hundred latte ruins on Guåhan alone, making them the most "conspicuous archeological survivals of the ancient [Chamorro] culture."[65] Currently, local and federal laws protect latte sites, and these ruins continue to inspire CHamorus today:

> Although the original integrity of the latte has lapsed, the latte stones of the Marianas have left a long-lasting imprint, not only on the historic landscape, but also within the minds of the indigenous Chamorro people. The latte stones of the Marianas have captivated the curiosity and imagination of virtually all segments of society, including the general public, artists, archaeologists, school children, teachers, tourists, politicians, political activists, and historic preservationists, to name just a few.[66]

Even though actual latte stone houses are no longer part of everyday CHamoru experience, the representational image of the latte is ubiquitous throughout contemporary Guåhan. The latte motif is used in many modern structures, such as the Guam International Airport, the University of Guam, the archbishop's and governor's residences, and the Guam Legislature, as well as at the entrances to villages and churches. Images of the latte can be found on government documents, business logos, souvenirs, bus stops, jewelry, T-shirts, license plates, and even tattoos. The latte remain powerful symbols of CHamoru cultural identity, architectural ingenuity, and Indigenous history. At the same time, latte also represent feelings of loss, trauma, absence, nostalgia, and longing.[67]

Many artists and architects have attempted to reenvision, reconstruct, and replicate latte stones and the latte house graphically and architecturally.[68] Various latte replicas have also been constructed on Guåhan. One of the most symbolic projects is a canoe house known as Guma' i Latte Sakman, which is being planned for Ypao Beach in Tumon Bay. Ten latte columns, each measuring twelve feet in height, will support an A-frame structure, which will be nearly forty feet high. This latte house is designed to house the outrigger canoe *Saina*.[69] In 2018, the first-ever course entitled Åcho' Latte Carving and Quarrying was offered at the University of Guam, taught by Kelly Marsh-Taitano and cultural practitioner Joe Viloria. The students study latte stone usage and symbolism, archaeological documents related to latte, and how to quarry and carve the latte.[70] Beyond attempts to literally reconstruct latte houses, others have attempted to reconstruct the latte in various figurative and symbolic forms:

> Within the present-day context, an awareness of the latte as a viable link to the past has inspired artists, activists, preservationists and the like to reconstruct the ancient latte in various forms. Creative artistic license and imagination can be seen in some of these attempts at reconstructing the ancient latte architecture.[71]

This act of rearticulating ancient latte architecture is visible in various formal elements of Onedera's poetry collections. In other words, poetry is a way for Onedera and other CHamoru writers to creatively and symbolically reconstruct the CHamoru house of story through Na(rra)tive architecture.

CHamoru customary architecture embodied CHamoru cultural values and identity. The latte stones formed the foundation of CHamoru housing, rooted its inhabitants to the land (Puntan's body), served as a reminder of Fu'una's sacrifice to birth the CHamoru people, and established a genealogical, ecological, and architectural belonging to the land. Despite the strength of these foundations, centuries of architectural colonialism destroyed these housing practices and replaced them with other structures, settlement patterns, and roads and bridges that embody the architecture of colonial, military, and religious control, power, and surveillance. These new buildings structured CHamoru life and often severed communal and familial links and kinship networks.

Reconstructing latte stones through poetry is an attempt to make the latte house whole again. As Rensel highlights, the term *housing* is "both noun—an object, something people have, make, live in—and verb—an activity, something people do."[72] Archaeologists claim that ancient CHamorus used stone for the foundation of their houses because stone resists rot and is strong enough to withstand typhoons and earthquakes. Perhaps CHamorus also used stone for another reason: to make sure there would be lasting signs by which future CHamorus might connect to our past if tragedy struck. The continued presence of latte reminds us of our strength and endurance; it reminds us of home. Perhaps the latte deliver a message to CHamorus: when we enter the ruins of a latte house, it is our responsibility to remember, to tell the story of the past, and to rebuild the house. The epigraph to this chapter asked what has become of the architects of the latte houses. Today, not only are CHamorus learning how to rebuild latte stone housing, but CHamoru writers are also becoming Na(rra)tive architects, constructing poetry from the ruins to rebuild a CHamoru house of story, belonging, healing, and strength.

CHAPTER 3

The Flying Proa

Outrigger Aesthetics, Migration, and Diasporic Indigeneity in Lehua Taitano's A Bell Made of Stones

> These Indians are no ways defective in understanding, for their flying proas in particular, which during ages past have been the only vessels employed by them, are so singular and extraordinary an invention that it would do honour to any nation, however dexterous and acute, since if we consider the aptitude of this proa to the navigation of these islands, which lying all of them nearly under the same meridian, and with the limits of the trade wind, require the vessels made use of in passing from one to the other to be particularly fitted for sailing with the wind upon the beam; or if we examine the uncommon simplicity and ingenuity of its fabric and contrivance, or the extraordinary velocity with which it moves, we shall in each of these articles, find it worthy of our admiration, and deserving a place amongst the mechanical productions of the most civilised nations where arts and sciences have most eminently flourished.
>
> —George Anson

Introduction

While the previous two chapters were rooted in the land and houses of Guåhan, this chapter will carry us to the vast transoceanic expanse of the CHamoru diaspora. We will explore the complex relationship between navigation traditions, outrigger canoe aesthetics, CHamoru migration, and Indigenous diasporic cultural identity. To orient our wayreading, I will provide an introduction to the history, theory, and praxis of Pacific voyaging traditions and canoe design, as well as the colonial history of suppressing Pacific navigation and mobility. Then I will wayread the content and forms of *A Bell Made of Stones* (2013), an experimental poetry collection by CHamoru writer Lehua M. Taitano. I will show how the theme of voyaging provides

200 BALLOU'S PICTORIAL DRAWING-ROOM COMPANION.

FLYING PROAS OF THE LADRONE ISLANDS.

The accompanying picture represents the peculiar boats (proas) used by the Ladrone islanders, with their slender hulls and huge triangular sails, managed by the natives with great adroitness. To the mariner accustomed to European rigs, a fleet of these queer craft hurrying along shore affords a singular spectacle. All the navigators who made known to us the existence of groups of islands in the Pacific, the Indian and other oceans, accompanied their narratives with descriptions of the canoes or other kinds of boats in use among the natives; and means are thus afforded for observing the various ways in which ingenuity is brought to bear on such matters. Whether each nation or tribe made its own discoveries, and applied its own inventive skill, or whether one borrowed ideas from another and modified them according to circumstances, can now hardly be known; but it is probable that both causes led to the production of the object in view. The proa we have delineated is used among the Ladrones and other eastern islands. In the account of Anson's voyage, this proa is spoken of with marked commendation. "Whether we consider its aptitude to the particular navigation of these islands, or the uncommon simplicity and ingenuity of its fabric and contrivance, or the extraordinary velocity with which it moves, we shall find it worthy of our admiration, and meriting a place among the mechanical productions of the most civilized nations." The proa seems to be constructed on a principle the very reverse of American vessels; for, while we make the head ot the vessel different from the stern, and the two sides alike, the proa has the head and stern alike, but the two sides different. There is one side of the vessel which is intended always to be kept to leeward, and this is flat, whereas the other side is rounded. To prevent her oversetting, which is liable to happen from her narrowness of beam, and the straitness of her leeward side, there is a frame extending from her to windward, to the end of which is fastened a log, shaped like a small boat, and made hollow. The weight of the frame is intended to balance the proa, and the small boat, by its buoyancy, prevents the oversetting. The body of the proa is made of two pieces joined endwise, and sewed together with bark—there being no iron used about her; it is always about two inches thick at the bottom, and about one at the gunwale. The proa generally carries six or seven men, two of them placed in the head and stern to steer the vessel alternately with a paddle, according to the direction in which it is going; the other men being employed in baling out the water which she accidentally ships, or in setting and trimming the sail. The peculiar construction of these vessels arises out of the sort of navigation for which they are intended. The Ladrones are a string of islands lying nearly north and south of each other, and the proas have scarcely to follow any other points of the compass than these two in maintaining intercourse between one island and another. Either end of the vessel may at pleasure make the head, and thus, by simply shifting the sail, it may go to and fro without ever "putting about" or turning round. By the flatness of their lee side and small breadth, they are able to be much nearer the wind than other vessels. They have been known to progress, when a brisk tradewind was with them, at the rate of twenty miles an hour, and their amazing swiftness has earned for them the name of "flying proas."

FLYING PROAS OF THE LADRONE ISLANDS.

WASHINGTON STREET, HOBOKEN, NEW JERSEY.

In our number of September 6th, we presented a general view of Hoboken, taken from the river, and accompanied it by a sketch of the place. We now add a view of Washington Street from the pencil of the same artist—Mr. Hill. Hoboken is laid out with great taste and liberality, and the streets are planted with shade trees. That in our view is the principal business street. The prominent buildings delineated are the Odd Fellows Hall and one of the armories. In front of the latter, a New York city company, on a target excursion, accompanied by Dodworth's band, is halted. During the fall, hundreds of corps come over from New York for target and battalion exercises. There is great military spirit in New York, and the emulation among the volunteer companies brings their drill as near perfection as possible.

THE LAKE OF GENEVA.

The Lake of Geneva, or Lake Leman, presented on the next page, is one of the most beautiful and celebrated of European lakes. The picture before us delineates as far as engraving can, one of the most striking portions of this vast inland mirror, reflecting the magnificent theatre of mountains that rise until their snow-capped summits blend with the very clouds. The buildings stretching along in the middle distance, add greatly to the picturesque effect of this truly magical scene. This lake lies between Switzerland and the Sardinian States. It is in the form of a crescent. Its length is forty-five miles, while its breadth varies from one to ten. It is 1230 feet above the sea, and its greatest depth is 984 feet. It is traversed by the Rhone from east to west, and receives the Dranse, Venoge and other small rivers. Its waters are noted for their deep cerulean blue color. They abound in fish. This magnificent sheet of water is never frozen over. It presents a very curious phenomenon at times, when it rises from one to five feet, this remarkable elevation lasting only about half an hour. It has formed the subject of many paintings and poems, but none of the latter attain the beauty of the well-remembered stanzas in Child Harold's Pilgrimage. During Lord Byron's stay in Switzerland, he took up his residence at the Campagne Diodati, in the village of Coligny. It stands at the top of a sloping vineyard, the windows inside presenting a fine view of the lake and the city of Geneva. To his evening excursions on the lake, we owe those stanzas commencing with an invocation to the lake:

"Clear, placid Leman! thy contrasted lake,
With the wild world I dwelt in, is a thing
Which warns me, with its stillness, to forsake
Earth's troubled waters for a purer spring.
This quiet sail is as a noiseless wing
To waft me from distraction; once I loved
Torn ocean's roar, but thy soft murmuring
Sounds sweet as if a sister's voice reproved,
That I with stern delights should e'er have been so moved."

FIGURE 8 "Flying Proas of the Ladrone Islands," 1856, in *Ballou's Pictorial Drawing-Room Companion*. Courtesy of the Guam Public Library System.

Taitano with a vessel through which to navigate the trauma of migration and to articulate a diasporic CHamoru identity. Furthermore, I will propose that Taitano's use of innovative visual typographies and formal poetic techniques evokes outrigger design and "moving islands" navigational techniques, or what I will frame as a "flying proa poetics."

CHamoru Navigation and the Flying Canoe

The first recorded contact between Europeans and Pacific Islanders occurred aboard oceangoing vessels. When Ferdinand Magellan and his galleons neared Guåhan, CHamorus swiftly raced toward them in outrigger canoes. Magellan's chronicler, Antonio Pigafetta, described how numerous outrigger canoes with lateen (triangular) sails deftly maneuvered "like dolphins jumping from wave to wave" and surrounded the galleons.[1] He called the canoes *parão*, a Portuguese word that became *proa* in English, and which possibly originated from the Malay word for "boat," *prahu*.[2] Because the CHamoru canoes seemed to skim the water and could travel as fast as twenty miles an hour, they came to be known around the world as "flying proas." Indeed, Europeans described the CHamoru proa as the best canoe in the world, and the Mariana archipelago was, at a certain point, referred to as "Islas de las Velas Latinas" (Islands of the Lateen Sails).[3] Of course, CHamorus had their own names for watercraft. Canoes without sails were known as panga; a small reef canoe was called galaide'; small and medium-sized outrigger canoes with sails were termed duduli, dudings, or lelek; and the largest oceangoing vessels were referred to as sakman.

CHamorus inherited and perpetuated a voyaging tradition that can be traced back four thousand years to the very invention of the sail and outrigger. The words for mast, sail, and outrigger are among the oldest words in Austronesian languages.[4] CHamoru canoe technology and seagoing art not only were essential to everyday commerce (such as pelagic fishing and trade), but also allowed CHamorus to traverse the open ocean and make landfall on distant, unsettled islands. Indeed, CHamorus became the first people to settle the western Pacific Ocean, inaugurating an "unparalleled seaborn expansion" throughout the Pacific.[5] As Vicente Diaz notes, CHamorus and other islanders navigated across Oceania "millennia before Europeans ventured from eyesight of their shores."[6]

CHamoru proa innovation included the development of outrigger design, asymmetrical hulls, and inverted lateen sails. Most European ships contained a symmetrical hull with differently shaped bow and stern; the CHamoru proa, however, had an asymmetrical hull with an identical (hence interchangeable) bow and stern. The leeward side of the hull was flat, and the windward side of the hull was rounded, with a frame extending outward upon it toward the outrigger float (a platform for cargo and passengers was sometimes built over the frame). The mast, which rested on the outrigger side as opposed to extending to the bottom of the hull, held the sail aloft. Since the bow and stern were identical, the proa tacked (switched directions across the wind) by means of moving the sail from one end of the canoe to the other—also known as shunting. Together, the asymmetrical hull, triangular sail, and outrigger design functioned to resist drift, keep the proa afloat, counterbalance winds, and maximize speed and mobility.[7]

The CHamoru proa was constructed with local, sustainable materials.[8] The sail was woven from pandanus. The hull was carved from the trunk of a breadfruit tree using a higam, or shell adze. The mast, yard, boom, and planks were made from different kinds of native hardwoods and bamboo. Planks were lashed together with coconut fiber rope, and seams were caulked with heated breadfruit sap or powdered quicklime mixed with coconut oil. Red, black, and white paints were sourced from red clay, burnt coconut-husk soot, and a mixture of coconut oil and quicklime. Shaped coconut husks were used as paintbrushes. The canoes were painted not only to protect them from weathering, but also for aesthetic reasons. CHamorus considered red and black beautiful colors; this is evidenced in the cultural aesthetic practice of etching designs onto the surface of their teeth and staining them red and black (a long process that involved great pain, yet also preserved teeth from rotting).[9]

In addition to constructing technologically sophisticated and aesthetically pleasing watercraft, CHamorus and other Pacific Islanders developed complex navigational techniques that involved reading the movements of stars, winds, currents, clouds, birds, fish, waves, and islands, as well as the fragrances of endemic flowers and plants.[10] They also used various kinds of visual star compasses and wave maps, as well as aural chants and stories. Besides being "fundamentally discursive and narratological," Pacific wayfinding is also fundamentally ethical.[11] For example, CHamoru navigation exemplifies the CHamoru cultural value of inafa'maolek (interconnectedness, reciprocity, sustainability, and mutual care) by highlighting the "deep and profound kinship between humans and the animal world, as well as the genealogical connections between humans and animals on the one hand with land and sea on the other."[12] Maintaining and respecting the integrity of the land, sea, and animals was important because their predictability allowed navigators to find their way. Additionally, respecting native trees and other natural resources was important because canoe builders relied on their consistent availability to make their tools and construct their vessels. Overall, the CHamoru voyaging and canoe tradition embodied CHamoru aesthetics, technologies, and ecological values, in addition to being a crucial aspect of CHamoru cultural identity.

When the Spanish authorities initiated their policy of reducción to control, convert, acculturate, and tax the CHamoru population, they further immobilized CHamorus by forbidding them from building outrigger canoes, sailing the open ocean, and fishing beyond the reef.[13] They even burned the

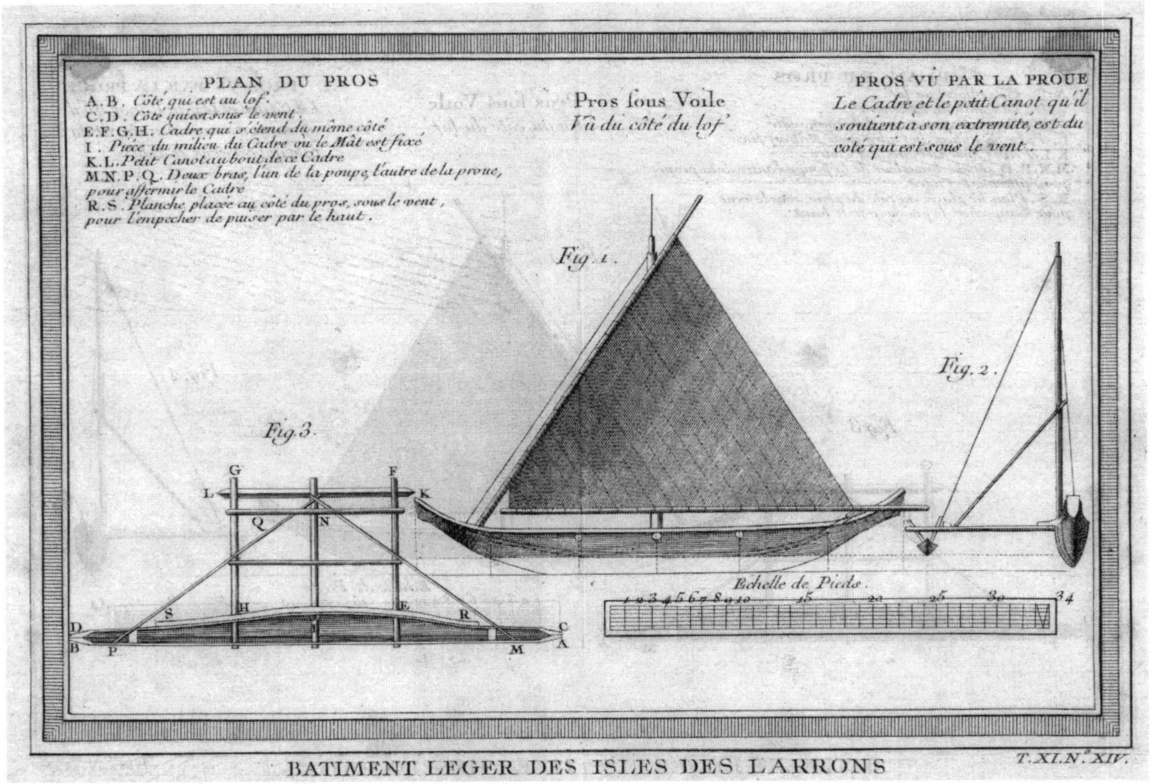

FIGURE 9 "Proa Design," from Antoine Prevost's *Histoire générale des voyages*, 1753. Courtesy of the Guam Public Library System.

canoes. Across the Pacific, canoe-building and voyaging traditions were "discouraged and criminalized by nineteenth-century European missionaries, traders, and colonial administrations who had a vested interest in maintaining a local tax-paying, church-going, and plantation-working population."[14] Once highly skilled ship builders, transoceanic navigators, and pelagic fishermen, CHamorus were severed from the knowledge of how to build and sail their ancestral canoes in just a few generations. The navigational stories, chants, songs, rituals, and maps were lost at sea. The sakman, the vessel that had carried CHamorus across the ocean to Guåhan millennia before European invasion, no longer flew across the waters.

George Anson, the commander of a British naval squadron that was sent to attack Spanish colonies during the War of the Austrian Succession in 1740, ended up in the Mariana archipelago, where he encountered a CHamoru proa. His crew captured and disassembled it to record its dimensions. Then they burned the canoe. A drawing and description of the proa was published in Anson's *Voyage Round the World* in 1748. By the time the book was published, the CHamoru population, which had continued to collapse, numbered less than two thousand. Anson was possibly "the last European visitor to see the flying proa in use."[15] The epigraph that opens this chapter, along with the drawing of the canoe, can be read as a memorial to the loss of CHamoru mobility and freedom, as well as the loss of a core component of CHamoru culture and identity.

A Bell Made of Stones and "Flying Proa Poetics"

Despite this history of loss, the themes of seafaring and voyaging feature prominently in Pacific literature.[16] The oceangoing vessel is represented as a symbol and icon of Indigenous Pacific genealogy, sovereignty, history, cultural identity, technology, and aesthetics. Navigation has come to signify a "transoceanic imaginary" and become a "master trope for Pacific literary production."[17] Lehua Taitano's *A Bell Made of Stones* (2013), one of the first poetry books published by a diasporic CHamoru writer, is an important contribution to the "maritime narrative legacy" of CHamoru poetry.[18]

Taitano was born in 1978 to a CHamoru woman, Catherine Flores Taitano, and a white American man, Ralph David Shelton. Her parents met when Shelton, an airman in the U.S. Air Force, was stationed at Andersen Air

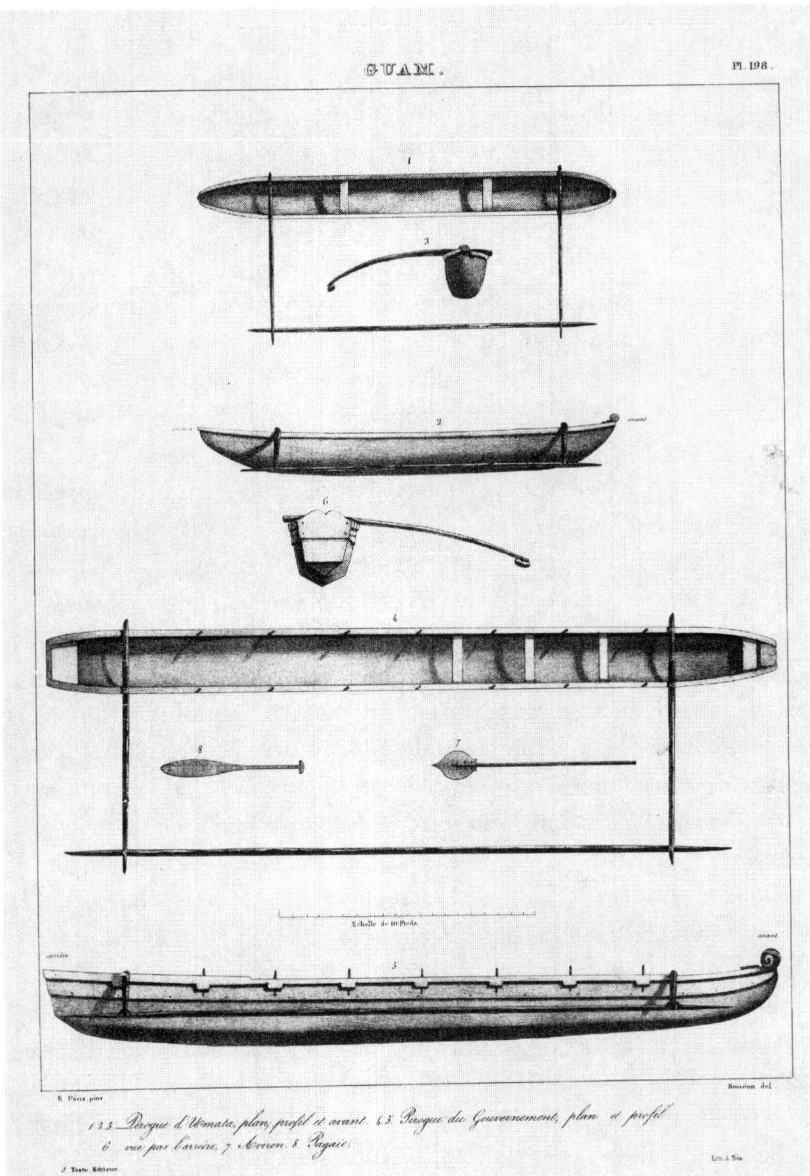

FIGURE 10 "Plans for Two Chamorro Canoes," illustration by Louis Auguste de Sainson, from Dumont d'Urville's *Voyage de la corvette l'Astrolabe*, 1830. Courtesy of Guam Public Library System.

Force Base in northern Guåhan. Their family lived near the base in the village of Yigo until they moved to Asheville, North Carolina, in 1982. Since then, Taitano has lived in various parts of the Appalachian region of North Carolina, as well as Missoula, Montana, and Santa Rosa, California. She graduated from the University of Montana's MFA Program in Creative Writing in 2010, and she is author of the poetry chapbooks *appalachiapacific* (2010) and *Sonoma* (2016). Her poetry, essays, and Pushcart Prize–nominated fiction have appeared in many national and international literary journals, and her second poetry collection, *Inside Me an Island*, was published in 2018. Taitano is also an interdisciplinary artist whose visual, installation, and collaborative art has been exhibited throughout the United States and the Pacific. Her work explores diasporic, queer, and Indigenous identities.

The cover of *A Bell Made of Stones*, designed by Allison Hanabusa, features a close-up detail of a deeply fissured red stone (figure 11).[19] Parts of the image are clear and defined, revealing the intricate texture of the stone, while other parts are intentionally blurred, creating a depth of field that points to the main fissure. A white circle composed of hyphens overlies this fissure, with the title of the book placed within the circle (the word "Made" is placed atop the darkest part of the fissure), and the author's name lying just outside it. The title refers to the latte stone megaliths (whose shapes resemble those of bells) that form the foundation of ancestral CHamoru houses, discussed in the previous chapter. The fissuring of the stone suggests that the author's home has been fractured. The circle of hyphens conjures a star compass used for navigation, foregrounding the major theme of the book: navigating diaspora and searching for home. The hyphenation of the circle reflects the idea that the author is trying to plot her hyphenated cultural identity. Overall, the cover visually articulates the themes of navigation, migration, and home.

Taitano launches her book with a letter addressed to an unnamed reader. The top of the letter is dated "April 2013" and the location is listed as "a little room / in California / with wind and eucalyptus" (*Bell*, 9). The first paragraph of the letter addresses the reader in an intimate tone:

> You are there, turning these words over in your hands, in your island heart. I am here, breathing salt air, sitting in a long slant of light, opening slowly to the story I wish to tell you. My only request: take these words out into the sun, into the wind, beside the ocean if possible. This space desires waves. (*Bell*, 9)

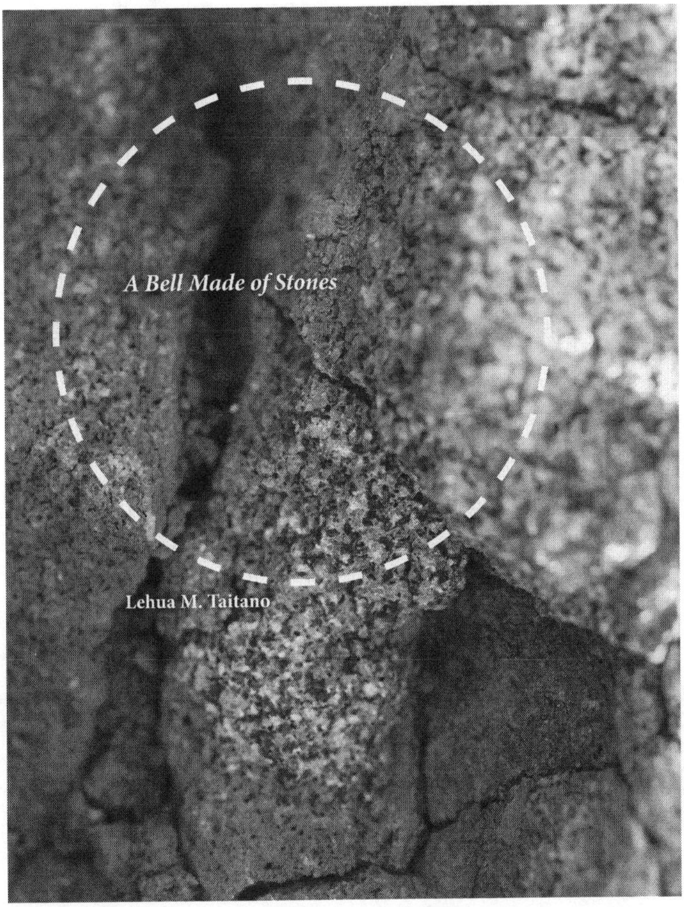

FIGURE 11 Cover of Lehua Taitano's *A Bell Made of Stones*, designed by Allison Hanabusa, 2013. Reproduced courtesy of Tinfish Press.

Beginning in California, the letter situates the speaker in a diasporic space. Using the epistolary form, it invites the reader to become the addressee and carry the book beside the ocean, suggesting that the reader is part of this journey. We can then interpret the "little room" as a metaphoric canoe house from which we will launch. For the speaker, the destination island is the reader's "island heart" and the space between is a space where waves (ocean waves and sound waves) connect the *I* and *you*, the *here* and *there*. Beyond addressing a general reader, the "you" with the "island heart" can also refer more specifically to CHamorus back home in the Marianas, CHamorus in the diaspora, or other Pacific Islanders. For any audience, the journey of the book is cast as an unfolding story.

Within Pacific migration and diasporic studies, voyaging and navigation are major themes and important conceptual frames through which to think about mobility and displacement. In the introduction to *Pacific Diaspora: Island Peoples in the United States Across the Pacific* (the cover of which also features a double-hulled Pacific canoe), Paul Spickard writes: "People have been moving around the Pacific Ocean for a very long time. The Pacific diaspora is thousands of years old."[20] Epeli Hau'ofa also points to how large, interconnected, and global the Pacific islands are, countering the conception of islands and islanders as small, insignificant, insular, and dependent. In his pivotal essay "Our Sea of Islands," he writes:

> The world of our ancestors was a large sea full of places to explore, to make their homes in, to breed generations of seafarers like themselves. People raised in this environment were at home with the sea. . . . They developed great skills for navigating their waters—as well as the spirit to traverse even the few large gaps that separated their island groups. Theirs was a large world in which peoples and cultures moved and mingled, unhindered by boundaries of the kind erected much later by imperial powers. From one island to another they sailed to trade and to marry, thereby expanding social networks for greater flows of wealth. They travelled to visit relatives in a wide variety of natural and cultural surroundings, to quench their thirst for adventure, and even to fight and dominate.[21]

This story of Indigenous mobility shows that migration and diaspora are essential components of Indigenous Pacific Islander identities and cultures. Or, as Hau'ofa poetically phrases it: "it is in their blood to be mobile."[22]

The period of free Indigenous mobility ended with the arrival of European imperialism in the sixteenth century, as colonial powers suppressed the voyaging traditions of Pacific Islanders in order to immobilize, control, and tax Indigenous populations.[23] These same forces also launched Pacific Islanders into new imperial trade routes and pathways.[24] For example, thousands of islanders (including Hawaiians, Sāmoans, and CHamorus) embarked on whaling ships in the nineteenth century, which carried them across the Pacific and into the Americas. Pacific Islanders participated in the whaling industry, the fur trade, the California gold rush, and even the American Civil

War.[25] During this era, other islanders were recruited by labor agents and later enslaved and sent to work the mines of Peru. Some estimate that one hundred thousand islanders from Melanesia became enslaved labor in Australia—an inhumane practice known as "blackbirding."[26]

Even though these colonial migrations continued through the first half of the twentieth century, the major wave of Pacific migration occurred in the decades after World War II. The presence of various colonial nations (including the United States, Japan, France, Chile, Britain, Germany, Australia, New Zealand, the Netherlands, and Indonesia) established new routes of migration. As Spickard describes: "The administrative, military, commercial, and missionary presence of all these outsider nations provided the links along which tens of thousands of Pacific Island people were set in motion."[27] In the decades following World War II, Pacific Islanders began to migrate to cities and metropolitan nations in search of economic, educational, and health care opportunities. Some of the factors that encouraged Pacific out-migration included enlistment in colonial militaries, land dispossession, unemployment, displacement by nuclear testing, high real-estate prices, lack of educational opportunities, and (in recent years) climate change.[28] This mass migration has resulted in the highest concentrations of Pacific Islanders now living in cities like Auckland, Honolulu, and Los Angeles. Some islands have more islanders living overseas than at home, and currently populated small islands are likely to experience future depopulation.[29] In this "new diaspora," Pacific Islanders have settled in other countries around the world to the point that there are now generations of islanders who were born outside their ancestral lands.[30]

Just as the Pacific diaspora has grown exponentially, scholarship on Pacific migration and diaspora has also increased. Much of the scholarship focuses on the historical, political, economic, and cultural contexts and impacts of migration.[31] Several scholars examine how migration affects home economies and kinship networks, especially in relation to remittances and family obligations.[32] Other scholars conduct ethnographic research, interviewing Pacific Islander migrants in various diasporic locations. This scholarship highlights the positive and negative lived experiences of Pacific Islanders in the diaspora, addressing issues of education, health, employment, family, longing, discrimination, and trauma. Scholars also focus on how migration has shaped and changed Indigenous cultural identities, especially in relation to family structure, language, cultural connection, and religion.[33]

Most of the aforementioned research focuses on Polynesian populations; however, there is a growing body of scholarship that examines the movement from and within Micronesia. The first major wave of Micronesian migration occurred in the 1980s and 1990s, after Compacts of Free Association were established between the United States and the Republic of Palau, the Republic of the Marshall Islands, and the Federated States of Micronesia, which granted citizens from these places access to reside and work in the United States and its territories. This opened pathways for Micronesian migrants to move and settle in Guåhan, Hawai'i, and the continental United States. Early research on Micronesian migration involved understanding the historical, political, colonial, and martial factors that led to out-migration.[34] As diasporic Micronesian communities settled, ethnographic studies emerged that examined how Micronesians adapted to and struggled in new environments, maintained ties with home, and articulated new diasporic cultural identities.[35]

Pacific migration and diaspora have been conceptualized as both a continuity of ancient voyaging traditions and a consequence of global imperialism, militarism, and capitalism. On the one hand, Pacific out-migration is understood as displacement, rupture, brain drain, depopulation, loss, disconnection, departure, and crisis; on the other hand, Pacific out-migration is understood as mobility, empowerment, cosmopolitanism, enlargement, horizon, transnationalism, circulation, and opportunity. Most often, both conceptions operate simultaneously to highlight the traumas and triumphs of Pacific diasporas. While different Pacific populations have unique experiences, it is clear that Pacific cultures, identities, families, histories, and politics have all been indelibly shaped by waves of migration. Sometimes Pacific Islanders let go of their home cultures and assimilate into the dominant society, and sometimes they continue to maintain their Indigenous identities by cultivating, revitalizing, and rearticulating Pacific customs, languages, and values despite pressures to acculturate.

Because Taitano opens the book in California, it is crucial to understand the significance of California and the specific history of CHamoru migration and diaspora. Historically, California has been a major destination for CHamoru migrants, and it is home to the largest CHamoru diasporic population in the United States, numbering around 45,000 as of 2010. The first CHamorus to settle in California arrived via the Pacific whaling industry, which flourished in the nineteenth century, when nearly thirty ships docked off Guåhan each year. Robert Underwood describes how these schooners "scattered Chamorros to many corners of the earth, and today on Guam many Chamorro families count a whaler or two as part of their heritage."[36] From the beginning of American occupation in 1898 to the start of World War II, hundreds of CHamorus enlisted in the navy and would become "the first Chamorros to leave in significant numbers and not return."[37] When CHamorus became U.S. citizens as a result of the Organic Act of 1950, enlistment in the armed forces increased exponentially. In turn, this increased the number of CHamorus migrating to and settling in California, especially in cities with or near military bases, such as San Diego, Long Beach, Vallejo, Alameda, and Fairfield.

While three-quarters of all diasporic CHamorus are associated with the armed services,[38] the remaining quarter out-migrated for education and economic opportunities, as well as for access to health care services. The introduction of jet travel made the trip from Guåhan to California much easier; the journey could be made in twelve hours, and the price of a one-way ticket in 1983 was $450. By 1990, 50,000 CHamorus lived in the United States; by 2000, the population had nearly doubled to 92,000.[39] As of 2010, an estimated 150,000 CHamorus have settled in all fifty states and even in Puerto Rico. Today, more CHamorus live in the diaspora than in the Mariana Islands.[40] Put another way, approximately six out of every ten CHamorus live in the diaspora. According to the 2010 U.S. census, CHamorus have become "the most geographically dispersed" of all the Pacific populations.[41]

Throughout the scholarship on CHamoru diaspora, migration is often characterized in voyaging and navigational terms. Faye Untalan Muñoz, for example, describes how the opportunity for travel and migration reignited a CHamoru "passion for traveling and exploration" that dated back to seafaring days.[42] Similarly, Underwood employs a metaphor of water to conceptualize migration: "What began in 1937 as a *trickle* of mess attendants had become by the 1970s a steady *stream* of visitors, movers, and emigrants."[43] Underwood also visualizes military service as a "vehicle of departure."[44] Lastly, Jesi Lujan Bennett discusses how "Chamorro migrants have created a *transpacific home*, where there is a *back and forth flow* of communication, goods, and bodies between the Mariana Islands and their current location."[45] Bennett points out how the CHamoru word for "airplane" is *batkon aire*, which literally translates as "air boat."[46] These oceanic and voyaging metaphors situate CHamoru migration as a continuation of traditional voyaging histories. This suggests that CHamorus still maintain agency in navigating the open waters of the diaspora and the ability to map their routes, make safe landfall, and navigate a trans-Pacific home.

The desire for trans-Pacific connection is encapsulated in the opening letter of *A Bell Made of Stones*. In it, Taitano describes a dream in which she walks down a dirt path toward a Spanish mission and finds her ancestors and their living bones. They speak to her, but she doesn't understand their language. Even though the maternal side of Taitano's family spoke both CHamoru and English when they lived on Guåhan, her father forbade them from speaking CHamoru when the family moved to North Carolina because he insisted it would prevent her from "fitting in" (*Bell*, 11). In "Chamorro Ambivalence and Diaspora: Beyond U.S. Racial Formations," Michael Perez notes that an "intergenerational language gap, whereby grandchildren do not speak the native tongue, is especially detrimental to cultural integrity . . . thereby marking a potential generational departure and virtual snipping of the indigenous umbilical cord."[47] The intergenerational linguistic gap, which is exacerbated by living in the diaspora far away from other CHamoru language speakers, alienates the poet from the CHamoru ancestors she meets in the dream. If they were trying to teach her a navigational chant describing how to return home, for example, she would have no way of knowing. Because she can't understand them, she remains silent and laments: "I have had my tongue cut out and then have been asked why I don't have more to say" (*Bell*, 11).

Besides not speaking the language of her ancestors, the speaker also worries that her ancestors won't recognize her because of her light skin color. She writes: "In my bare feet I am Chamorro. And white, yes" (*Bell*, 9). Taitano's migration story differs from those described in most of the scholarship that focuses on CHamoru migrants because her family is mixed-heritage (or, as Taitano phrases it, composed of "disparate parts" [9]). Taitano feels anxiety about not being recognized by her ancestors because she does not have a phenotypically "brown face" (9). This anxiety is extended to experiences in the United States in which she doesn't appear to be either brown or white "enough" to fit into recognizable racial categories. Michael Perez speaks to this struggle when he posits that "Chamorros remain relatively invisible within the context of the US 'melting pot' [because of their] relatively small population size and their 'racial' similarities with other 'brown faces' on the US mainland."[48] Of course, this invisibility is even more complicated if you are a mixed-heritage CHamoru who may not share racial similarities with other "brown" ethnic minorities. Taitano conceives this uncomfortable space as a hyphenated space: "This is the hyphen inside of me talking. Fused, spliced, separated, compounded. . . . These are my intersections of half-ness. Of -lessness" (*Bell*, 11). The speaker's feelings relate to what Perez describes as the CHamoru "marginal existence across multiple dimensions of culture, nationality, and otherness. These dimensions involve experiences with US minority status and racism, intragroup antagonism, and being at the margins of Chamorro and American cultures."[49] Indeed, Taitano's experience as a diasporic, mixed-heritage CHamoru living between languages, cultures, racial categories, and geographic locations makes her feel ambivalent and further displaced.

Previous scholarship on migration frames CHamoru migrants as ambitious people who seek upward mobility through military employment and economic or educational opportunities. Untalan Muñoz has noted how CHamoru migrants "want change, want to improve their living conditions, and are willing to make the necessary sacrifices."[50] Underwood adds that to some, migration "seemed obligatory if one was to experience the full joys of life that awaited the Chamorro in California."[51] Through her poetry, Taitano shares an aspect of CHamoru migration that we do not often discuss: the trauma of migration (or, to connect it to voyaging, the trauma of being lost at sea). For example, the first poem after the epistolary preface poignantly captures this emotion with six words in the middle of an otherwise blank page: "inside me an island / shaped hole" (*Bell*, 13). Here the journey is cast as an interior journey; however, the destination island is, emotionally, absent. This short poem alludes to two well-known lines in Pacific literature. In Albert Wendt's poem "Inside Us the Dead," the phrase "inside me the dead" acts as a navigational chant-like refrain through which the author recounts his multiple ancestors, genealogies, and geographies, which remain "woven into [his] flesh like the music / of bone flutes."[52] Taitano's poem also echoes the title of Epeli Hau'ofa's essay "The Ocean in Us," in which he articulates the importance of the ocean as a metaphor for how islanders are connected culturally, politically, economically, geographically, and spiritually. The essay ends:

> The sea is as real as you and I, it shapes the character of this planet, it is a major source of our sustenance, and it is something that we all share in common wherever we are in Oceania: these are all statements of fact. Above that level of everyday experience, the sea is our pathway to each other and

> to everyone else, the sea is our endless saga, the sea is our most important metaphor, the ocean is in us.[53]

While Wendt and Hau'ofa envision the presence of ancestors and the fullness of the ocean inside islanders, Taitano complicates this vision by highlighting how migration has created a hole where an island should be, thus speaking, as I will show, to how diasporic islanders might rebuild transoceanic connections. We might call this a diasporic etak through which CHamorus ask: How do we navigate home when home, our destination island, is an island-shaped absence?

The very next poem in *A Bell Made of Stone* is titled "asamplingfromtheguamvisitorsbureau" (*Bell*, 9; figure 12). As the title informs us, this poem collages (and edits) text from the website of the Guam Visitors Bureau. The poet uses the website to locate Guåhan in space: "the island: 6,000milesfromsanfrancisco / 3,800mileswestofHonolulu / 1,500milessouthofjapan." Before discussing this poem, we must pause to note that many poems in the book omit the spaces between words. One effect of this poetic technique is that it foregrounds the visuality of the words, in the sense that they are not simply relaying information but also embodying meaning in their visual form. Put another way, the words become a visual puzzle, asking the reader to slow down and parse the jumble of letters to make sense of—*to navigate*—the poem. On one hand, we can interpret this to mean that the form embodies the difficulty of navigating the Pacific diaspora; on the other hand, we can understand this form as embodying the speaker's desire to reduce the distance between geographical spaces. The fact that Taitano looks to a tourism website to locate and learn about Guåhan, the "island shaped hole" in her heart, shows her distance and disconnection from her home island. As Michael Perez has noted, turning to the Internet to search for information and connection is a common part of the way that diasporic CHamorus try to "remain culturally connected to one another via communication technology, mass media, long-distance familism and cultural continuity."[54] The Internet is one space through which diasporic CHamorus map the location of their cultural identity.[55]

Besides omitting spaces between words, Taitano also composes with a typewriter. *A Bell Made of Stones* appears to be a scanned original of a manuscript that was produced on an actual typewriter. In the prefatory letter, Taitano explains that she wrote the poems on an old seafoam-colored typewriter that she bought at a flea market in a small Appalachian town. To her,

asamplingfromtheguamvisitorsbureau.
theisland: 6,000milesfromsanfrancisco
3,800mileswestofhonolulu
1,500milessouthofjapan
wascreatedfrompeaksoftwoancientvolcanoes
thatsankintothesea
(Agana)
population: canbedividedintothreeethnicgroups
originalinhabitantsmakeup
approximately
37%
politicalstatus: one(1)non-votingcongressional
delegatetothehouseofrepresentatives
history: bycanoe
clanandcaste
matrilineal
isolatedfromtherestofthe world
magellan
broughtcatholicismandawesternway
newera
japaneseforcesassumedcontrol
u.s.troopsreclaimed
organic.
gettingthere: gateways
accommodations: regionalhotelchainshavebeachfront
language: englishandchamorro
climate: providingexcellentopportunitiesforwatersports
attractions: petroglyphs
lattestones(pillars)
spanishruins
wwIImemorials
totransformdishesintoachamorromeal,
requestfinadene
apiquantsauce
usually,familystylefinadenehasmoreheat
traveldocuments (entryandexitformalities):
citizens
of
most other
countries
musthave
avalid
passport

FIGURE 12 "asamplingfromtheguamvisitorsbureau," by Lehua Taitano, 2013. Reprinted courtesy of Lehua Taitano and Tinfish Press.

the "gridded keys" are islands "afloat yet firmly stationed in their neat rows, resting at neat angles" (*Bell,* 9). The word *keys* signifies not only the units of the typewriter and low islands or reefs, but also objects that open a lock, map legends, systems of tones or harmonies, and even sets of instructions to decipher codes. Interestingly, the speaker points out that her typewriter's key for the letter *A* sticks so that "words like American and Chamorro are rendered with hiccups and enjambments" (9). Even though the keys are metaphorically supposed to provide (or unlock) instructions, directions, and explanations, the fact that one key "sticks" foregrounds the ambivalence that Taitano feels as a CHamoru in diasporic and cultural flux. And if the typewriter is the sea and the keys are islands, then each stroke is the poet's attempt to voyage across the great distances of memory, diaspora, cultural identity, and home. Taitano describes how each stroke, "each imprint, each metal sound, reverberates its dull clack, its certain hollow ache. A stamping. Each poem is visual evidence of this echo. The surfacing and submergence of islands of sound" (11). Since the poet envisions the text of the poems as "islands of sound," then we can also wayread the page as an ocean of silence. Furthermore, if each poem is "visual evidence" of her echo (locations), then each poem can be wayread as a navigational map.

Engaging with the visuality of Taitano's work reveals deeper meanings embedded in the form and structure of the poems and the book itself. In *Trans-Indigenous: Methodologies for Global Native Literary Studies,* Chadwick Allen shows how the technologies and aesthetics of Pacific voyaging can shape a literary text's "complex formal structures and multiple structural patterns."[56] He illustrates how navigational intentionality and repeatability are embodied in the formal patterning of the individual poems and the overall structure of the poetry collection *Star Waka,* by Māori poet Robert Sullivan. Allen charts the "regularized variation in the number and length of lines within poems and of stanzaic patterning within, between, and among poems across the sequence."[57] He also details how the "structures of specific subsections, poems, stanzas, and lines in each sequence" interact with the "macrostructure of each poetic sequence" to create regular, repeating patterns of relationship.[58] Allen focuses on a sequence of visual poems in *Star Waka,* which are textually and typographically shaped into waves, pitches, stars, islands, horizons, maps, and a compass. Allen proposes that through this visuality, the poems "evoke primary tools for Indigenous open-water navigation."[59] He demonstrates how poetic forms (poem, line, stanza, punctuation, typeface, and blank space, as well as sequencing, numbering, and patterning) combine to embody aspects of navigational technologies and aesthetic forms of oceangoing canoes. This method can be applied to Taitano's work as well, I will argue, in both its overall structure and a series of poems titled "maps."

Structurally, *A Bell Made of Stones* is not your average 6-by-9-inch paperback; instead, the book has a large 8.5-by-11-inch format, which makes it feel much more like an atlas than a poetry collection. This poetic atlas contains twenty-one individual poems and five serial poems. The collection spans nearly ninety pages, but the text of the poems only appears on the recto pages (the right-hand side or front of the page), while the verso pages (left-hand side or back of the page) contain no poetic text. At the same time, the recto pages contain no page numbers, while the verso pages contain double page numbers (12–13, 14–15, etc.) located at the bottom right side near the gutter. I contend that the asymmetrical macrostructure of the book reflects the asymmetrical design of the CHamoru outrigger. We can imagine the blank verso page as the flat leeward side of the canoe, and the textualized recto page as the windward side with the outrigger of text. Similar to the proa, the asymmetrical design of *A Bell Made of Stones* functions to counterbalance the text and the blank space so that each poem appears to hover, or fly, above the ocean of the page.

The serial poem "maps" is composed of six sections and explores the main theme of migration and diaspora. The different sections are dispersed throughout *A Bell Made of Stones*, mirroring the scattering of the CHamoru population. The first poem in the series, "maps1," comprises a single stanza of eighteen lines with no spaces between the words (*Bell*, 13; figure 13). The poem opens with the speaker spinning a globe to look for Guåhan. She explains a navigational "trick" to find the island.

After we decipher the signs, we learn the navigational trick: locate and place your index finger and thumb on larger, recognizable (reference) islands like Japan and the Philippines; then, Guåhan will be at the angle where your fingers intersect. Even though this "trick" is supposed to help the speaker find Guåhan on a map, it still makes her feel "lost at sea." Perhaps she feels this way because Guåhan is so small that it sometimes does not even appear on maps, or maybe because she is lost in the diaspora ("I spun the globe too long") without a cultural navigator to guide her home, or maybe because the view is from above and not at the level of the ocean.

~~ma-ps.1~~

mapsl.

ispunaglobe
toolongsoit
appea redid
idnotknowwh
ereiwasfrom
evenwithatr
ickwhichist
ofindjapanf
irstandthep
hilippinesse
condandscan
therightang
ledintersec
tiontwofing
ersmeetingm
akeiwaslost
atseayesi'v
eheardital1

FIGURE 13 "mapsl," by Lehua Taitano, 2013. Reprinted courtesy of Lehua Taitano and Tinfish Press.

The scholarship on CHamoru migration focuses mainly on adult migrants and does not study how migration affects CHamoru children.[60] Some CHamoru children are born on Guåhan and forced to move with their families at a young age, while others are born elsewhere after their parents' migration. Some are able to periodically visit their ancestral home islands, while some are not. The second poem of the series, "maps2," captures a traumatic moment in Taitano's life as a diasporic child (*Bell*, 49; figure 14). The map-poem is set in a North Carolina classroom. The teacher, Mrs. Bradley, is calling students to the front of the room to point out where they are from on a world map. Sadly, the speaker has a difficult time finding Guåhan. Instead of helping her navigate, Mrs. Bradley pulls the speaker by her ear away from the map and embarrasses her in front of the entire class.

The feeling of invisibility is further embodied in "maps3," which consists entirely of the title of the poem in the middle of an otherwise blank page. At first, the blank space evokes absence, distance, and silence. However, when wayread within a Pacific context, the blank space also evokes connection and relation. Albert Wendt discusses space through the Sāmoan concept of va: "va is the space between, the betweenness, not empty space, not space that separates but space that relates, that holds separate entities and things together in the Unity-that-is-All, the space that is context, giving meanings to things."[61] In this way, "maps3" can also be understood as the space between arrival and departure, origin and destination, home and diaspora, silence and story.

After we contemplate the space of "maps3," "maps4" arrives four pages later and presents the names of villages on Guåhan (including Taitano's home village of Yigo), as well as names of military bases and installations, such as "AFB" (Andersen Air Force Base) and "AFB munitions storage area" (*Bell*, 53; figure 15). When you hold the text at arm's length, the constellation of names visually resembles an aerial view of part of Guåhan's landmass. Even though the poem conjures a feeling of hope because the island has been found, it also conjures a sense of incompletion because the shape is only partial.

At this point in reading, I assumed the rest of the landmass would be textually shaped in "maps5"; yet the very next section we encounter is "maps6." I retrace my inter-poem journey across the ten pages between "maps4" and "maps6" just to make sure I didn't skip over "maps5." Since I don't sight the poem, I return to the table of contents and find that "maps5" is located thirty maps2.

mrs.bradleywas
hernameanditbe
arsrepeatingth
oughshe'slongd
eadiwillshouti
t:MRS.BRADLEY!
washernameands
hepulledmebymy
ea ra wa yfrom
themapofthewor
ldinfrontofthe
whitekidswheni
searchedbutcou
ldnotfindmybel
oveddotmybelov
edsplotchshesa
idlehuayouarew
astingourtimea
nditwasthenikn
ewiwasonlyhalf
visible .

FIGURE 14 "maps2," by Lehua Taitano, 2013. Reprinted courtesy of Lehua Taitano and Tinfish Press.

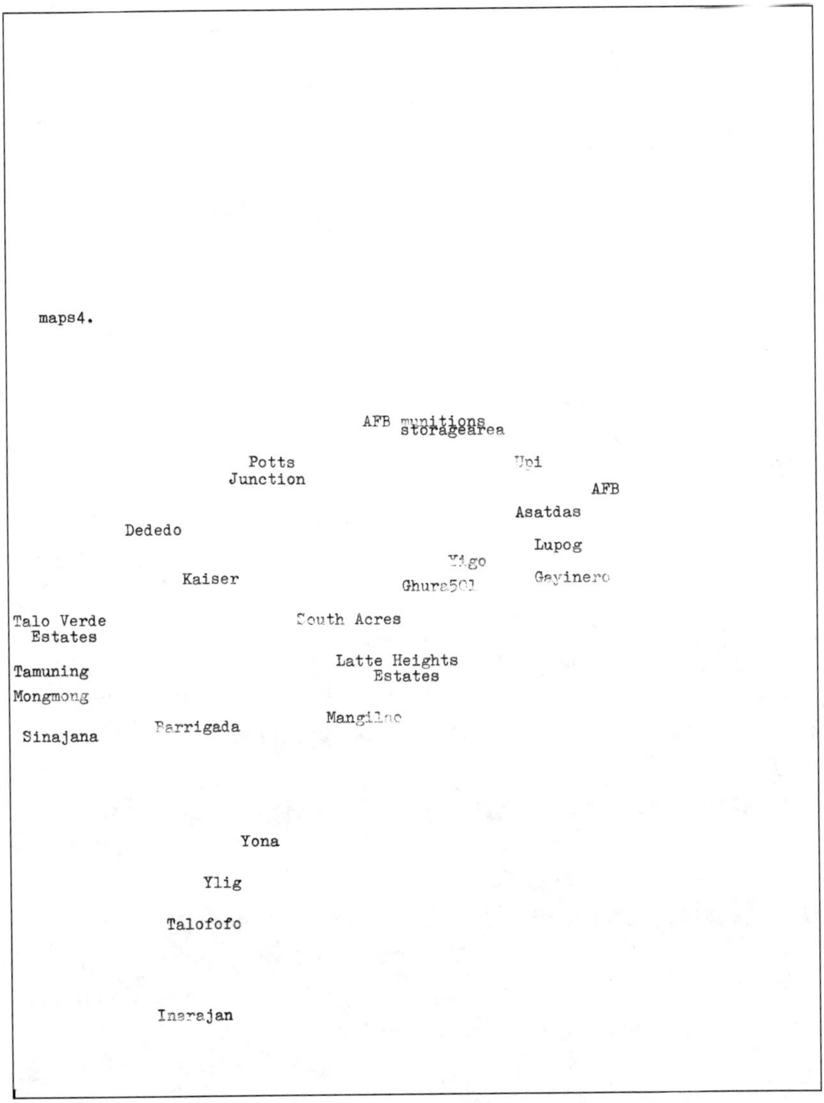

FIGURE 15 "maps4," by Lehua Taitano, 2013. Reprinted courtesy of Lehua Taitano and Tinfish Press.

pages *before* "maps4." How did I miss this misplaced map? I turn to "maps5" and realize I missed it because the title is not on the actual page. As anticipated, "maps5" does complete "maps4," as it lists names of other villages and military bases on Guåhan (*Bell*, 23; figure 16).

When you combine the fourth and fifth maps together, this completes the textual replica of the shape of Guåhan. The effect of serializing the poem-maps and misplacing part of the expected sequence is disorientation. The missing map page stirs up anxiety that we have lost our way. The dividing of the map into two sections and its dispersal in the book subtly alludes to a familiar ancestral story that explains how Guåhan's landmass was formed into its current shape. The story goes: One fateful day, a giant sea creature began eating away at the middle of the island, threatening to bite it in half. The men hunted the creature but it cleverly eluded them. So the women wove their hair together to make a throw net and sang songs to lure the creature. When the beast surfaced, they cast their wide net over it and saved Guåhan.[62] Perhaps the beast represents the vehicles of migration (literally, ships and airplanes; and figuratively, military service and educational and economic opportunities) that have divided the island in the sense that more than half of the CHamoru population now lives off-island. Moreover, the fragmentary nature of these two maps may also highlight the fragmentary (and fissured) identity of the CHamoru diasporic experience.

The map-poem series ends with "maps6," which once again situates the wayreader in cyberspace (*Bell*, 95; figure 17). Although the exact website is not explicitly stated, we can infer that it is one that calculates distance and directions when you input an origin and a destination. The poem opens by listing the total distance from North Carolina to Guåhan: 12,879.58 miles. The rest of the poem, however, fails to provide navigable directions.

The fact that the poet lists her full address in North Carolina yet only the village name of Yigo suggests that she no longer remembers her full home address. For many migrants, as Underwood writes, "Guam is only a faint memory."[63] The strike-through visually expresses the poet's disappointment—and perhaps even anger—at being so far from home and not knowing if or when she will ever return. Even though the Internet acts as a vehicle for diasporic CHamorus to stay connected to their home and culture, it does not fully satisfy the desire for connection and belonging.

Looking at the six poems that comprise the map series, each poem has a different visual appearance. The first two contain a single stanza but are

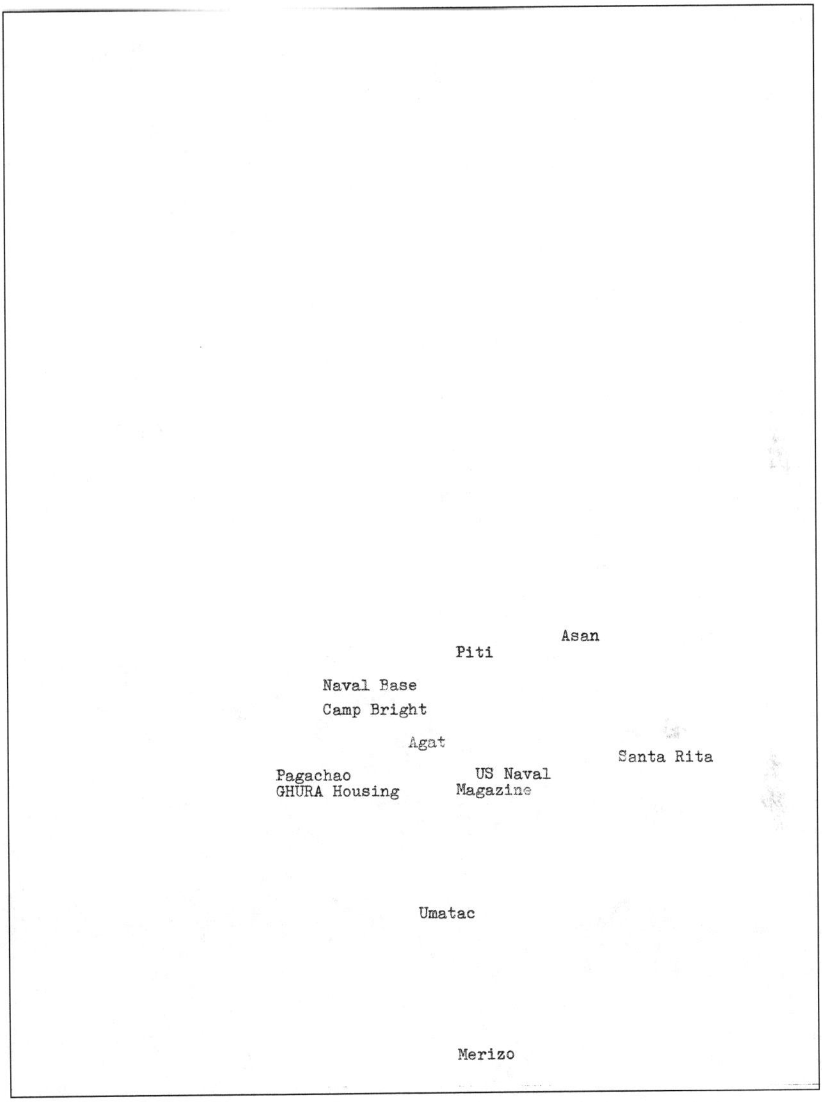

FIGURE 16 "maps5," by Lehua Taitano, 2013. Reprinted courtesy of Lehua Taitano and Tinfish Press.

maps6.

totaldistance
(as the crow flies):
12,879.58 miles

~~sorry,-we-could-not~~
~~calculate-directions~~

~~from179carolinabluebirdloop~~
~~arden,northcarolina~~

~~to-Yigo,-Guam~~

FIGURE 17 "maps6," by Lehua Taitano, 2013. Reprinted courtesy of Lehua Taitano and Tinfish Press.

placed on different parts of the page; the third is blank; the fourth and fifth contain individual words spaced throughout the page; and the sixth is made of several shorter stanzas separated into columns. Wayreading the different poetic forms from page to page makes the words appear to be moving (or flying) islands of sound. The concept of etak, then, can be understood as more than a navigational technology to measure time/space; it can also be understood as an Indigenous aesthetic that shapes the form of the poem.

Conclusion

In the 1960s, anthropologists debated whether Pacific Islanders made landfall through intentional, noninstrumental navigation or through drifting and accidental discovery. Some of these anthropologists sought out the last remaining Pacific canoe builders and navigators in order to learn the craft and see if they could replicate ancient oceanic voyages.[64] Even though voyaging traditions disappeared throughout the Pacific during the colonial era, the practice survived on some islands, including Puluwat and Satawal in Micronesia. In the early 1970s, Micronesian navigators led journeys to the Mariana Islands. This sparked region-wide interest and led to the most well-known revitalization voyage: the 1976 journey of the sixty-foot, double-hulled canoe the *Hokule'a* from Hawai'i to Tahiti, led by Satawalese navigator Pius "Mau" Piailug (affectionately known as "Papa Mau"). The *Hokule'a* was a "performative equivalent replica" of an ancient Polynesian voyaging vessel.[65] Its name means "Star of Gladness," referring to the zenith star (also known as Arcturus) of the Hawaiian Islands. During subsequent decades, canoe-building and navigational arts have been revitalized throughout Oceania. Despite centuries of suppression and cessation, "the dignity of the seagoing past of the Islanders has been rescued," as David Lewis has phrased it, and "they are regaining a new self-respect as inheritors of this illustrious past."[66]

Voyaging revitalization was launched in Guåhan in the mid-1990s, when Manny Sikau, from Puluwat, taught navigation to the Traditional Seafaring Society at the University of Guam. He taught their members the techniques of etak, the stars of the star compass, and the cartography of the local archipelagoes. He also taught them the features of pookof, such as ocean swells, seamarks, cloud formations, and bird routes. The Traditional

Seafaring Society then purchased a twenty-two-foot Micronesian outrigger canoe called *Quest.* They sailed it more than five hundred miles from Puluwat to Guåhan in 2001, with several shorter voyages across the Marianas the next year.[67] In 2008, a group named Traditions About Seafaring Islands built a thirty-three-foot sakman and named it *Saina,* which means "elder" or "ancestor." The following year, the crew sailed *Saina* to the island of Rota, forty-five miles north of Guåhan. This was the first CHamoru proa built in Guåhan and sailed in the waters of the Mariana archipelago in over 250 years. Inspired by this voyage, the *Ayuyu,* a seventeen-foot proa, and the *Hurao,* a twenty-foot proa, were built in 2012.[68] The revitalization of CHamoru voyaging even expanded beyond the Mariana Islands. In 2011, CHamorus in San Diego who were part of the group Sakman Chamorro Project built a forty-seven-foot sakman named *Che'lu,* which means "friend," "brother," or "sister." The navigators of *Che'lu* shipped the canoe from San Diego to Guåhan for the Festival of Pacific Arts in 2016.[69]

These contemporary revitalization efforts have reconnected CHamorus to their island neighbors across Micronesia, and to other CHamorus across the diaspora. The return of the flying proa has given Pacific Islanders a sense of pride in the accomplishments and ingenuity of our ancestors. It reminds CHamorus of the great distances we have traveled—our roots and routes. The stories of CHamoru voyaging customs and practices, the stories of the violent colonial history that suppressed these traditions, and the stories of the return of CHamoru canoes will help CHamorus navigate the future. As Mario Reyes Borja, carver and navigator of the *Che'lu,* poignantly stated: "This is a story that highlights the work of our hands, our understanding of nature, and our determination as a people. This is a story that gives credit to our ancestors for the simple gift that they gave us. . . . This is Our Sakman Story."[70]

In addition to revitalizing voyaging and navigational practices, CHamorus have also been creating spaces of cultural connection in the diaspora. According to the research done by Jesi Lujan Bennett, one of the oldest CHamoru diasporic organizations is the Sons and Daughters of Guam Club in San Diego, founded in 1953. The club includes a gathering house, pavilion, bar, and outdoor kitchen, and its two-and-a-half-acre property hosts fiestas, nobenas (rosaries), fundraisers, CHamoru language classes, senior meals, and cultural events.[71] As Bennett illustrates, "The Guam Club gives Chamorros a place to make connections to people . . . while also keeping kinship bonds strong in a new geographical and cultural context."[72] Another organization founded in San Diego is Che'lu (Chamorro Hands in Education Links Unity). Since the early 2000s, Che'lu has organized educational initiatives and offered language classes, public health programs, and cultural workshops. They were also involved in the building of the sakman. At their location in San Diego, they have a "Guma' Chamorro," a replica of a CHamoru house with latte stones. Che'lu also hosts the annual Chamorro Cultural Festival, first started in 2010 and celebrated every March to correspond with "Mes Chamoru" (Chamorro Month) in Guåhan. CHamorus from all over the United States and even some from Guåhan travel to the festival. Bennett describes its importance: "Within the transpacific home, gatherings of Pacific Islanders are an important means of maintaining collective identities and links to home islands. . . . Having a gupot brings Chamorros together from far and wide in order to take care of social and cultural obligations."[73] In CHamoru culture, the gupot is a gathering, celebration, party, feast, or holiday in which family, friends, and the community come together and cultivate relations. The *diasporic gupot* is important for establishing and maintaining cultural ties while CHamorus are far from their ancestral island. Today, there are CHamoru organizations in California, Oregon, Washington, Texas, Arizona, Nevada, Florida, the Midwest, Hawai'i, Washington, D.C., and more. There are even diasporic CHamoru groups on social media, such as the Faces of the Chamorro Diaspora Facebook page.[74] Taken together, these groups create a kinship network across vast geographical distances in order to help CHamorus navigate the diaspora, as well as to connect diasporic CHamorus to each other, to CHamoru culture, and to the Mariana Islands.

Through her poetry, Lehua Taitano similarly guides us through the blank and fragmented maps of the diaspora to show that an important part of CHamoru identity is discovering ways to stay connected to the islands, cultures, and language of CHamoru ancestors, even when one is far from home. *A Bell Made of Stones* attempts to navigate the strong currents of the diaspora by developing a transoceanic imaginary. The text itself becomes a vessel that carries Taitano toward home and circulates her story back across the ocean and to other archipelagic spaces. According to Vicente Diaz, master navigator Papa Mau often spoke about how having "a clear image of the destination island in one's head was indispensable for a successful voyage. This visual clarity was needed, he explained, because out at sea, the navigator will be challenged so vigorously by the elements."[75] Tragically, some diasporic CHamorus only have a faint memory of the Marianas, and they often have no teacher to guide them. Taitano's map-poems embody this ambivalence in both their primary themes and their forms. Though she drifts in the diasporic sea and feels only half-visible, Taitano's CHamoru identity is not extinguished. This embodies a key insight articulated by Michael Perez:

> Despite the seemingly disheartening terrain, Chamorros continue to endure as a people in spite of their locations at the edges of US racial and ethnic relations. Notions of indigeneity are therefore not limited to being authentically located in a given place. Rather they are located in space across various sites. Chamorros are Chamorros precisely because of their indigeneity, diasporic transnationality, resistance, consciousness, and articulation.[76]

Throughout *A Bell Made of Stones*, Taitano articulates a diasporic Indigeneity that is routed across various locations, memories, and stories while also remaining rooted in Guåhan and CHamoru cultural identity. Poetry becomes a map, a compass, a navigational chant, and a transoceanic letter home. Poetry is the space between, where the poet can locate herself and her song (*Bell*, 99):

> . . . cry out f
> or the flightless to stret
> ch roots, for the husk of
> things set adrift. Canoe i
> n the sea, cry out, sing.

CHAPTER 4

Singing Forward and Backward

Kåntan Chamorrita, CHamoru Intertextuality, and Spoken-Word Poetry

> Poetical expression came naturally to the [ancient Chamorro], and songs, chants, and epics set to poetical cadence and (often) to rhyme, were the medium by which a complete, practical, sometimes pragmatic but always honorable, cultural heritage was comprehended and preserved and transmitted—almost as if it had been engraved in tablets of stone.
>
> —William Peck

Introduction

Let us now turn our canoes back toward the northwestern Pacific, catch the trade winds, and return home to Guåhan. This last chapter explores the most well-known surviving form of CHamoru orature: kåntan chamorrita, a call-and-response, extemporaneous, communal oral poetry that was displaced and suppressed by colonial forces. I will explore how the themes, aesthetics, and values of the kåntan chamorrita have become rearticulated through different CHamoru literary, musical, and expressive forms, exemplifying CHamoru cultural and aesthetic vitality. I will argue that the kåntan chamorrita is also rearticulated in both contemporary CHamoru spoken-word and written poetry. Specifically, I propose that the spoken-word poetry movement on Guåhan evokes the kåntan chamorrita through its focus on oral performance, communal composition, and public competition. I will discuss a collaborative poem, "Self-Guamination" (2011), by two poets, Ryan Leon Guerrero and Walla Wai, of the youth spoken-word poetry team known as Team Guåhan, which is part of the Sinangån-ta youth poetry group. Moreover, I will argue that the dialogic, call-and-response form of the kåntan chamorrita is rearticulated in written poetry as a "CHamorucized intertextuality." I illustrate this point by putting into conversation two poems by CHamoru poets from different generations, Anne Perez Hattori's "Thieves" (1991) and Michael Lujan Bevacqua's "My Island Is One Big American Footnote" (2009). Overall, I will show how contemporary written and spoken-word poetry rearticulates the aesthetic, cultural, and political values of the kåntan chamorrita in order to weave a community of voices.

Kåntan Chamorrita: Customary CHamoru Orature

Oral literature was an integral part of customary CHamoru culture. As in other Indigenous cultures, CHamoru oral literature was an essential vessel for the intergenerational transmission of language, customs, genealogy, knowledge, religion, spirituality, navigation, history, politics, and cultural identity.[1] It is through oral storytelling, as Katherine Aguon has noted, that "the Chamorro learned how to become Chamorro."[2] The importance of CHamoru oral literature continued throughout the twentieth century; for example, the "Chamorro Literature" entry in *The Pacific Islands: An Encyclopedia* (2000), written by Keith Camacho, describes how the "richest sources of Chamorro literature are to be found in oral traditions, ranging from legends and folk tales to a variety of musical forms."[3]

The most documented form of ancestral CHamoru orature is commonly referred to as kåntan chamorrita.[4] This form is often described as "call-and-response impromptu verses."[5] Ethnomusicologist Kim Bailey described the kåntan chamorrita as

> ancient folk songs, arranged in quatrains of two octosyllabic couplets, which, according to some writers, are composed on a single melody, the variations depending on the individual style of performance. The distinctive features are spontaneous improvisation and a dialogue performance between two or more people, depending on the occasion or function.[6]

In other words, a poet sings a four-line verse, with each line containing eight syllables and the second and fourth lines rhyming. Then a second poet repeats the last two lines and adds a new couplet, rhyming their last line with the previous poet's last line. This call-and-response continues until one poet can no longer improvise new lines. The "quintessence of the genre," as

Bailey puts it, is the "imaginative interpretation of the subject through use of figurative expressions, in rhyme and meter."[7] Kåntan chamorrita contains "special hidden meaning" through symbols and layered allusions, as well as other poetic artistries such as "raunchy idioms, complex metaphors, [and] terse (almost short-hand) code expressions."[8] In order to master the kåntan chamorrita, one must be able to "sing both forwards and backwards."[9]

The kåntan chamorrita form complemented and contributed to the communal structure of customary CHamoru life. For example, when village communities gathered to thatch the roofs of homes, the weavers would sing and perform kåntan chamorrita. The following verse from "chamorrita higai" (thatching chamorrita) emphasizes this communality:

Manhihigai hit pa'go	We are thatching now
Para ta afte in gima'-ta	To put a roof over our home
Para i leheng-ta para u fa'maolek	For the care of our shelter
Para todu i familia-ta.	For all of our family.[10]

CHamorus composed and sang kåntan chamorrita during activities that involved collaboration, transformation, and interconnection, such as weaving mats, nets, ropes, and clothes. They also composed kåntan chamorrita while planting, cultivating, and harvesting crops, and while grinding corn, husking rice, and cooking. They even utilized this communal poetic form for courting, conflict resolution, and entertainment. During seasonal fish runs, families would line the entire coastline from Hagåtña all the way to Tomhom to cast their throw nets, cook, share food, and sing the kåntan chamorrita:

> For miles up and down the shoreline, the calls and responses of the lead singers would be heard. Sometimes a neighborhood group would respond. Sometimes women in the group would band together to try to outsmart the men through their verse innovations. Rhyming phrases would be thrown back and forth, sometimes for hours, with different people joining in and calling out challenges or responding to the rhyming of others.[11]

Beyond pragmatic and everyday communal relations, CHamorus utilized the kåntan chamorrita form to perform the CHamoru creation story. On the day that CHamorus made their pilgrimage to Laso Fu'a (Fu'a Rock), twelve poets from different villages would stand in a circle and recite verses to retell the story of Puntan and Fu'una.[12] They added music, dance, and gestures to "clarify the metaphorical content of the myth [and] supplement and embellish what the words failed to express."[13] In addition, the poets used "small bells, seeds or shells in a box and the playing of a half moon or media luna."[14] Overall, the kåntan chamorrita was an integral part of everyday and spiritual life that could be performed while fishing or as "an allegorical pantomime and public enactment of myth."[15]

The aesthetic form and social function of the kåntan chamorrita embodies the deepest value of CHamoru cultural identity: inafa'maolek. The reciprocal nature of kåntan chamorrita is manifest in both its call-and-response "reciprocal speech-making" form and in the communal situations in which the songs would be sung.[16] In all aspects of CHamoru life, the kåntan chamorrita "[brought] people together, encourage[d] cooperation, allow[ed] for friendly competition, and form[ed] the basis for spontaneous and humorous interaction."[17] Overall, the kåntan chamorrita threaded together every aspect of CHamoru life and formed the literary foundation of CHamoru cultural identity.

Unfortunately, the practice of kåntan chamorrita was displaced and suppressed by Spanish and American colonialism. As a result of Spanish military conquest and missionary conversion, many of the communal practices in which the kåntan chamorrita thrived were destroyed or forbidden. Living under the surveillance of priests and soldiers meant that CHamorus could no longer express themselves as freely as before. Acculturation within the new religion and education system meant that the most prevalent themes of the kåntan chamorrita disappeared from the storytelling repertoire. As Michael Clement Sr. has noted, CHamorus "could think no more of their warriors, race, country or nation, nor could such lyrics enter their poetry again."[18] Similarly, Elizabeth Diego foregrounds how CHamoru "debate, chants, stories, and songs met their fate as these practices were attacked by the missionaries who preached that the exercises contradicted Christian principles. Slowly those who were converted abandoned their traditional practices as they became increasingly convinced that their oral culture had no utilitarian use."[19] In 1817, the king of Spain declared that Spanish would be taught in the Marianas, and Spanish became the language of business, education, and government. The introduction of Spanish changed the CHamoru language by introducing many Spanish loanwords, phrases, and sounds (indeed, *kåntan* itself is derived from the Spanish word for "song").[20] However, the Jesuit priests learned the CHamoru language to better acculturate and convert the CHamoru population; CHamoru, therefore, became the language of the church.[21] The priests even appropriated the kåntan chamorrita form:

> The Jesuits began immediately to apply the same technique of making couplets and debating to teach Christian doctrine to young Chamorro boys and girls. . . . Through poetry, debate, and miracle plays, the Jesuits supplanted the ancient beliefs . . . with stories and symbols of Jesus and Mary. . . . Eventually this changed the way Chamorros expressed themselves through poetry, song and debate.[22]

While the ancestral themes of the kåntan chamorrita were displaced and a foreign language forcefully introduced, CHamorus still spoke their native language at the end of the nineteenth century, and the kåntan chamorrita form was "nurtured in and around the Church community" and "stayed in the fields and family enclaves around the island."[23]

American colonial language policies and the introduction of American education and media were the main forces that further displaced the kåntan chamorrita. CHamoru language scholar Kenneth Gofigan Kuper exposes how the U.S. Navy "implemented various policies and incentives aimed at eradicating the Chamoru language [and] forcing Chamorus to use English as the language both inside and outside the home."[24] New laws established English as the official language of Guåhan, its government, and its school system.[25] The CHamoru language was banned in public buildings, baseball fields, classrooms, and playgrounds, and students were punished if they were caught speaking CHamoru at school. The American authorities even burned CHamoru-English dictionaries. Services in the Catholic church, a bastion of CHamoru language, began to be performed in English, and American priests replaced Jesuit priests.[26] After World War II, the island shifted to a wage economy, and many of the new jobs in the military, tourism industry, and consumer sectors required applicants to speak English. Additionally, many foreign workers arrived, especially from the Philippines, for the reconstruction of the island. This created a situation in which different groups needed to "communicate with each other, and in this case, English became the lingua franca . . . [because] all business was conducted in English."[27] English-only policies continued in the postwar school system, and administrators created English-speaking clubs and encouraged parents to speak English at home.[28]

As English was gaining traction on the island, many CHamorus began to seek educational and economic opportunities off-island, thus reducing the number of CHamoru speakers at a time when English was becoming more prevalent. For diasporic CHamorus, success in the United States also meant they had to learn English and encourage their children to speak English.[29] In addition to out-migration, outmarriage also contributed to language loss:

> Unions between Chamorro women and stateside men also had implications in the dynamics of cultural change. Whereas in the past Chamorro women had generally acculturated foreign husbands to Chamorro society, the new orientation towards American national identity seemingly negated this dynamic and generally insured that such households would be exclusively English speaking zones.[30]

All these factors combined to make English the language of educational success and economic progress, as well as the major language at church, in the home, and across the CHamoru diaspora.

At the same time that the English language was colonizing governmental, educational, economic, and domestic spaces, it was also colonizing the public spheres of print, music, film, and television. The main publication on the island during the naval era was the English-language monthly magazine the *Guam Recorder* (1924–40), a print outlet for the navy. Many articles and editorials published in the *Guam Recorder* reinforced "the English language as hierarchically better than Fino' Chamorro [Chamorro language] in all aspects of life and at the same time, devalue[d] Fino' Chamorro of any worth, purpose, utility, or meaning."[31] The establishment of another print media outlet, the *Guam Daily News*, in 1950 didn't change the situation because it was also published in English. Alongside English-language print media, two movie theaters opened in Hagåtña in the 1930s and screened American Westerns. In 1944, Armed Forces Radio began broadcasting American music on Guåhan, and it was the only station broadcasting for the next decade. As music historian Michael Clement Jr. explains:

> Through Armed Forces Radio, Chamorros listened to the likes of the Glenn Miller Orchestra, Frank Sinatra, Perry Como, Bing Crosby and the Andrews Sisters, along with every other kind of music that was nationally popular in the United States. No music had a bigger impact on Chamorros than coun-

> try and western. Country music, particularly the cowboy tunes featured in western films, were already popular before the war. . . . Now, with more cash and access to radios, Chamorros fell in love with the songs of artists like Kitty Wells, Patti Page, Hank Snow, Gene Autry, Tex Ritter, Eddy Arnold, Ernest Tubbs, and Hank Williams.[32]

The first local television station, KUAM, was established in 1956, and it "presented idyllic images of American suburbia, consumer excess, and harmonious nuclear families that presented a stark contrast to the large extended family system that regulated daily life for Chamorros. The combined impact of such images was to present Chamorro [culture] as abnormal."[33] Television not only promoted the English language and American culture, but it also became the dominant form of entertainment. Judy Flores observed that the kåntan chamorrita had been "overwhelmed by radio, television and the ubiquitous boom box (portable stereo) . . . always set at high volume—preclud[ing] any possibility of Kantan Chamorrita performance."[34] The postwar decades saw intensified efforts to acculturate CHamorus through an expanded American education system as well as the proliferation of English-language American music, literature, print media, and television, all of which acted to further situate English as the language of progress and success and to cast CHamoru as the language of failure and backwardness.[35] The suppression of Indigenous language is a key component of colonialism and a profound trauma, especially considering that CHamoru language is considered the "umbilical cord of the culture" and "the single most obvious expression of Chamorro identity."[36]

The culmination of this history is what Kuper refers to as CHamoru "linguicide." According to the census data, only 18 percent of Guåhan's population speaks CHamoru, and 44 percent of the population lives in households in which only English is spoken.[37] Furthermore, a majority of those who speak CHamoru are elders, which means that the language is endangered.[38] This has impacted the kåntan chamorrita. Laura Souder noticed in the 1990s:

> The Kantan Chamorrita is sung almost exclusively by Chamorro men and women over fifty years old. While the art form has not disappeared entirely, its continuity is threatened because younger Chamorros have not carried on the tradition. There are master singers of the Kantan Chamorrita in each of the twenty-three villages on Guam, but with fewer than fifty master singers

> islandwide, the chant's survival has become of increasing concern to those who appreciate its cultural significance.[39]

The traumatic decline and loss of the CHamoru population, religion, education system, communal practices, and language, and the hegemonic presence of English-only policies, print, music, and film, have all contributed to the decline of the kåntan chamorrita, as CHamoru language was the main vehicle of the oral tradition.

Sinangån-ta: CHamoru Spoken-Word Poetry

In this section, I will argue that contemporary CHamoru spoken-word poetry is a rearticulation of the kåntan chamorrita tradition. I situate my argument within scholarship that shows how the kåntan chamorrita has survived within the CHamoru recitation of the rosary, contemporary CHamoru music, and CHamoru poetry. Several scholars argue that after Spanish missionization, the Catholic rosary became the rearticulated site of the kåntan chamorrita. The rosary is a devotional prayer to the Virgin Mary, and it is recited "for a number of Saints, important liturgical holidays such as Christmas, as well as during life events such as when someone passes away."[40] In CHamoru, the rosary for the dead is often referred to as lisåyo; it lasts eighteen days, the first nine consisting of public prayers and the second nine consisting of private prayers:

> The first nine days are called *lisåyon linahyan* (group rosary) which begins the evening immediately after the death and includes the burial of the deceased individual. During this period, the rosary prayer is said every evening, usually at the home of an immediate family member or at a local Catholic parish. Refreshments are then served afterward. After the first nine days, the rosary then shifts into another phase called *lisåyon guma'* (home rosary) which is held only for the immediate family.[41]

According to Jessica Ann Unpingco Solis, the rosary practice has remained a "cultural space where Chamorro culture is perpetuated through the use of the Chamorro language to pray and sing [and] reliance on kinship ties to support these events."[42] The rosary is a space of inafa'maolek, offering healing and kinship during times of mourning. CHamorus who led the rosary prayer were known as techas. Judy Flores suggests that the techas recited the rosary in kåntan chamorrita style, characterized by a "particularly nasal, high-pitched singing monotone, which was joined in response by the congregation."[43] Similarly, anthropologist Laura Thompson infers that the shrill voice of the techa and the style of the rosary are more closely linked to the kåntan chamorrita style than to any Hispanic oratory tradition.[44]

Scholars have also interpreted CHamoru music that emerged during American colonialism as evoking aspects of the kåntan chamorrita. For example, Judy Flores argues that twentieth-century CHamoru singers commonly "borrowed" imported melodies and added their own CHamoru lyrics, or they would loosely translate and sing popular American songs in CHamoru. She speculates: "Perhaps the tradition of borrowing melodies is based on the traditional use of one melody with slight variations on which to create the impromptu verse in *Kantan Chamorrita*."[45] Michael Clement Jr. further affirms that the "practice of borrowing and adapting foreign influences into Chamorro music" is consistent with kåntan chamorrita aesthetics and "deeply rooted in strategies of appropriation and resistance to colonial hegemony."[46] Flores also proposes that the kåntan chamorrita continues in CHamoru-language songs "through the use of ribald humor, layers of meaning, and one-upmanship through the call-and-response song format."[47] Clement Sr. comments that the "competitive extemporaneous poetry of teen-age rap, utilizing stock phrases and mnemonics in poetry-dictated meter, sung to a simple rhythmic ground . . . represent[s] the evolution of [kåntan chamorrita] singing."[48] All in all, scholars have shown that the kåntan chamorrita is audible in "new transformations of Chamorro music."[49]

Lastly, I draw inspiration from a chapter in Kisha Borja-Kicho'cho' and Anghet Hoppe-Cruz's thesis, discussed in chapter 1, which argues that the kåntan chamorrita tradition is rearticulated in contemporary CHamoru women's resistance poetry. Their chapter, entitled "*Fanggi'i* i Linachi Siha—Sinangan Inaguaguati yan i Lina'la' Minesngon: 'Kantan Chamorrita' siha gi Siklon benti i Unu (*Writing* the Wrongs—Poetry as Resistance and Survivance: 'Kantan Chamorritas' in the 21st Century)," argues that since the kåntan chamorrita tradition was most often practiced by CHamoru women, it is rearticulated in written poetry by CHamoru women who carry on the tradition.[50] They highlight how contemporary written "resistance" poetry by CHamoru women that deals with difficult issues, like colonialism, militarism, and other traumas, is related to the kåntan chamorrita; indeed, the latter also "served the function of expressing, in a culturally acceptable way, thoughts that otherwise would have been difficult or sensitive."[51] Specifically, Borja-Kicho'cho' and Hoppe-Cruz share their own resistance poetry in dialogue with resistance poetry by CHamoru women writers Anne Perez Hattori and C. T. Perez to highlight how "the Chamorro woman is at once culture-bearer, culture preservationist, and agent of change."[52] Perhaps we can imagine the weaving of the kåntan chamorrita as similar to the braiding of the aerial roots of the banyan tree.

Weaving my own analysis into this scholarship, I suggest that the oral, communal, and competitive aspects of the kåntan chamorrita are also evident in the recent movement of CHamoru spoken-word poetry, which is "performance-based poetry that is presented as a narration, as if the poet were engaged in a conversation."[53] These narrations are considered poetic because they are recited in a rhythmic and rhyming oral form, often drawing parallels to hip-hop and rap. Spoken-word poetry is most often performed at a poetry slam, which is an "interactive event that showcases poetry and its crucial component, performance."[54] During the slam, the poet performs original work (no longer than three minutes) without props, costumes, or musical instruments. Five judges (sometimes selected before the slam, sometimes chosen from the audience) score each performance on a scale of one to ten. There are usually several rounds of competition before a final champion is chosen. Slams can also include singers, dancers, actors, storytellers, and comedians.

In 2007, poets Melvin Won Pat-Borja, Kie Susuico, Fanai Castro, and Jovan Tamayo established the first youth poetry slam competition on Guåhan. In consultation with renowned CHamoru chanter and spoken-word poet Jay Baza Pascua (whose work I have written about elsewhere), they named the series of events Sinangån-ta, which translates as "our spoken words."[55] The founders aimed to "provide the community with a forum for mutual education and free expression, to resurrect the art of poetry and place it into a lively setting."[56] Additionally, Sinangån-ta conducted writing workshops for youth at high schools, the University of Guam, and other community and nonprofit organizations, with the goal of forming a slam team that would represent Guåhan in national and international poetry competitions. One of the co-founders, Susuico, considers spoken-word poetry to be "a modern form of storytelling rooted in indigenousness, a link to the customs and beliefs of the first peoples to settle these islands now known as the Marianas."[57] Fellow co-founder Castro also notes: "The fact that the audience can be actively involved by making noise if they hear something that they like or dislike evokes the system of call and response that is characteristic of Chamorro oral narration, challenging all participants to listen and think critically."[58] The multicultural mix of talented poets who have participated and developed the spoken-word network on Guåhan include John "Meta" Sarmiento, Nichole Rose Quintanilla, Gee Quintanilla, Arielle Taitano Lowe, J-Rae Tedtaotao, Dominic Taimanglo, Carlos Anderson, and Shane Salas, to name a few.

In 2011, the Sinangån-ta Poetry Collective put together a youth poetry team, dubbed Team Guåhan, to compete in the Brave New Voices International Poetry Slam Festival, a national competition for youth spoken-word poetry sponsored by the national organization Youth Speaks Inc. Four youth poets from Guåhan, along with their coaches, traveled to San Francisco, California, to compete. Perhaps we can consider this competition as analogous to a kåntan chamorrita competition, in which poets from different villages would compete and the winners would bring their villages and clans great prestige.[59] Even though Team Guåhan did not win the Brave New Voices competition, they performed several crowd-pleasing poems, most notably a group poem titled "Self-Guamination," performed by Ryan Leon Guerrero and Walla Wai. While I was not in attendance for the competition, the performance was recorded by an audience member and posted on YouTube.[60] During the performance, the two poets stand side by side, sometimes alternating lines and phrases, and sometimes speaking the same lines and phrases simultaneously. Throughout, they vary their vocal registers and rhythms and attempt to embody the emotions, actions, and rhythms of the poem with hand gestures and body movements. Additionally, the audience responds during the poem with cheers and applause, more than once forcing the poets to stop the performance until the crowd noise subsides. Since its original posting in 2011, the YouTube video of "Self-Guamination" has been viewed more than 35,000 times. Their performance, along with the contributions of all the poets who competed and coached, brought great pride to Guåhan and to the CHamoru diaspora.

"Self-Guamination" exposes and critiques the colonial history of Guåhan from the Spanish to the American colonial eras. The poem begins with Spanish military conquest and Catholic missionary conversion:

In 1668 silence sailed from Spain
and invaded the shores of Guam
The Spanish hushed the Chamorro culture with rifles
and the sounds of extinction were deafening
They justified genocide with bibles
Burnt down huts, destroyed villages,
and called it . . . Catholicism
they forced us to our knees to praise a foreign GOD
as if chanting to our ancestors was anything less than spiritual
The Spanish brought disease, soldiers, and missionaries to our island
colonization was their mission.[61]

"Silence," the first subject of the poem, is figured as a force that sailed and invaded Guåhan, symbolizing the silencing effect of colonialism as it "hushed" the CHamoru culture through the deafening "sounds of extinction" (gunshots and other violent sounds). As the end of the above passage mentions, even the spiritual chanting (possibly a reference to kåntan chamorrita) was replaced with prayers to a foreign god. While we can interpret the meaning by reading the transcribed spoken-word poem, we can only wayread the connection to the kåntan chamorrita by paying attention to how the poem is vocalized. Based on the video, the spoken performance can be transcribed in this way:

Wai:
In 1668 silence sailed from Spain
Together:
and invaded the shores of Guam
Leon Guerrero:
The Spanish hushed the Chamorro culture with rifles
Together:
and the sounds of extinction were deafening
Wai:
They justified genocide with bibles
Burnt down huts, destroyed villages,
and called it . . .
Together:
Catholicism

Leon Guerrero:

They forced us to our knees to praise a foreign GOD
as if chanting to our ancestors was anything less than spiritual

Wai:

The Spanish brought disease, soldiers, and missionaries to our island
colonization was their mission.

As is evident, the poets' voices interweave to create a sonic landscape that replicates a call-and-response narration. The tone of their voices captures the emotions of the passage, ranging from anger to rage to loss. Their hand and bodily gestures emphasize the stressed syllables of their words and sometimes enact the movements described in the poem (e.g., they gesture downward when describing how their ancestors were made to kneel, and gesture upward when mentioning the foreign god). As the poem continues, the poets testify about the abuses and trauma caused by Spanish and American colonialism.

Later in "Self-Guamination," the poets turn away from trauma to highlight the strength and survival of the CHamoru people. They assert that the "foundation of strength . . . to keep the Chamorro culture living and breathing" is oral stories, because these have the power to "break free from this tyranny" of silence. Indeed, the poem reaches a narrative and emotional climax when the poets testify about the power of contemporary poetry:

Wai:

But with the strength we inherit from our ancestors
We will engage in this war to preserve our past

Leon Guerrero:

Using our vocal cords as slings and our vocal tones as stones

Together:

they are thrown,

Wai:

not to break bones,

Together:

but to break the silence of our people

Leon Guerrero:

to all of you this is just a poem,

Wai:

but to us, it's the chance to bring justice to our home.

The young poets imagine themselves as continuing the legacy of Indigenous survival and resiliency. For them, spoken-word poetry preserves the past by retelling stories and reanimating history in the present. The dialogue phrasing and the long vowel rhymes—*tones, stones, thrown, bones, poem,* and *home*—further emphasize the interwoven quality of the poem. Slings and stones were traditional weapons used by CHamorus against the Spanish military, and the youth poets view their voices and words as similar narrative weapons. However, the poets are not advocating armed conflict; instead they are insisting that CHamorus must break their silence and speak out against oppression. As they note in the final couplet, spoken-word poetry is more than just an aesthetic object, it is an opportunity to advocate for justice.

Another important aspect of this poem that one would not know from simply witnessing the performance is that Walla Wai is not CHamoru; his ethnic background is Pohnpeian-Hawaiian.[62] Moreover, some members of the Sinangån-ta Poetry Collective and Team Guåhan are not CHamoru (for example, one of the most active members and coaches is John "Meta" Sarmiento, who is of Filipino descent, born and raised on Guåhan). According to the 2010 U.S. census, the population of Guåhan was about 160,000. The CHamoru population comprises about 70,000 people; Asians comprise around 60,000; Native Hawaiian and other Pacific Islanders around 20,000; whites around 11,000; African Americans around 1,500; and Hispanics/Latinos around 1,200. To break this down further within the Asian and Pacific Islander categories, in relation to the poets I mentioned: there are around 3,000 Pohnpeians and Hawaiians in the 2010 census count, and around 42,000 Filipinos (who make up the second largest ethnic demographic on Guåhan).[63] While I have briefly discussed Micronesian and Japanese migration to Guåhan in chapters 2 and 3 respectively, there is a growing body of scholarship on Filipino migration to Guåhan that highlights how this migration began during the Spanish era and continued through the post–World War II era, with Filipinos serving as a labor force in both the military and tourism industries.[64] As Vicente Diaz (who is Filipino-Pohnpeian, born and raised on Guåhan) has noted, the island became known as "'Guam U.S.A.'—gateway to America for Asian and other immigrants looking for a piece of the mythical pie, or at least an American passport and U.S. citizenship."[65] While the historical tensions and conflicts between Indigenous CHamorus and Asian and other Pacific Islander settlers on Guåhan have been emphasized, there are other scholars, such as Josephine Faith Ong, Kristin Oberiano, and

Tabitha Caser Espina, who focus on cross-cultural, decolonial solidarity.[66] I mention this important work here because I believe that "Self-Guamination," the collaborative performance by Leon Guerrero and Wai, and the multicultural composition of the Sinangån-ta Poetry Collective represent a decolonial communality through poetry. Paul Lyons describes this kind of coalition as "Native/non-Native collaboration against Empire within the arts. Such collaborative friendships . . . become a usable inheritance, and have an uncanny power to continue generating effects."[67] Diaz also encourages this kind of collaboration, perhaps alluding to the kåntan chamorrita, when he insists: "Sing together. Belt it out with our different accents. For if the history of relations between Chamorros and Filipinos is one of a shared struggle within colonial and neocolonial realities, then it is we who should be orchestrating the history, not allowing it to play us."[68] I suggest that spoken-word poetry, as a rearticulated kåntan chamorrita tradition, has the generative effect of bringing together CHamorus, Asians, and other Pacific Islanders who call Guåhan home and who believe in the decolonial power of literary collaboration against empire.

CHamoru Intertextuality: Anne Perez Hattori and Michael Lujan Bevacqua

While the connection between the kåntan chamorrita, the rosary, music, and spoken-word poetry makes logical sense because they are all oral forms, in this section I will argue that CHamoru written poetry can also be a rearticulation of the kåntan chamorrita through the use of intertextuality. This argument is rooted in a genealogy of scholars who have drawn a connection between traditional Indigenous orature and contemporary Indigenous written literature since the 1970s.[69] For example, Kenneth Rosen has proposed an "oral/written continuum," suggesting that when you read written Native literature, "you can still hear the old singer's refrain, the incremental repetition that served as so powerful an aid to the memories of so many generations, and you can still discern the communal beat beneath the varied tones and tempos of the individual artists."[70] In a similar vein, other scholars have conceptualized written literature not as a betrayal of, or the demise of, authentic Indigenous oral expression but instead as an extension, development, or evolution from oral to textual literature.[71] Beyond theorizing a genealogical relationship between oral and written literature, scholars have also examined how oral aesthetics have shaped textual aesthetics. For example, Susan Berry Brill de Ramirez foregrounds the presence of oral strategies and structures in written Native literature, such as voice shifts, repetition, parallelism, unexpected transitions, mythic time, lack of closure, omission, episodic structure, interconnectedness, and circular forms.[72] Also, Kimberly Blaeser highlights oral aesthetics in Native written literature, including the use of nonlinguistic sounds, stock characters, a fixed grammar of themes, dialectical discourse, riddles, neologisms, formulaic diction, repetitive phrases, and allusions to sacred reality. She even suggests that written literature can elicit audience participation—similar to an oral performance—through the use of absence, contradiction, ambiguity, satire, shock, humor, abrupt transitions, unusual juxtapositions, pronoun shifts, repetitions, and the lack of closure.[73] Helen May Dennis posits that Native writers utilize "a series of textual strategies . . . includ[ing] the nuanced use of voice and the creation of the implicit reader as confidante and addressee" to retain the flavor of oral literature.[74]

Scholars of Pacific Islander literature have similarly theorized that contemporary written Pacific literature emerged genealogically from the rich tradition of Pacific orature. As Subramani highlights:

> The tradition which has given considerable stimulus to the literature in English is the indigenous oral literature. Oral literature, where cultural transmission takes place by word of mouth, in face-to-face contact, and which depends for its survival on memory and habits of thought and action, belongs to the pre-literate stage but continues to be added to up to the present day.[75]

One formal aspect of oral poetry that Subramani believes transferred to written verse is "a spontaneous song-like effect" involving the presence of phonic and rhythmic effects, simple chant-like metrical units, and even distribution of repetitions and lexical variants.[76] Additionally, Peggy Fairbairn-Dunlop grounds the written literature of Sāmoa within the traditional Sāmoan oral storytelling tradition known as fāgogo:

> Samoans relish the spoken word. The development of Samoan writing must be set against this tradition of language to be understood. The love of words, building up into logical argument and woven into intricate plots, allusion

> and innuendo, are all here. The development of an indigenous written literature has been slow, following a pattern evident in other developing countries moving from an oral to a written literacy.[77]

In terms of aesthetics, Fairbairn-Dunlop claims that written literature follows the "natural rhythm of the spoken voice."[78] Epeli Hau'ofa has also written about the connection between written words and oral literature in Tongan writing:

> My main reason for writing is to develop a personal style that echoes the sounds of the spoken words in the islands. Like most Pacific Islanders, I was nurtured throughout my pre-pubescent years mainly on the spoken word. . . . When I string words together on a piece of paper, what I actually do is to connect sounds, each of which should flow naturally and easily from the preceding sounds. I believe that this is exactly the way that island masters of the spoken word use their language. The style that I have developed is an attempt to translate into writing the cadences of sounds as produced in the islands by story-tellers, preachers, orators, people in supplication, people giving orders, arguing, quarreling, gossiping, and so forth.[79]

Hau'ofa poignantly describes writing as "silent story-telling" and a reader as "a listener to stories told silently by invisible tellers."[80] Beyond viewing oral literature as the foundation of contemporary written literature, Hawaiian scholar ku'ualoha ho'omanawanui details how aesthetic elements in contemporary Hawaiian poetry, such as dualistic pairings, linked assonance, complementary elements, opposites, repetition, chant, rhyme schemes, connectors, closing lines, and other mnemonic devices, are drawn from customary Hawaiian orature. Whereas one might have otherwise considered written literature a sign of assimilation and the demise of traditional orality, many scholars instead insist that oral literature forms the foundation of contemporary Native written literature, and that the themes, forms, and techniques of oral literature are rearticulated and audible (so to speak) in textual, written literature.[81] My contribution to this scholarship is to add intertextuality as a rearticulation of the call-and-response aesthetics of the oral tradition. Specifically, I discuss here two poems by CHamoru poets from different generations—Anne Perez Hattori's "Thieves" (1991) and Michael Lujan Bevacqua's "My Island Is One Big American Footnote" (2009)—to show how intertextuality between the poems embodies the call-and-response of the kåntan chamorrita.

Anne Perez Hattori is a CHamoru historian, activist, writer, and professor. She earned a master's degree in Pacific islands studies and a doctorate in history from the University of Hawai'i, Mānoa. Her monograph, entitled *Colonial Dis-ease: US Navy Health Policies and the Chamorros of Guam, 1898–1941*, was published in 2004. She has also written numerous essays related to the history of American colonialism, health care, hospitals, midwifery, leprosy, and hookworm in prewar Guåhan. She has been a professor of history, Micronesian studies, and CHamoru studies at the University of Guam.

Her poem "Thieves" appeared in *Storyboard 5* (1995).[82] The title refers to the name with which Magellan christened Guåhan and the Mariana Islands: "Islas de los Ladrones" (Islands of the Thieves). Magellan considered CHamorus to be thieves after a misunderstanding and dispute over trade.[83] As a result, he and his men disembarked from their galleons, burned several homes, and murdered seven CHamorus. Hattori's poem begins with a reflection on this violent encounter and its colonial and missionary aftermath:

Thieves, they called us.
Religious converts, they made us.
Said we were sinful,
naked, savage, primitive
Playmates of Satan,
native souls blackened and corrupted
by immoral appetites.

("Thieves")

Hattori points to how the colonizing "they" (referring to explorers, missionaries, and administrators) classified the CHamoru population as corrupted savages and immoral sinners. This ideological and rhetorical dehumanization was used to justify forceful ("they made us") Catholic conversion. The irony lies in the fact that even though CHamorus were called "thieves," it was the missionaries and Spanish colonials who were the true thieves.

The next stanza in Hattori's poem moves forward in history to the period of U.S. colonialism after 1898. At that time, Chamorros became racialized as "impure" and "inauthentic":

Exterminated, they called us.
Half-castes, they branded us.
Said we were impure,
racially—culturally—spiritually
casualties of inauthenticity
native blood contaminated and polluted
by casual miscegenation.

("Thieves")

This stanza captures the degrading anthropological idea that "pure" CHamorus were exterminated by contact, disease, acculturation, and miscegenation. As a result, the CHamorus who survived the first wave of colonialism and conversion, along with their descendants, were seen as "impure" because of mixed bloodlines, Catholic religious practices, and other cultural changes brought on by Spanish acculturative efforts.[84] The poem goes on to address American perceptions of CHamorus in terms of intellectual development:

Infantile, they called us.
Wards of the state, they made us.
Said we were immature,
UNeducated, UNdeveloped, UNcivilized
Victims of illiteracy,
native intelligence retarded and muted
by indifferent laziness.

("Thieves")

The U.S. Navy and Congress viewed CHamorus as childlike wards lacking literacy, intelligence, education, economics, government, and even civilization, thus justifying their colonial territorialization of Guåhan. Hattori's capitalization of the prefix *UN* not only creates a sonic stress on the first syllable but also semantically invokes the United Nations, and the fact that Guåhan is still on the UN's list of "non-self-governing territories."

The final stanza of "Thieves" points to how centuries of colonial acculturation have forged an image of CHamorus in which they were once seen as in need of religion, civilization, and governmental wardship, and are now seen as severed from Indigeneity:

Now they tell us
we are simply, sadly, contemptibly
OVER-developed
OVER-modernized
OVER-theologized
OVER-Americanized.
UNDER-Chamorricized.

("Thieves")

Throughout the poem, Hattori catalogues the colonial stereotypes about CHamorus during different historical eras. At first, CHamorus were conceived of as savage and needing to be missionized and civilized. Then they were seen as impure, inauthentic, and intellectually incapable of self-governance. By the end, CHamorus are viewed as overmodernized and acculturated, tragically "UNDER-Chamorricized." With a sense of deep irony, Hattori alludes to the many aspects of CHamoru culture and identity that were stolen by the true thieves, including the connection to CHamoru language and the kåntan chamorrita. Formally, we can see that Hattori uses many techniques associated with oral literature, including rhyme, anaphora, parallel grammatical structure and rhythm, juxtaposed oppositions, repetition, and chant-like metrical units.

Fourteen years after Hattori's poem was published, another CHamoru scholar, historian, activist, and writer, Michael Lujan Bevacqua, published the poem "My Island Is One Big American Footnote" (2009).[85] While he attended the University of Guam, Bevacqua took several courses from Hattori.[86] He would graduate with a bachelor's degree in art and literature and a master's degree in Micronesian studies. He then traveled to California to attain a doctorate in ethnic studies from the University of California, San Diego. His dissertation, "Chamorros, Ghosts, Non-voting Delegates: GUAM! Where the Production of America's Sovereignty Begins" (2010), explored the subjects of decolonization, self-determination, and sovereignty on Guåhan. When he returned home, he taught for many years at the University of Guam, where he led the efforts to establish the Chamorro Studies Program. Throughout his career, he has organized CHamoru studies and activist conferences; produced and written documentary films about CHamoru culture, language, and politics; served on the boards of nonprofit organizations serving the CHamoru community; conducted oral interviews with CHamoru elders; edited anthologies, zines, and academic journals; translated songs and other texts into CHamoru; authored multiple academic essays, comic books, plays, poems, works of fiction and nonfiction, and newspaper columns; taught CHamoru language and history classes; created culturally grounded and CHamoru-language products and educational materials; and actively engaged with CHamoru cultural revitalization efforts. Currently, he is the co-chair of Independent Guåhan, the task force of the Commission of Decolonization that advocates for the sovereign independence of Guåhan.

"My Island Is One Big American Footnote" is just one of his many impressive cultural works. Bevacqua's poem not only explores and critiques colonial representations of Guåhan and CHamorus, but it also intertextually cites Hattori's poem "Thieves," and her scholarship, specifically her monograph *Colonial Dis-ease.*

At first glance, Bevacqua's poem appears to comprise a single line and a mere five words: "Guam, Where America's Day Begins!!!" ("My Island," 120; see figure 18). This phrase is actually a well-known slogan on Guåhan, coming from the fact that Guåhan lies west of the international date line and is a day ahead of any other state or U.S. territory. In the 1970s, the Guam Visitors Bureau developed the slogan to market the island as the next major tourist destination in the Pacific after Hawai'i.[87] Even though the slogan started as a tourism ploy, you can now see the phrase on T-shirts, websites, advertising, and articles, and you can hear it spoken during public events and political speeches. In his dissertation, Bevacqua argued that the slogan ideologically articulates Guåhan "not as a point of inequality or exploitation, but rather as a point of celebratory exceptionality." By repeating the slogan, CHamorus "embody America and claim to finally be a secure piece of it."[88]

Even though the "main text" of Bevacqua's poem is only five words long, *three* footnotes are appended to the slogan, and the footnoted text inhabits *three entire pages.* The first footnote begins: "Life in the colonies, the borderlands, the territories sucks. Sucks like nationally strategic words and verbs used to keep my ethnicity selfishly un-determined . . . it sucks like carefully crafted, beautifully bound footnotes that no one bothers to read or quote" ("My Island," 120). The use of the prefix *un-* connects this poem intertextually to Hattori's "Thieves" and its use of the same prefix ("UNeducated, UNdeveloped, UNcivilized"). Similar to Hattori, Bevacqua describes how

My Island Is One Big American Footnote
Michael Lujan Bevacqua

Guam, Where America's Day Begins!!![1,2,3]

---

[1] **Life in the colonies, the borderlands, the territories sucks.**
Sucks like nationally strategic words and verbs used to keep my ethnicity selfishly un-determined
It sucks like cluster/mustard bombs buried in your land or landing on your head.
It sucks like carefully crafted, beautifully bound footnotes that no one bothers to read or quote.

My island is one big American footnote,
Sitting black/brown as day on the bottom of every red whitewashed and blue page
Through textual treaties or wars these narrow margins are our new, now, old or eternal homes.
Whether we liked it or not (Wanted it or not) our bloods were mixed with colonially supplied inks and our lives recast, set typed and dyed woven into tyrannical threads of foreign flags that call us to war with familiar terms of friendliness, unity, warmth, love of life, yet that same textual flag will blind a budget, or an international summit to our superfluous "footnoted" needs.

Footnotes? Small islands of text really,
Off the margins, somewhere between margins of national importance we sit there, ideologically spaced/almost erased like far-flung chick-peas etched/embossed on these pages of strategic seas by a constitutional, conscious and colonial disease,
Colonial *dis-ease.*
We cannot be incorporated for insane and inconsistent reasons
A hundred years ago it was because our skins were different.
Then it became because we spoke different languages
Or our lack of rights and liberties was integral to military strategy,
Now it is because we would receive too much power if we became a fair and equal part of the union.
We are the territorial thoughts that are too precious to let go, but not precious enough to bring into the fold.
Not critical enough to really think on, and not real enough to think critically about.

Welcome to the footnotes, like the foothills of some forever inferior land.
Because when you look up upon the wealth of words, verbs, periods, commas and paragraphs of the text, their completeness of thought, their unlimited potential, their self-referential existence (while yours seems so conditional,

[120]

FIGURE 18 "My Island Is One Big American Footnote," by Michael Lujan Bevacqua, 2009. Reprinted courtesy of Michael Lujan Bevacqua.

Guåhan and the CHamoru people are simply footnotes to the American empire and how Guåhan is reduced to a "small island of text [that] no one bothers to read or quote [because it is simply] conditional, contextual, so dependent on the [main] text" ("My Island," 120). The footnotes sit "on the bottom of every red whitewashed and blue page [at the] margins of national importance" (120). Furthermore, Bevacqua describes how these margins are infected with "constitutional, conscious and colonial disease, / Colonial *dis-ease*." (120). This is another intertextual moment in the poem, as Bevacqua references Hattori's aforementioned monograph. Those diseased CHamorus who live in the footnotes are indeed "excesses that don't really belong in this 'glorious' document of democracy and freedom" (121). Bevacqua's creative and subversive reconceptualization of the footnote exposes the colonial rhetoric of the slogan. In other words, with the exposure of the colonial relationship between the *footnote island* of Guåhan and the *main text* of the United States, Guåhan no longer signifies a celebratory footnote to American democracy but is instead seen as marking "Where America's Empire Begins."[89]

In addition to defining the footnote as a symbol of colonial subjugation, Bevacqua also imagines the footnote's potential agency. He asks, "So what does my footnote do?" ("My Island," 122). Besides being evidence of U.S. imperialism, the existence of the footnote encourages the poet to speak out (or up, as it were) to the main text. From under the hegemonic text, the footnoted voice of the CHamoru rises to challenge its marginal position at the "bottom of any flag/budget/page" (122). In the final footnote, the speaker exclaims: "Release us to flutter beyond these American borders and margins! / Leave us to determine self-fully! A text of our own!" (122). By highlighting the voice from the footnote island, Bevacqua reimagines the signifying power of Guåhan.

Hattori's poem "Thieves" critiqued the many colonial and dehumanizing representations that have suppressed and stolen CHamoru identity and representational agency for centuries. While her poem critiques these representations and exposes who the real thieves are, it does not speak back. Nearly fifteen years later, Bevacqua reads Hattori's poem and, I argue, responds with "My Island Is One Big American Footnote." His poem takes up the same theme: representational theft and power. Guåhan has had its power stolen and is represented as a mere footnote to America, something that is not worthy of its own text but instead only worthy of existing in the political/

textual margins. While intertextually referencing Hattori's poem and recontextualizing its theme, Bevacqua also responds by adding his own verse: the voice of the footnote, the CHamoru voice speaking back, demanding representational power, demanding a sovereign text of its own.

With this theoretical context in mind, we can see how Hattori's poem casts out the initial call, the first verse, while Bevacqua's poem takes up the challenge by repeating the theme, intertextually weaving together the two poems, and "throwing" his own verse. Thus we can think of intertextuality as rearticulating the oral call-and-response technique in written form. This intergenerational and intertextual call-and-response creates a communal situation in which both poets protest colonial regimes of representation used to dominate, control, and suppress CHamoru identity, culture, history, and politics. In the face of this power, these poets weave a written kåntan chamorrita to advocate for CHamoru empowerment and self-determination. Through their poetic, communal interweaving, they prove that Guåhan is more than an "Island of Thieves," more than a footnote to American empire. They prove that Guåhan is where the voice of CHamoru empowerment begins!

Conclusion

The kåntan chamorrita was once the most important and prevalent form of CHamoru literature. Its dialogic call-and-response form embodied the communal values of CHamoru cultural identity, bringing people together during many group activities, from feasts to funerals, planting to harvesting, weaving to thatching. Tragically, the history of religious, educational, cultural, and media colonialism, in addition to the history of CHamoru linguicide, has led to the marginalization and endangerment of the themes, contexts, and language of the kåntan chamorrita tradition. However, if we closely wayread contemporary CHamoru poetry, we can witness how the kåntan chamorrita has been rearticulated in creative and profound ways.

Inspirationally, there have been efforts to preserve and revitalize the CHamoru language, the kåntan chamorrita, and CHamoru oratory. In 1979, a CHamoru mandate was passed into law, requiring CHamoru language to be taught in public elementary schools. CHamoru language classes expanded to high schools in 1992, and they are now taught at the Guam Community College and the University of Guam.[90] In 2005, the nonprofit organization

Chief Hurao Academy was created as the first "full-immersion" CHamoru language program on Guåhan.[91] In 2019, the first full CHamoru immersion program was established in the public schools as a public-private partnership between the Guam Department of Education (through its CHamoru Studies and Special Projects Division) and Chief Hurao Academy. Housed at Pedro C. Lujan Elementary School, the program, known as Faneyåkan Sinipok, welcomed its first two kindergarten classes.[92]

CHamoru orature has been revitalized and rearticulated alongside CHamoru language revitalization efforts. One of the first contemporary chanters was Jesse "Tåno'" Rivera, who became active in the 1990s, often opening cultural ceremonies with his chants and traveling with other CHamoru cultural delegations to perform throughout the Pacific. He opened his chants with his signature phrase, "Guahu Taotao Tåno," which translates as "I am a person of the land." His chants focused on themes of CHamoru heritage, CHamoru practices (like fishing, hunting, canoe building, and sailing), respect for elders, and CHamoru nationalism.[93] CHamoru chant and dance groups also emerged in the 1990s. The most prominent was Guma' Pålu Li'e (House of the Seeing Mast), later known as I Fanlalai'an (The Place of Chant), founded by Leonard Iriarte.[94] Using precolonial CHamoru words, the chants take up various themes related to CHamoru culture, customs, and history. As described by Judy Flores: "Their group chants are usually structured with a lead chanter who calls the tone and cadence with a beginning phrase. The group joins in with a repetition of the leader's phrase or a group response. The rhythm is Micronesian in style, with body slapping, stomping, and repeated vocal sounds to create the cadence."[95] In a poignant connection to chapter 3, it should be noted that the chanters often adorn their bodies with red, white, and black shells, flowers, and feathers—the same colors that CHamorus painted traditional canoes. Today, there are several CHamoru dance and chant groups, such as Inetnon Gefpa'go, each with its own stylistic rearticulations, and there are even CHamoru dance, chant, and performing arts courses offered at the University of Guam. CHamoru artists such as Dakota Camacho, founder of Guma' Matao, are innovatively interweaving CHamoru chant and dance with hip-hop and avant-garde performance.[96]

In the 1980s, a group of kåntan chamorrita singers, along with the Guam Council of the Arts and Humanities, the Chamorro Studies Program of the Department of Education, and several faculty from the University of Guam, began to revitalize the art form by offering apprenticeships to youth.[97]

Through a grant from the Folk Arts Program of the National Endowment for the Arts, kåntan chamorrita poets (including Clotilde Gould, Asuncion Cruz, Marcella Aguon, Angelina Anderson, Maria Crisostomo, Lourdes Taitague, Floren Paulino, and Vicente Meno) were able to teach apprentices in replicated home settings, and performances were held throughout the island.[98] Another important endeavor was an oral history project conducted by Flora Baza Quan through the Government of Guam Department of Parks and Recreation Historical Preservation Program. As a result of these efforts, the Chamorro Heritage Foundation was established in association with the Guam Economic Development Agency. With the support of these new cultural agencies, the kåntan chamorrita singers attended and participated in the 1988 South Pacific Festival of the Arts in Australia, and in the 1992 festival in the Cook Islands. As a result, Allan Nazareno noted, the "attendance at arts festivals in the Pacific region created more interest from the international community and its acceptance as an indigenous art form."[99] In 1990, the group received the Governor's Arts Awards for the Performing Arts, and, in 2000, the Guam Council of Arts and Humanities Agency honored them as Masters of Chamorro Tradition.[100] The support for and interest in these projects offers "hope that this poetic tradition will rise in popularity as a means of cultural expression. With continued community interest and support, the revitalization of the Kantan Chamorrita can be of tremendous value to the preservation and development of Chamorro language and culture."[101] Taken together, these contemporary practices articulate an imaginative communality in which today's CHamoru poets braid their poems together to create a new communal situation (on the page and on the stage). From this empowered space, these poets rearticulate and revitalize CHamoru culture, literature, dance, and performing arts.[102] Moreover, this braiding heals what was once deemed severed by connecting contemporary CHamoru poets to Indigenous aesthetics, weaving songs and voices, singing forward and backward.

CONCLUSION

Prutehi yan Difendi

CHamoru Literature as Decolonial Activism

Throughout the journey of this monograph, we have navigated vast expanses of CHamoru "time/space/self/narrative" in order to experience and understand the diversity, complexity, resiliency, and vibrancy of CHamoru culture, identity, and literature from Guåhan. As I have shown, CHamorus have an impressive aesthetic tradition, including the oral form of kåntan chamorrita, latte stone housing architecture, and outrigger canoe design. These precolonial aesthetic practices and the CHamoru values they embodied were reified as the "authentic," "pure," and "traditional" CHamoru art and aesthetics. Similarly, precolonial CHamoru customs, practices, and values defined what most people would understand as authentic, pure, and traditional CHamoru culture and identity. Because Guåhan has experienced more than three centuries of colonization by three different imperial nations, CHamoru language, beliefs, customs, practices, identities, and aesthetics have dramatically changed. Thus, anthropologists and historians have claimed that authentically Indigenous CHamoru culture no longer exists. Similarly, literary scholars have argued that contemporary CHamoru literature is degraded and inauthentic because it is often composed in a written form as opposed to an oral form, predominantly in English as opposed to CHamoru, and in a foreign genre as opposed to an Indigenous genre. This discourse of inauthenticity, I suggest, is based on an understanding of CHamoru culture and literature as static essences that once existed in a "pure" and "authentic" state before colonialism, modernity, and globalization. As a result, CHamoru people and writers are seen as in danger of being lost in the currents of cultural and literary assimilation.

I countered this fatal impact cultural and literary theory by arguing that CHamoru culture is a dynamic, moving entity composed of enduring core values, customs, and practices that are continually transformed and rearticulated within various historical contexts and under various political pressures. Relatedly, I contended that CHamoru literature is a dynamic phenomenon comprising an enduring aesthetic genealogy that has also been transformed and rearticulated by every successive generation of CHamoru authors. To navigate this complex terrain, I developed and enacted an interpretive literary methodology that I term wayreading, inspired by Pacific Islander, Native American, and global Indigenous literary studies. Wayreading maps CHamoru culture, identity, and literature as dynamic, transformative, and resilient—*as moving islands of articulated Indigeneity and aesthetics.* Wayreading roots our interpretation of a text within Indigenous histories, cultural practices, and epistemologies. Wayreading prioritizes analyzing contemporary Indigenous literature through the lens of customary Indigenous aesthetics—such as canoeing, tattooing, weaving, or carving—not only in terms of how they function as a theme within a text, but also how they function as a primary structural logic. Lastly, wayreading involves being attentive to how Indigenous literature contributes to movements of liberation, revitalization, decolonization, and self-determination.

While I foregrounded the anticolonial, decolonial, and postcolonial themes of CHamoru poetry throughout this study, I will conclude our voyage with a few examples of CHamoru literature as decolonial activism. Contemporary CHamoru literature has developed hand in hand with the CHamoru decolonization movement because literature is one space through which CHamorus revitalize Indigenous identity and cultural pride, as well as advocate for ecological protection, land reclamation, and political liberation from colonialism, militarism, and capitalism. As Monique R. Carriveau Storie phrases it, CHamoru literature is "simultaneously a cultural artifact (a product of a culture) and a cultural agent (an influence on a culture)."[1] To provide examples of CHamoru poetry as a "cultural agent," I will focus on two poems by CHamoru authors from two different generations, Frederick B. Quinene and Melvin Won Pat-Borja, whose poetry became part of direct political action and public testimony.

Frederick B. Quinene was born on Guåhan in 1942. He graduated from the University of Guam, served in the U.S. Navy, and worked for decades in education, health, prisons, and youth affairs. However, he is most known for his poems; in 1986, he was named the first poet laureate of Guam by the governor at the time, Ricardo Bordallo, through Executive Order 86–14. The order reads in part:

> WHEREAS, poetry, compositions characterized by great beauty of expression, is a most appropriate way to celebrate Guam's unique, rich cultural heritage; and
> WHEREAS, literary publications of poetry, will remain in the hearts and minds of the present and future generations of the People of Guam; and . . .
> WHEREAS, Fred Quinene has been blessed with the gift of a poetic pen, and possesses the ability to write beautiful, lyrical sonnets; and
> WHEREAS, this gift, should not go unnoticed, and is most certainly a source of pride for all of Guam . . .[2]

Throughout his life, Quinene has written hundreds of poems related to family, love, culture, identity, food, and politics. However, his work was not gathered into a book until 2018, when his first and only collection, *An Islander's Voice*, was published by the University of Guam Press.[3] The book includes sixty-four poems (around one hundred pages total) written in English and CHamoru. In the introduction, the executive director of the press, Victoria-Lola Leon Guerrero, highlights how Quinene's poetry "expresses his deep love for Guam. He writes about the island and the CHamoru culture with pride. . . . It is from this place of love that he also critiques important political and historical issues, and has always been vocal about Guam's colonization and relationship with the United States."[4]

While his collection as a whole deserves its own study, I will focus on the poetry that Quinene read as testimony to the U.S. Congress, as an example of CHamoru literary and decolonial activism. On December 12, 1989, a hearing for H.R. 98, the Guam Commonwealth Act, was held in Honolulu at the Hawai'i State Capitol building before the House of Representatives Subcommittee on Insular and International Affairs, which is part of the Committee on Interior and Insular Affairs. To understand that moment, it is important to understand Guåhan's political "quest for commonwealth." As mentioned previously, the 1950 Organic Act granted U.S. citizenship to residents of Guåhan and a degree of civilian self-governance. However, the federal legislation did not install elections for governor of Guam (who was appointed), provided no representation in Congress, and offered no local control over federal law on Guåhan. Moreover, a few months after the Organic Act was passed, a security clearance was imposed by the Pentagon, which stifled economic development. The clearance was not lifted until 1962, and it was not until 1972 that residents of Guåhan were able to elect their own governor and a (nonvoting) delegate to the House of Representatives. To push for additional political gains and rights, the Guam Legislature established official commissions to deliberate on political status options, organize possible plebiscites, and negotiate with the federal government. In 1973, they determined that the most realistic path forward was to advocate for a "commonwealth" status. Historian Frank Quimby remarked:

> Because US administrations had accepted commonwealth pacts with [Puerto Rico and Northern Marianas], Guam leaders assumed [commonwealth] represented a new transitional or interim status in the US territorial relations hierarchy—above unincorporated but below incorporated—which could limit US federal power and enhance local control of island affairs. Commonwealth was seen as a solution that allowed continued US sovereignty while addressing local autonomy issues, such as the application of US law, military land acquisition policy and preservation of Chamorro culture.[5]

After several years of stalled and unproductive negotiations, a new political status commission was established in 1975 and a plebiscite held in 1976. A majority of voters chose "status quo with improvements," though at the time "commonwealth" was not included as an option. A month later, Congress authorized Guåhan's legislators to draft a constitution; however, voters on the island ended up rejecting the drafted constitution. Some argued that it was more important to first resolve the political status debate before drafting a constitution. Thus, the Commission on Self-Determination was established in 1980. The commission held a plebiscite in 1982 and "commonwealth" received the most votes (49 percent of the overall votes). In a runoff with the second choice of "statehood," "commonwealth" was chosen by 73 percent of the voters. For several more years, the commission worked with the public and with the federal government to draft the Guam Commonwealth

Act, which was completed in 1986, under the administration of Governor Bordallo. Summarized by Quimby:

> The final version of the measure called for mutual consent on key self-government aspects of a federal-territorial commonwealth relationship, including the application of federal law to the island, and provided the local government authority over immigration, labor law and the Exclusive Economic Zone. The bill prohibited the federal use of eminent domain power to acquire land for military bases, and required the return of excess Defense Department lands to the local government and consultation with Guam officials before major changes to force levels or base missions. The measure would also provide Guam greater authority to negotiate commercial agreements directly with Asian-Pacific states and a greater role in awarding commercial air carrier routes into Guam.[6]

The voters of Guåhan approved the bill with revisions in 1987, and the proposed legislation received its first hearing by the House Interior Subcommittee on Territorial and Insular Affairs in 1989.[7]

Enter Guåhan's poet laureate. Quinene traveled to Honolulu, along with many others from Guåhan, to present testimony in support of the Commonwealth Act. Instead of a traditional congressional testimony, Quinene decided to recite two of his original poems. The first poem, titled "The Quest for a Commonwealth," comprises eleven quatrains (forty-four total lines) with a rhyme scheme of *abcb* (perhaps echoing the kåntan chamorrita form). The poem opens with a question: "What is the real relationship / of Guam to the U.S. of A.?"[8] The next lines answer this vital question: "No matter what is really said / Guam is still a colony today." This first rhymed quatrain is surprisingly direct about Guåhan's colonial status, especially when you consider that Quinene was reciting the poem aloud to a congressional committee. The next quatrain crafts a compelling metaphor for Guåhan's quest for commonwealth:

> Guam has remained all these years
> Nothing but the spoils of war,
> Her seeking greater self rule is
> Not unlike reaching for a star.
>
> *("Quest")*

The next several stanzas are addressed to "Uncle Sam," mainly in the form of questions that ask whether or not he will change the political status of Guåhan, which is reaching for a higher level of self-government. After these questions, Quinene becomes more critical in stanzas 7 and 8:

To this day Congress still refers
To Guam as her possession,
Isn't it unconstitutional to own
People no matter what the reason?

Please be generous to this land
Grant her people true dignity.
Cease your role of master to slave
In terms of no uncertainty.

("Quest")

Drawing an analogy between slavery and territorial possession is a dramatic and striking figuration. Clearly, Quinene is appealing to the morality of the United States as a democratic nation that abolished slavery and claims to represent the ideals of liberty and freedom. Since he refers to both Guåhan and the United States with feminine pronouns, we can see how he is casting the two countries as motherlands, perhaps in order to highlight Guåhan's matriarchal Indigenous culture and to appeal to the U.S. as Lady Liberty. The poem ends with a related, final question:

Shouldn't you now Uncle Sam
Prove to the world again,
For justice you'll allow all
Their true desire to attain?

("Quest")

Throughout his powerful poem, Quinene challenges and critiques the United States for suppressing CHamoru rights and self-government for Guåhan, and he appeals to the American ideals of democracy, situating Guåhan's struggle within a longer genealogy of freedom and liberation struggles.

Quinene's second poem, titled "What Am I," comprises seventeen quatrains (sixty-eight lines total), in the same *abcb* rhyme scheme. The poem also opens by addressing "Uncle Sam," reciting the American colonial history of Guåhan from 1898 to 1989, perhaps to educate the U.S. congresspeople and committee members who may not have knowledge of this history. Even though the speaker knows this history, he states: "But I still don't know what I am." The speaker is experiencing an identity crisis because he is a U.S. citizen, yet also a colonized subject. The seventh stanza reads:

> You say you do not colonize
> Yet I feel Guam is a colony.
> You say I am your citizen,
> Then why is it I don't feel free?
>
> *("What Am I")*

The poem then goes on to discuss how Uncle Sam gives Guåhan "all kinds of goods" and education, yet the speaker still feels "stripped of dignity" and "depressed." He begs Uncle Sam for recognition and self-determination, appealing again to democratic ideals and the political maturation of the people of Guåhan. He concludes:

> I do believe my Uncle Sam,
> That I am mature enough right now,
> that I can decide my destiny,
> for you yourself have shown me how.
>
> *("What Am I")*

Despite Quinene's poetic testimony, as well as the many other testimonies by CHamoru politicians, activists, and community organizers in support of the Commonwealth Act, the U.S. Congress had concerns with a few of the bill's major provisions. In the following years, the commission worked with a federal task force to address them. On October 29, 1997, there was a second hearing before Congress in Washington, D.C. While Quinene was not able to attend this hearing in person, he submitted three poems as his testimony, which are included in the written record. Quinene once again submitted "Quest for a Commonwealth," along with two new poems: "I Love Justice" and "Ignominy." Both poems are in the same rhymed quatrain form, and they continue the theme of pointing out the hypocrisy and political irony of the fact that Guåhan is a part of America yet still colonized.

Throughout, Quinene searingly critiques America while at the same time passionately appealing to the United States and its democratic ideals of freedom to support CHamoru self-determination and commonwealth status for Guåhan. His last words in the congressional record echo his previous testimony:

> Shouldn't you now Uncle Sam
> prove to the world again,
> for justice you'll allow all
> their true desire to attain?[9]

Unfortunately, even the testimonies in 1997 did not lead to a change in Guåhan's political status. Neither the George H. W. Bush nor the Clinton administration fully supported the Commonwealth Act. As Quimby pointed out, the bill was rejected for several reasons related to voting, constitutionality, and sovereignty: "The bill would authorize the exclusion of US citizens (the settler population), based on ethnicity, from a vote on ultimate status, which federal officials said conflicted with constitutional protections against non-discriminatory voting. Other provisions, they argued, ran counter to strategic defense interests and territorial policy."[10] Ultimately, the Commonwealth Act never made it out of committee. Quinene included the above four poems in his poetry collection *An Islander's Voice*. In a powerful connection to chapter 2, Quinene's book cover features him standing next to a latte stone (figure 19), suggesting that the latte is giving him strength to speak, that he is speaking to honor his ancestors, that he is figuratively rebuilding CHamoru culture and identity, and that his book is also a CHamoru house of story. Sadly, Quinene passed away in 2019, at the age of seventy-seven. Even though Guåhan is still on a quest for self-determination, Quinene's poetic voice continues to inspire the next generation of CHamoru poets.

Another poignant example of CHamoru poetry as decolonial activism occurred in the twenty-first century as a response to the military buildup proposal in 2006, which I mentioned in chapter 1 but will briefly summarize here. This "mega-buildup" would include the construction of facilities to house and support the transfer from Okinawa to Guåhan of 8,600 marines and their 9,000 dependents, as well as 7,000 transient navy personnel, 600–1000 army personnel, and 20,000 foreign workers.[11] Additionally, the buildup would establish an air and missile defense task force, a live firing

FIGURE 19 Cover of Frederick Quinene's *An Islander's Voice*, 2018. Reproduced courtesy of the University of Guam Press.

range complex, and the creation of a deep-draft wharf in Apra Harbor for nuclear-powered aircraft carriers.

For this proposed military project, the Department of Defense prepared an environmental impact statement to assess the potential environmental, social, and cultural impacts.[12] The draft environmental impact statement (DEIS) of the military buildup was released in November 2009 and made available online and in print at various locations on Guåhan.[13] The statement comprised nine volumes and 11,000 pages. Some of the impacts described include limiting access to Pågat (the richest site of ancient CHamoru artifacts and latte stones on Guåhan) to build the live firing range complex, eliminating hundreds of acres of jungle rich with medicinal plants to construct permanent military facilities and a camp for foreign laborers, removing more than seventy acres of living coral reef from the ocean floor to build a deep-draft wharf, and producing over eight tons of hazardous waste. The DEIS also noted that the increase in population would increase instances of violence, crime, prostitution, and rape; moreover, it would put an unsustainable stress on affordable housing, social services, education, health care, and utility services such as water, power, and sewage.[14] Residents of Guåhan were given a ninety-day period to read, decipher, and comprehend the DEIS in order to submit online commentary or voice their opinions (or "testify") for three minutes or less at public hearings held throughout the island.[15]

The first DEIS public hearing was held on January 7, 2010, at Southern High School in the village of Santa Rita, which is in the southern part of Guåhan, near the naval base. In fact, the history of Santa Rita began when villagers from the ancient village of Sumay were evicted and relocated so that the U.S. military could make room for the construction of the naval station.[16] Enter CHamoru poet Melvin Won Pat-Borja, who was teaching creative writing at Southern High School at the time. Won Pat-Borja was born on Guåhan in 1981. He graduated from Southern High School, and then went on to attend the University of Hawai'i at Mānoa, where he majored in secondary education. While living in Hawai'i, he was introduced to slam poetry and spoken word. He was a member of Hawai'i's national slam team, and he won the finals as Grand Slam Champion in 2005. He also co-founded the nonprofit organization Youth Speaks Hawai'i, for which he coached the youth team for the Brave New Voices International Youth Poetry Slam Festival. In 2007, he returned to Guåhan and co-founded the Sinangån-ta Youth Movement (discussed in chapter 4). In addition to his work as a poet and educator, Won Pat-Borja is also an accomplished hip-hop and rap artist.[17]

This background brings us back to the first DEIS hearing at Southern High School in 2010. Won Pat-Borja, who was also actively engaged in CHamoru activism and the demilitarization movement, signed up to testify at the hearing. He represented the organization We Are Guåhan, a "multi-ethnic collective of individuals, families and grassroots organizations" that emerged in

November 2009 to "inform and engage our community on the various issues concerning the impending military build up." As stated on the group's website: "We Are Guåhan aims to unite and mobilize our people to *protect and defend* our resources and our culture. We Are Guåhan promotes peaceful, positive and prosperous change for our island."[18]

Throughout the promotional and activist materials that We Are Guåhan produced, the group often used the phrase "prutehi yan difendi," which translates as "protect and defend," as a rallying message to the community. This phrase (and its Indigenous and decolonial ethos) comes from a well-known poem, "Inifresi" (1991), by cultural activist, CHamoru language scholar, and educator Bernadita Camacho-Dungca.[19] Camacho-Dungca was born in 1940. She earned a bachelor's degree in linguistics and anthropology from the University of Hawai'i at Mānoa, a master's degree in education from the University of Guam, and a doctorate in education from the University of Oregon. Her dissertation was titled "Use of Telecommunication in the Delivery of a Staff Development Telecourse for Educators of Exceptional Children in Guam and Saipan: A Descriptive Study of Its Use and Suggestions for Improving Its Effectiveness" (1987). When she returned to Guåhan, she became instrumental in training the first CHamoru language teachers in the Department of Education and building the degree program for CHamoru teachers in the School of Education at UOG, where she taught for over forty years. Her death in 2016 was mourned island-wide.[20]

The "Inifresi" has become the most well-known CHamoru poem. The title translates as "Pledge" or "Offering." Briefly examining this poem will illustrate the power of literature to respond to colonial and military oppression. The poem reads in its entirety:

Ginen i mås takhelo' gi Hinasso-ku
i mås takhalom gi Kurason-hu,
yan i mas figo' na Nina'siña-hu,
Hu ufresen maisa yu' para bai hu
Prutehi yan Difendi
i Hinengge,
i Kottura,
i Lengguåhi,
i Aire
i Hanom yan i Tåno' Chamoru

ni' Irensiå-ku direchu ginen as Yu'os Tåta.
Este hu afitma gi hilo' i Bipblia yan I Banderå-hu,
i Banderan Guåhan.[21]

The speaker pledges to "prutehi yan difendi" (protect and defend) the hinengge, kottura, lengguåhi, aire, hanom, and tåno' (beliefs, culture, language, air, water, and land). The source of this pledge comes from "i mås takhelo' gi Hinasso-ku" (the depths of the speaker's mind), "i mås takhalom gi Kurason-hu" (the bottom of her heart), and "i mas figo' na Nina'siña-hu" (the totality of her strength). The pledge is affirmed on the "Bipblia" (Bible) and "Banderan Guåhan" (Guam flag).[22] The Bible represents the strong (and perhaps ironic) connection between CHamoru culture and Catholicism.[23] The Guåhan flag, which was created in 1917, is often associated with CHamoru nationalism.[24] The fact that the poem is entirely in the CHamoru language is also a politicized linguistic act since one of the main goals of the U.S. colonial education system on Guåhan has been to eliminate the CHamoru language.

In 1998, "Inifresi" was read at a CHamoru-language event to students at the University of Guam. Because English was the official language of Guåhan, this event in and of itself held cultural and political significance. A week later, the governor of Guam at the time, Carl T. C. Gutierrez, issued Executive Order No. 98–28, which adopted "Inifresi" as the official "Chamorro Pledge of Allegiance." The executive order described how "the public recitation of 'Inifresi' will foster deeper appreciation for the Chamorro people, culture, language and our Guam homeland," and that it should be recited "in any public and private event where the 'American Pledge of Allegiance' might also be recited."[25] Not only does the order recognize the inspirational quality of Camacho-Dungca's poem and the important role of art in inspiring cultural pride, it also reaffirms the idea that poetry can have political power, as evident in the consideration of "Inifresi" as equivalent to the American pledge of allegiance.

It was in the spirit of the "Inifresi" that Won Pat-Borja walked up to the microphone and, instead of delivering talking points, performed a spoken-word poem titled "No Deal" as his three-minute testimony (which differed dramatically from the other testimonies).[26] Though the poem was performed orally, the author sent me a text copy via personal communication. The poem was composed without line breaks, so it appears as prose when I quote it here.

"No Deal" opens in a classroom, with the speaker in the poem, a teacher, being asked a question by a student: "Sir, what if we protest and unite as a people, and in the end they just do whatever they want?"[27] At first the teacher is rendered speechless by his student's fear, but then he responds:

> I am not naïve to the reality of the situation, I understand that the federal government has done worse things and gotten away with it, like smallpox blankets, like nuclear testing in the Marshall Islands, like dropping bombs on Vieques, like holding the sovereign queen of Hawai'i at gunpoint to sign the annexation. ("No Deal")

The teacher draws these transnational connections to expose the abuses of U.S. colonialism and to insist that CHamorus are not alone in this struggle. Won Pat-Borja asserts that CHamorus can find strength in their ancestral claims because "for centuries [Chamorros] have been the guardians and caretakers" of Guåhan. This genealogical insistence dispels the belief that Guåhan is merely, as Won Pat-Borja memorably phrases, "part of a perverse manifest destiny."

Won Pat-Borja suggests that the hopelessness the student feels, mirroring the hopelessness that many residents felt after the DEIS was released, causes some to believe that "the best course of action is to make a deal" ("No Deal"). However, Won Pat-Borja resists making a deal, thinking of the long-term genealogical effects the military buildup will have on CHamorus: "I cannot go home and look my son in the eyes and tell him that I love him knowing that behind closed doors, I am making a deal, I cannot look at my students and tell them I care about their future if I am making a deal—I am not here to make a deal." While the teacher refuses to make a deal regarding the military buildup, he also points out the fact that many CHamorus have made deals with the military:

> We are loyal servants fighting for your freedom of action, fighting so that you can let the federal government label Guam sovereign US soil and impose the largest military relocation in history. We are so loyal that we enlist more sons and daughters into America's armed services to fight and die than anywhere else in the world. We have paid your ultimate sacrifice time and again. ("No Deal")

Not only is Guåhan a strategic location for American military bases, it has also become an invaluable resource for military recruiters. CHamorus have enlisted and died in the U.S. armed forces at some of the highest rates in the nation. During the Vietnam War, Guåhan had one of the highest killed-in-action rates per capita. In 1980, the Department of Defense estimated that 5 percent of Guåhan's population was in the military, which was twelve times the national average. During the Iraq war, most recruitment officers struggled to meet their quotas; however, Guåhan's recruiters excelled: four of the army's twelve most successful recruiters were based in Guåhan.[28] The military is the major employer on Guåhan, and there are three JROTC programs in the public schools, as well as an ROTC program at the University of Guam (ROTC stands for the Reserve Officers' Training Corps, a group of college- and university-based programs to train commissioned officers for the U.S. armed forces; JROTC is the "junior" program for high schools and middle schools). A key reason for recruiting success is economic: 25 percent of the population is defined as poor, and around 40 percent receives food stamps.[29] Many CHamorus see the military as their only opportunity to gain economic, social, and political capital. Out of the relationship between CHamorus and the military emerged the description of Guåhan as a "recruiter's paradise."[30]

Beyond economic pressures, scholars have noted that CHamorus enlist in such high numbers due to historical and psychological factors related to World War II. As I described earlier in this monograph, the U.S. military invaded Guåhan on July 21, 1944, and a three-week battle for the island ensued, which would ultimately end Japanese rule. A commemoration known as Liberation Day was created a year later. This annual event was seen as a time of rebirth and forgiveness, emphasizing "notions of spiritual salvation, national sacrifice, and cultural obligation."[31] The first liberation celebrations resembled Catholic rituals, as opposed to civic or military ceremonies, and the themes of salvation and liberation became intertwined, reflecting the "interconnected nature of spirituality, identity, and nationality in postwar Guam."[32] Liberation Day underwent a shift in the 1950s and 1960s, when the key commemorative theme became CHamoru loyalty to America, and the actual event became more civic and secular, with parades, marching bands, and floats. Young women even competed to become "Liberation Day Queen" by selling fundraising tickets. Over the years, Liberation Day has shaped the collective memory of the CHamoru people.[33] Some scholars believe that the rhetoric of salvation and liberation inscribed by Liberation Day ignited CHamoru "indigenous codes of indebtedness,"[34] thus partially explaining CHamoru enlistment patterns and "the high levels of public and phatic patriotism, military and civilian loyalty and devotion."[35] In other words, the CHamoru soldier "willingly and loyally shoulders the indigenous sacrifice" because military service is considered payment toward the CHamoru debt for "liberation" from the brutality of Japanese occupation.[36]

With these contexts in mind, let us return to Won Pat-Borja's poem-testimony. The speaker of the poem mentions Guåhan's high enlistment rates to show the cruel irony that even though CHamorus sacrifice their lives in the military, Guåhan continues to be exploited by the U.S. military for the sake of its geopolitical ambitions. Won Pat-Borja explores this irony when he asks how the U.S. government can consider CHamorus "Americans" if they "add insult to injury by burdening us with 8,600 marines all of whom Okinawa has lost its patience for, a nuclear aircraft carrier that will cost us a coral reef, over 20,000 foreign workers to make it all happen, and an army ballistic missile system to defend it all" ("No Deal"). In the next moment of the poem, the teacher powerfully proclaims: "The hands of your Presidents are drenched in the blood of our fallen—the same presidents that we are not allowed to vote for." Evoking the Insular Cases, Won Pat-Borja exposes the truth that the entirety of the U.S. Constitution does not apply to Guåhan since it is an unincorporated territory. Moreover, the sacrifice of CHamoru soldiers does not change the colonial truth that CHamorus do not have the right to vote for the president who decides their fate. Angered at this injustice, Won Pat-Borja concludes the poem with volcanic rhetoric:

> Let the record show that in the face of oppression and injustice, the people of Guam refuse to live a life absent of liberty, that we refuse to accept anything less than justice, that we refuse to sell Guam to the highest bidder. And should we die fighting your war machine, let your history books show your children the struggle that we fought to find freedom in a country filled with hypocrisy. Let the record show that Guåhan stood up and said, Uncle Sam, sorry, but *No Deal*. ("No Deal")

Throughout Won Pat-Borja's passionate testimony, audience members at the public hearing cheered loudly, sometimes muffling his words. As he exclaimed, "No Deal," with strength and conviction, the audience erupted into cheers. Won Pat-Borja's poem offers hope that CHamorus can find the strength to refuse to live under such an unjust and oppressive situation, and to continue to "prutehi yan difendi" Guåhan.

At subsequent public hearings for the military buildup, other poets (including Kisha Borja-Kicho'cho') also used their time to read poem-testimonies, which we can imagine as another form of kåntan chamorrita.[37] These poetic testimonies stood out from the other public comments because their recitations were so rhythmic and rhetorically compelling. The poetic testimonies were also more personal than some of the testimonies that were more data-driven. Won Pat-Borja's poem became a "cultural agent" in that it influenced others to take a stand against the further militarization of Guåhan. In all, over 10,000 comments were submitted at the public hearings and through the online portal, a majority of which rejected the military buildup. The activism succeeded in protecting the sacred area Pågat, and in both delaying and reducing the military buildup.[38]

In the time since then, Won Pat-Borja moved to and lived in Hawai'i for a few years to earn a master of arts degree in Pacific islands studies from the University of Hawai'i at Mānoa (the same program attended by C. T. Perez, Kisha Borja-Kicho'cho', and Anghet Hoppe-Cruz). His thesis, co-authored with Filipino poet and activist Jason Mateo, is titled "Cultivator: Pacific Tongues Educators' Guide to Cultivating an Active Artistic Oceanic Community of Writers, Spoken Word Performers, Leaders, Educators, and Students of All Ages" (2015). In 2016, he joined Guåhan's Commission on Decolonization, and the next year he traveled to New York to testify to the Special Committee on Decolonization of the United Nations.[39] In 2019, he was appointed executive director of the Commission on Decolonization.

Unfortunately, the activism was not able to stop the buildup entirely. As I write this in October 2020, the U.S. military is moving forward, though with adjustments to the plan. Now, the number of marines to be transferred from Okinawa to Guåhan is 5,000, and the live firing range complex that was originally proposed for Pågat is being built in an area of northern Guåhan known as Litekyan (Ritidian), which not only is a wildlife refuge, an ancestral CHamoru village with latte stones and burial sites, and a habitat for medicinal plants used by traditional healers, but also is close to the Northern Guam Lens Aquifer, the main source of drinking water for the island.[40] A contract for the live-fire training complex has already been awarded ($78 million to Black Construction), and the clearing of hundreds of acres of limestone forest has begun.[41] Protests are ongoing as CHamorus continue to struggle to "prutehi yan difendi" the sacred lands and waters.

Throughout the history of CHamoru and Pacific literature, the interplay between the poetics of political speech and activism and the politics of creative production is apparent. As Hawaiian poet and activist Haunani-Kay Trask once wrote: "Life is a confluence of creativities: art is a fluid political medium, as politics is metaphorical and artistic."[42] In general, most CHamoru and Pacific literature can be conceived as decolonial literary activism in the sense that literature functions to decolonize hegemonic representations of CHamoru and Pacific history, culture, and identity in the imagination of the reader, as well as to offer new imaginaries for a decolonial future. At the same time, there exist a number of CHamoru-authored texts that have entered into the public and political realms, enacting a decolonial activism in which literature travels beyond the page and becomes a tool through which to inform and engage the community on political issues, to unite and mobilize different groups, and to rally and inspire people.

This spirit of literary activism was captured in the 1987 anthology *Chamorro Self-Determination: The Right of a People / I Derechon i Taotao*. In the preface, the editors Laura Torres Souder and Robert Underwood write:

> Inspired by their own heritage and motivated by their own history, today, many Chamorros are articulating issues pertaining to their existence as a people. They articulate, define and seek redress to issues not merely as participants in an American body politic, but as members of an indigenous people whose cultural institutions predate any of the social, economic, and political institutions, which currently hold sway on Guam. This spirit has fueled the movement for Chamorro self-determination, inspired the artistry of the island's creative community, and motivated the quest for the return of stolen lands.[43]

The CHamoru spirit is fueled by the articulation of cultural pride and vitality as Indigenous people. One venue for this articulation has been CHamoru literature. As the editors point out, there is a symbiotic relationship between CHamoru activism and the CHamoru artistic and creative community. In this way, political and social activism are inextricably linked to literary and aesthetic creation, which in turn revitalize Indigeneity.[44] This spirit is also celebrated in Keith Camacho's entry "Chamorro Literature" in *The Pacific Islands: An Encyclopedia* (2000):

FIGURE 20 "Fishing for the Village," illustration by J. A. Pellion, from Freycinet's *Voyage autour du monde*, 1824. Courtesy of the Guam Public Library System.

> The future of Chamorro literature as an integral part of the contemporary culture of the Mariana Islands appears bright. The current momentum, linked to an insurgence of cultural pride and consciousness, encourages young people and elders to put their thoughts and experiences on paper as well as to make use of film and music. The growth of mass media opportunities and popular cultural resources in the islands will undoubtedly contribute to the flourishing of written literature as a vehicle for the expression of Chamorro culture and identity.[45]

I hope I have proven not only that the body of CHamoru literature is "measurably more than previously believed," but also that it represents a vibrant chorus of Native voices singing and writing our survival, resiliency, and vitality.[46] Furthermore, by wayreading CHamoru literature, I hope to have proven how contemporary CHamoru texts articulate the complexities of CHamoru cultural identities and aesthetics. Given my own limitations, I also hope this study will lead scholars to pay attention to the many other texts of CHamoru literature that have yet to receive critical attention, especially in the genres of fiction, nonfiction, and playwriting, by authors with genealogical ties to the Northern Mariana Islands, and by nonnative writers who now call the Marianas their home.

I will conclude by arriving, once again, on the shores of the Marianas. Imagine CHamoru families lining the entire coastline during the seasonal fish run to cast their nets, cook, and share food. Imagine countless generations of off-island CHamorus returning, finally, aboard flying canoes. Imagine our taotaomo'na emerging from the roots of the banyan trees to join us for the gupot. Imagine the jungle without snakes, and the birds released into the wild. Imagine hearing their songs echo throughout Pågat and Litekyan. Imagine thatching roofs together for a new guma' latte, a new house for all our stories. Imagine Puntan and Fu'una watching over us. Imagine weaving an endless kåntan chamorrita, forward and backward, that will honor our ancestors and inspire our descendants. Imagine our communal song map that will guide us to a decolonized, demilitarized, and sovereign future. Imagine our collective navigational chant that will guide us home. *Ekungok.*

NOTES

PREFACE

1. The fifteen volcanic islands of the Mariana archipelago include Guåhan, Rota, Aguijan, Tinian, Saipan, Farallon de Medinilla, Anatahan, Sarigan, Guguan, Alamagan, Pagan, Agrihan, Asuncion, Maug, and Farallon de Pajaros. The combined land area of the archipelago is nearly 400 square miles. In 1832, French explorer Jules-Sébastian-César Dumont d'Urville classified the Pacific into three "culture areas": Micronesia, Polynesia, and Melanesia. The name Micronesia derives from the Greek *micros* (small) and *nesos* (island). The region comprises thousands of islands in the Pacific, including the island groups of Kiribati, Nauru, the Marianas, the Marshalls, Palau, Yap, Chuuk, Pohnpei, and Kosrae. For a political history of Micronesia, see David Hanlon, *Remaking Micronesia: Discourses over Development in a Pacific Territory, 1944–1982* (Honolulu: University of Hawai'i Press, 1998). For an explanation of the Pacific culture areas, see Michelle Keown, *Pacific Islands Writing: The Postcolonial Literatures of Aotearoa / New Zealand and Oceania* (Oxford: Oxford University Press, 2007).
2. *Lali: A Pacific Anthology* (1980) and *Nuanua: Pacific Writing in English Since 1980* (1995) are considered the first major anthologies of contemporary Pacific literature: Albert Wendt, ed., *Lali: A Pacific Anthology* (Auckland: Longman Paul, 1980); and Albert Wendt, ed., *Nuanua: Pacific Writing in English Since 1980* (Auckland: Auckland University Press, 1995). A vast majority of the writers in *Lali* and *Nuanua* were from islands in Polynesia and Melanesia that were former British colonies served by the University of the South Pacific in Fiji. The only writers from the region of Micronesia were ones from Kiribati (a former British colony) who attended schools in Fiji. Wendt noted that, while he was aware of writers in Hawai'i, Australia, and New Zealand, he did not include

work from these places because writers there were already editing their own anthologies. Guåhan and the Mariana archipelago are not mentioned.

3. Craig Santos Perez, *from unincorporated territory [hacha]* (Kane'ohe, Hawai'i: Tinfish Press, 2008; reprint, Richmond, Calif.: Omnidawn Publishing, 2017).
4. Craig Santos Perez, *[hacha]*, 7.
5. See Craig Santos Perez, *from unincorporated territory [saina]* (Richmond, Calif.: Omnidawn Publishing, 2010); *from unincorporated territory [guma']* (Richmond, Calif.: Omnidawn Publishing, 2014); and *from unincorporated territory [lukao]* (Richmond, Calif.: Omnidawn Publishing, 2017).
6. For example, CHamoru literature is *not* studied in the following texts: Raymond Pillai and Ruth Finnegan, eds., *Essays on Pacific Literature* (Suva: Fiji Museum, 1978); Norman Toby Simms, *Silence and Invisibility: A Study of the Literatures of the Pacific, Australia, and New Zealand* (Washington, D.C.: Three Continents Press, 1986); John D. McLaren, *New Pacific Literatures: Culture and Environment in the European Pacific* (New York: Garland Publishing Incorporated, 1993); Mark Williams, *Post-colonial Literatures in English: Southeast Asia, New Zealand, and the Pacific, 1970–1992* (New York: G. K. Hall, 1996); and Vilsoni Hereniko and Rob Wilson, eds., *Inside Out: Literature, Cultural Politics, and Identity in the New Pacific* (Lanham, Md.: Rowman & Littlefield, 1999). It was not until Michelle Keown's 2007 monograph *Pacific Islands Writing: The Postcolonial Literatures of Aotearoa / New Zealand and Oceania* that CHamoru literature was cited in a single paragraph. I quote the paragraph in full: "The literature of Guam: The final locus of literary activity in the 'American Pacific' to be discussed here is Guam, a Micronesian island, annexed by the US in 1898, which remains an unincorporated US territory. In comparison to Hawai'i in particular, Guam features few publishing opportunities for local writers: the literary journal *Storyboard*, established in 1991, is the only regular local forum for the publication of contemporary creative writing, although Micronesian oral literature has been collected and disseminated in schools throughout Guam and the Trust Territory of the Pacific Islands. Named after an Indigenous art form from Belau (Palau) in which stories are presented visually, *Storyboard* published art, poetry, fiction, and non-fiction in English and other Pacific languages, particularly those of Micronesia, thus serving a similar 'regional' function as *Mana* at USP, or the UHP journal *Mānoa* and *The Contemporary Pacific* (established in 1989). Members of various US Micronesian territories have also published sporadically outside Micronesia, and a number of anticolonial poems and stories by writers from the 'American Pacific' (including Guam, the Marshall Islands, American Samoa, and Belau/Palau) were published in the 1992 literary anthology *Te Rau Maira* (ed. Crocombe et al.). In addition to the anticolonial material discussed in Chapter 3, this anthology includes a wide range of lyric poems and stories exploring the spiritual significance of the natural world, and celebrating the endurance into modern times of 'traditional' Micronesian cultural practices such as oratory, ritual dance, and weaving." Keown, *Pacific*

Islands Writing, 132–33. USP stands for the University of the South Pacific and UHP stands for the University of Hawai'i Press.

7. My testimony was published in *Diálogo: An Interdisciplinary Studies Journal* 19, no. 1 (Spring 2016): 153–56.

INTRODUCTION

1. Austronesia refers to Indonesia, Malaysia, the Philippines, and Taiwan. Robert F. Rogers, *Destiny's Landfall: A History of Guam* (Honolulu: University of Hawai'i Press, 1995), 37.
2. As Laurel Anne Monnig notes, ancient CHamoru culture "shared numerous cultural similarities with other Pacific, especially Micronesian, peoples described at the time." Laurel Anne Monnig, "'Proving Chamorro': Indigenous Narratives of Race, Identity, and Decolonization on Guam" (PhD diss., University of Illinois at Urbana-Champaign, 2007), 62. For more examples of the representation of "ancient" CHamoru culture, see Rogers, *Destiny's Landfall*; Lawrence Cunningham, *Ancient Chamorro Kinship Organization* (Agat, Guam: L. Joseph Press, 1984); Lawrence Cunningham, *Ancient Chamorro Society* (Honolulu: Bess Press, 1992); S. Russell, *Tiempon i Manmofo'na: Ancient Chamorro Culture and History of the Northern Mariana Islands* (Saipan: Commonwealth of the Northern Mariana Islands Division of Historic Preservation, 1998); Dominica Tolentino, "Ancient Chamorro Kinship and Land Tenure," *Guampedia*, http://www.guampedia.com/ancient-chamorro-kinship-and-land-tenure/; and Department of Chamorro Affairs, *Chamorro Heritage: A Sense of Place—Guidelines, Procedures, and Recommendations for Authenticating Chamorro Heritage* (Agana, Guam: Department of Chamorro Affairs, Research, Publication and Training Division, 2003).
3. Rogers, *Destiny's Landfall*, 1.
4. Rogers, 15.
5. See Frank Quimby, "The Matao Iron Trade Part 1: Contact and Commerce," *Guampedia*, updated September 27, 2020, accessed November 5, 2020, https://www.guampedia.com/the-matao-iron-trade-part-i-contact-and-commerce/. See also Frank Quimby, "The Hierro Commerce: Culture Contact, Appropriation and Colonial Entanglement in the Marianas, 1521–1668," *The Journal of Pacific History* 46, no. 1 (June 2011).
6. For a more detailed history of Spanish colonization in the Pacific, see Francis X. Hezel, "From Conversion to Conquest: The Early Spanish Mission in the Marianas," *Journal of Pacific History* 17 (1982): 115–20; Francis X. Hezel, "From Conquest to Colonization: Spain in the Marianas, 1690–1740," *Journal of Pacific History* 23 (1988): 137–55; and Rainer F. Buschmann, Edward R. Slack Jr., and James B. Tueller, eds., *Navigating the Spanish Lake: The Pacific in the Iberian World, 1521–1898* (Honolulu: University of Hawai'i Press, 2014).
7. Cynthia Ross Wiecko, "Jesuit Missionaries as Agents of Empire: The Spanish-Chamorro War and Ecological Effects of Conversion on Guam, 1668–1769,"

World History Connected, October 2013, accessed May 28, 2014, http://worldhistoryconnected.press.illinois.edu/10.3/forum_wiecko.html. For an examination of CHamoru resistance to these policies, see David Atienza, "CHamoru 'Adaptive Resistance' During the Spanish Conquest and Colonization in the Mariana Islands" (paper presented at the 4th Marianas History Conference, Guam, 2020).

8. For historical and political context on the war of 1898, see Louis A. Perez Jr., *The War of 1898: The United States and Cuba in History and Historiography* (Chapel Hill, N.C.: University of North Carolina Press, 1998); Amy Kaplan, *The Anarchy of Empire in the Making of U.S. Culture* (Cambridge, Mass.: Harvard University Press, 2005); Bonnie M. Miller, *From Liberation to Conquest: The Visual and Popular Cultures of the Spanish-American War of 1898* (Amherst: University of Massachusetts Press, 2011); and Hsuan Hsu, "Circa 1898: Overseas Empire and Transnational American Studies," *The Journal of Transnational American Studies* 3, no. 2 (2011).
9. Paul Lai argues that the Insular Cases signaled "a rupture in the previous logic of territorial acquisition. Overseas imperialism is not simply an extension of westward continental expansion but a new perspective that allowed for unincorporation as opposed to the two choices of incorporation or colonial control." Paul Lai, "Discontiguous States of America: The Paradox of Unincorporation in Craig Santos Perez's Poetics of Chamorro Guam," *The Journal of Transnational American Studies* 3, no. 2 (2011): 5. For more on the dynamics of territorialization, see Kaplan, *Anarchy of Empire*; Arnold H. Leibowitz, *Defining Status: A Comprehensive Analysis of United States Territorial Relations* (Boston: Martinus Nijhoff, 1989); and Kal Raustiala, *Does the Constitution Follow the Flag? The Evolution of Territoriality in American Law* (New York: Oxford University Press, 2009).
10. For scholarship on various aspects of the "naval era" of Guåhan, see Anne Perez Hattori, *Colonial Dis-ease: US Navy Health Policies and the Chamorros of Guam, 1898–1941* (Honolulu: University of Hawai'i Press, 2004); Penelope Bordallo Hofschneider, *A Campaign for Political Rights on the Island of Guam, 1899–1950* (Saipan: CNMI Division of Historic Preservation, 2001); Robert A. Underwood, "American Education and the Acculturation of the Chamorros of Guam" (PhD diss., University of Southern California, 1987); Christine Taitano DeLisle, "Navy Wives / Native Lives: The Cultural and Historical Relations Between Naval Wives and Chamorro Women in Guam, 1898–1945" (PhD diss., University of Michigan, 2008); Vicente Diaz, "Paved with Good Intentions . . . Roads, Citizenship and a Century of American Colonialism in Guam" (paper presented at the Centennial of the Spanish-American War Summer Seminar, Obermann Center for Advanced Study, University of Iowa, 1998).
11. Mark R. Peattie, *Nan'yō: The Rise and Fall of the Japanese in Micronesia, 1885–1945* (Honolulu: University of Hawai'i Press, 1988), 16. See also Wakako Higuchi, "Japanisation Policy for the Chamorros of Guam, 1941–1944," *The Journal of Pacific History* 36, no. 1 (2001): 19–35.

12. See Peattie, *Nan'yō*.
13. See Howard P. Willens, *An Honorable Accord: The Covenant Between the Northern Mariana Islands and the United States* (Honolulu: University of Hawai'i Press, 2002); and Don A. Farrell, "The Partition of the Marianas: A Diplomatic History, 1898–1919," *ISLA: A Journal of Micronesian Studies* 2, no. 2 (1994): 273–301.
14. See Vivian Dames, "Rethinking the Circle of Belonging: American Citizenship and the Chamorros of Guam" (PhD diss., University of Michigan, 2000).
15. Rogers, *Destiny's Landfall*, 51–52. For a discussion of Guam's "eras," see "Guam's Seven Historical Eras," *Guampedia*, October 10, 2019, accessed August 26, 2020, https://www.guampedia.com/guams-seven-historical-eras/.
16. Gwen Kirk and Lisa Natividad, "Fortress Guam: Resistance to U.S. Military Mega-Buildup," *The Asia-Pacific Journal* 8, issue 19, no. 1 (May 10, 2010): accessed April 15, 2014, http://japanfocus.org/-Gwyn-Kirk/3356; Catherine Lutz, "US Military Bases on Guam in Global Perspective," *The Asia-Pacific Journal* 8, no. 30 (July 26, 2010): accessed April 15, 2014, http://www.japanfocus.org/-catherine-lutz/3389.
17. Guam is one of the last remaining colonies on the United Nations List of Non-Self-Governing Territories. See United Nations, "United Nations and Decolonization," United Nations (website), accessed December 14, 2014, http://www.un.org/en/decolonization/nonselfgovterritories.shtml.
18. Rogers, *Destiny's Landfall*, 1.
19. Michael Lujan Bevacqua, "My Island Is One Big American Footnote," in *The Space Between: Negotiating Culture, Place, and Identity in the Pacific*, ed. Marata Tamaira (Honolulu: Center for Pacific Islands Studies, 2009), 120–22.
20. Elizabeth A. Paulino Diego, "Reclaiming Identity in Articulating What It Means to Be Chamorro: A Phenomenological Study of the Indigenous Peoples of Guam" (PhD diss., Gonzaga University, 2010), 73.
21. For a discussion of the meanings and origins of *Guamanian*, see Robert A. Underwood, "On Being ~~Guamanian Guamese Guamite Guamian~~ Chamorro," *Xanadu II*, Spring 1982, 1–13.
22. For discussions about this controversy, see Mary Therese Cruz, "(Re)Searching Identity: Being Chamorro in an American Colony" (PhD diss., University of Hawai'i, Mānoa, 2012), 3.
23. Diego, "Reclaiming Identity," 73–74. Different names and spellings often denote different political identities. For example, *Chamoru* is seen as reflecting a more Indigenous identity than *Chamorro*, while *I Taotao Tåno'* is seen as the most Indigenous choice. See Cruz, "(Re)Searching Identity," 3; and Gina E. Taitano, "Chamorro vs. Chamoru," *Guampedia*, accessed January 30, 2015, http://guampedia.com/chamorro-vs-chamoru.
24. Kumision i Fino' CHamoru yan Fina'nå'guen i Historia yan Lina'la' i Taotao Tåno' (Commisson on CHamoru Language and the Teaching of the History and Culture of the Indigenous People of Guam), "Utugrafihan CHamoru, Guåhan

(Guam CHamoru Orthography)," Commission on CHamoru Language (website), revised and updated April 2019, accessed June 12, 2020, https://kumisionchamoru.guam.gov/wp-content/uploads/2019/04/Orthography-as-of-April-9-2019.pdf.

25. Rogers, *Destiny's Landfall*, 14.
26. See Guam Exec. Order No. 2010–06 (2010), accessed February 20, 2015, http://documents.guam.gov/sites/default/files/EO-2010-06.pdf. Like the *Chamoru* versus *Chamorro* distinction, many people consider Guåhan to be the Indigenous name for the island.
27. Underwood, "On Being," 1.
28. For more examples of the representation of "ancient" CHamoru culture, see Rogers, *Destiny's Landfall*; Cunningham, *Ancient Chamorro Kinship Organization*; Cunningham, *Ancient Chamorro Society*; Russell, *Tiempon i Manmofo'na*; Tolentino, "Ancient Chamorro Kinship and Land Tenure"; and Department of Chamorro Affairs, *Chamorro Heritage.*
29. Diego, "Reclaiming Identity," 75. See also Michael Lujan Bevacqua, "CHamoru World View," *Guampedia*, updated December 17, 2019, accessed August 20, 2020, https://www.guampedia.com/chamorro-world-view/.
30. Diego, "Reclaiming Identity," 64.
31. Monnig, "Proving Chamorro," 62.
32. See Robert A. Underwood, "Hispanicization as a Socio-historical Process on Guam" (unpublished paper, Richard F. Taitano Micronesian Area Research Center, 1979).
33. See Vicente Diaz, *Repositioning the Missionary: Rewriting the Histories of Colonialism, Native Catholicism, and Indigeneity in Guam* (Honolulu: University of Hawai'i Press, 2010).
34. Diego, "Reclaiming Identity," 93.
35. Monnig, "Proving Chamorro," 69.
36. Diego, "Reclaiming Identity," 108.
37. Laura Thompson, *Guam and Its People* (1947; repr., New York: Greenwood Press, 1969), 35.
38. Rogers, *Destiny's Landfall*, 84.
39. Rogers, 84.
40. See Diego, "Reclaiming Identity," 106. See also Underwood, "American Education." To facilitate cultural Americanization, the naval administration also deported Spanish priests and prohibited Catholic practices (which were replaced with patriotic American celebrations) in order to disrupt the grip of the church. See Anne Perez Hattori, "Colonialism, Capitalism and Nationalism in the US Navy's Expulsion of Guam's Spanish Catholic Priests, 1898–1900," *The Journal of Pacific History* 44, no. 2 (2009): 281–302.
41. See Anne Perez Hattori, "Navy Blues: US Naval Rule on Guam and the Rough Road to Assimilation, 1898–1941," *Pacific Asia Inquiry* 5, no. 1 (Fall 2014): 13–30.

42. Keith L. Camacho, *Cultures of Commemoration: The Politics of War, Memory, and History in the Mariana Islands* (Honolulu: University of Hawai'i Press, 2011), 44.
43. Higuchi, "Japanisation Policy," 21.
44. Higuchi, 21.
45. Higuchi, 24. See also Naoto Sudo, "Colonial Mirror Images of Micronesia and Japan: Beyond the Tug of War between 'Americanization' and 'Japanization,'" *Postcolonial Text* 1, no. 1 (2004).
46. Higuchi, "Japanisation Policy," 27.
47. Underwood, "American Education," 181.
48. Diaz, *Repositioning the Missionary*, 13.
49. Vicente M. Diaz, "Deliberating 'Liberation Day': Identity, History, Memory, and War in Guam," in *Perilous Memories: The Asia-Pacific War(s)*, ed. T. Fujitani, Geoffrey M. White, and Lisa Yoneyama (Durham, N.C.: Duke University Press, 2001), 161.
50. See Robert A. Underwood, "The Role of Mass Media in Small Pacific Societies: The Case of Guam," *Pacific Islands Communications Journal* 10, no. 3 (1981): 60–72.
51. Laura Marie Torres Souder, *Daughters of the Island: Contemporary Chamorro Women Organizers on Guam* (Lanham, Md.: University Press of America, 1992), 41.
52. See Michael Lujan Bevacqua, "The Exceptional Life and Death of a Chamorro Soldier: Tracing the Militarization of Desire in Guam, ~~USA~~," in *Militarized Currents: Toward a Decolonized Future in Asia and the Pacific*, ed. Setsu Shigematsu and Keith L. Camacho (Minneapolis: University of Minnesota Press, 2010); and Keith L. Camacho and Laurel A. Monnig, "Uncomfortable Fatigues: Chamorro Soldiers, Gendered Identities, and the Question of Decolonization in Guam," in Shigematsu and Camacho, *Militarized Currents*, 147–79.
53. Underwood, "American Education," 362.
54. "Fatal impact" has been a major trope in Pacific historiography and cultural studies. See, for example, Alan Moorehead, *The Fatal Impact: An Account of the Invasion of the South Pacific, 1769–1840* (London: Harper Collins, 1966).
55. Michael Perez, "The Dialectic of Indigenous Identity in the Wake of Colonialism: The Case of Chamorros of Guam" (PhD diss., University of California, Riverside, 1997), 142.
56. M. Perez, "Dialectic of Indigenous Identity," 134.
57. M. Perez, 71.
58. Diego, "Reclaiming Identity," 134.
59. Monnig, "Proving Chamorro," 119.
60. For a history of the emergence of the international Indigenous rights movement, see José R. Martínez Cobo, *Study of the Problem of Discrimination Against Indigenous Populations*, United Nations Subcommission on Prevention of Discrimination and Protection of Minorities, E/CN.4/Sub.2/1986/7 and Add.4

(1987); Ronald Niezen, *The Origins of Indigenism: Human Rights and the Politics of Identity* (Berkeley: University of California Press, 2003); Lotte Hughes, *The No-Nonsense Guide to Indigenous Peoples* (London: New Internationalist / Verso Books, 2003); S. J. Anaya, *Indigenous Peoples in International Law* (New York: Oxford University Press, 2004); K. S. Coates, *A Global History of Indigenous Peoples: Struggle and Survival* (New York: Palgrave Macmillan, 2004); D. Maybury-Lewis, *Indigenous Peoples, Ethnic Groups, and the State*, 2nd ed. (Boston: Allyn & Bacon, 2002); R. J. Perry, *From Time Immemorial: Indigenous Peoples and State Systems* (Austin: University of Texas Press, 1996); H. Minde, ed., *Indigenous Peoples: Self Determination, Knowledge, Indigeneity* (Utrecht: Eburon Delft, 2008); L. Rodriguez-Pinero, *Indigenous Peoples, Postcolonialism, and International Law: The ILO Regime (1919–1989)* (New York: Oxford University Press, 2005); P. Thornberry, *Indigenous Peoples and Human Rights* (Manchester: Manchester University Press, 2002); and Jeffrey Sissons, *First Peoples: Indigenous Cultures and Their Futures* (London: Reaktion Books, 2005). For a brief history of decolonization in the Pacific, see Stewart Firth, "Decolonization," in *Remembrance of Pacific Pasts: An Invitation to Remake History*, ed. Robert Borofsky (Honolulu: University of Hawai'i Press, 2000), 314–32. For a look at decolonization in the context of literature, see Keown, *Pacific Islands Writing.*

61. For a history of this period in Micronesia, see Hanlon, *Remaking Micronesia.*
62. For a history of CHamoru decolonial activism, see Dames, "Rethinking the Circle." See also Michael Lujan Bevacqua, "Chamorros, Ghosts, Non-Voting Delegates: Guam! Where the Production of America's Sovereignty Begins" (PhD diss., University of California, San Diego, 2010).
63. Monnig, "Proving Chamorro," 115.
64. Laura Marie Torres Souder, "Preface," in *Chamorro Self-Determination: The Right of a People / I Derechon i Taotao*, ed. Laura Marie Torres Souder and Robert A. Underwood (Mangilao, Guam: Chamorro Studies Association and Micronesian Area Research Center, University of Guam, 1987), vii–viii.
65. Souder, "Preface," in Souder and Underwood, *Chamorro Self-Determination.*
66. Monnig, "Proving Chamorro," 158.
67. Monnig, 31.
68. Diego, "Reclaiming Identity," 256.
69. Carmen Artero Kasperbauer, "The Chamorro Culture," in *Kinalamten Pulitikåt: Siñenten i Chamorro / Issues In Guam's Political Development: The Chamorro Perspective* (Agana, Guam: Political Status Education Coordinating Commission, 1996), 26.
70. Cruz, "(Re)Searching Identity," 31–32.
71. M. Perez, "Dialectic of Indigenous Identity," 72–73.
72. A few key sources that consider Indigenous identities include Rona Tamiko Halualani, *In the Name of Hawaiians: Native Identities and Cultural Politics* (Minneapolis: University of Minnesota Press, 2002); Eva Marie Garroutte, *Real*

Indians: Identity and the Survival of Native America (Berkeley: University of California Press, 2003); and Hereniko and Wilson, *Inside Out*.

73. Vicente M. Diaz and J. Kēhaulani Kauanui, "Native Pacific Cultural Studies on the Edge," *The Contemporary Pacific* 13, no. 2 (2001): 315–42.
74. James Clifford, "Indigenous Articulations," *The Contemporary Pacific* 13, no. 2 (Fall 2001): 472.
75. Clifford, 472.
76. Clifford, 478.
77. Vicente M. Diaz, "Simply Chamorro: Telling Tales of Demise and Survival in Guam," *The Contemporary Pacific* 6, no. 1 (Spring 1994): 31.
78. Diaz, 52–53 (italics added).
79. Diaz, 32 (italics added).
80. Cruz, "(Re)Searching Identity," 126 (italics added).
81. F. García, *Life and Martyrdom of the Venerable Father Diego Luis De San Vitores of the Society of Jesus* (1683; repr., Madrid: Ivan García Infanzen, 1994), 171, quoted in Judy Flores, "Kantan Chamorrita Revisited in the New Millennium," in *Transnationalism and Modernity in the Music and Dance of Oceania: Essays in Honour of Barbara B. Smith*, ed. H. Lawrence (Sydney: University of Sydney, 2001), 21.
82. Jacques Arago, *Narrative of a Voyage Round the World, in the Uranie and Physicienne Corvettes, Commanded by M. de Freycinet During the Years 1817, 1818, 1819, and 1820* (London: Treuttel and Wurtz, 1823), quoted in Flores, "Kantan Chamorrita Revisited," 21.
83. William Peck, *I Speak the Beginning: Anthology of Surviving Poetry of the Northern Mariana Islands* (Saipan: Commonwealth Council for Arts and Culture, 1982), i.
84. Michael R. Clement Jr., "Kustumbre, Modernity and Resistance: The Subaltern Narrative in Chamorro Language Music" (PhD diss., University of Hawaiʻi at Mānoa, 2011), 49–51. See also Kasperbauer, "Chamorro Culture."
85. Katherine B. Aguon, "The Guam Dilemma: The Need for a Pacific Island Education Perspective," in *Kinalamten Pulitikåt: Siñenten i Chamorro / Issues in Guam's Political Development: The Chamorro Perspective* (Agana, Guam: Political Status Education Coordinating Commission, 1996), 92.
86. Keith L. Camacho, "Chamorro Literature," in *The Pacific Islands: An Encyclopedia*, ed. Brij V. Lal and Kate Fortune (Honolulu: University of Hawaiʻi Press, 2000), 520.
87. For an overview of the development of contemporary Pacific literature, see Keown, *Pacific Islands Writing*.
88. Jeannine E. Talley, "Editor's Comments," *Storyboard: A Journal of Pacific Imagery*, no. 4 (1996): 5. Based at the University of Guam, *Storyboard* put out issues that date from 1991 to 2001, 2006, and 2009 to the present. The first literary journal to emerge from the University of Guam was *Xanadu*, published once in 1966, and featuring work by students and faculty members of CHamoru and

non-CHamoru descent. Between 1981 and 1983, the journal was resurrected as *Xanadu II*.

89. Karen L. Nero, "Missed Opportunities: American Anthropological Studies of Micronesian Arts," in *American Anthropology in Micronesia: An Assessment*, edited by R. Kiste and M. Marshall (Honolulu: University of Hawai'i Press, 1999), 256. In contrast, university journals such as *Kovave* (University of Papua New Guinea), *Mana* (University of the South Pacific, Fiji), and *Mānoa* and *The Contemporary Pacific* (University of Hawai'i at Mānoa) created spaces for Pacific writers to publish their literary and critical works. In addition, Mana Publications released a series of regional anthologies edited by Albert Wendt that featured writers from Fiji, the Solomon Islands, the New Hebrides, Vanuatu, and Western Sāmoa.

90. Mark E. Skinner, "Contemporary Micronesian Literature: A Preliminary Bibliography" (MA thesis, University of Hawai'i, Mānoa, 1990).

91. The story of the comic strip *Juan Malimanga* is worth mentioning here. Gould was a member of two CHamoru activist organizations, the People's Alliance for Responsible Alternatives (PARA) and the Organization of People for Indigenous Rights (OPI-R). They led a demonstration to protest the English-only policies of Guåhan's major newspaper, *The Pacific Daily News* (*PDN*). The demonstration caused the newspaper to rescind its colonial language policy. The *PDN*, in collaboration with the Chamorro Studies Division of the Department of Education, of which Gould was the director, ended up publishing the CHamoru-language comic strip and *Fino' Chamorro*, a short daily language lesson.

Originally, the *PDN* asked Gould to translate the well-known *Peanuts* comic strip, but Gould instead proposed to create a comic strip with CHamoru and local humor. Juan Malimanga and his sidekicks, Kika and Nano, made their first appearance in the *PDN* in May 1981. Malimanga is based on the CHamoru folktale character Juan Malo, who was a trickster-type figure who lived during the Spanish era and continually outwitted the colonial administrators. For more on Gould, see Dominica Tolentino and Faye Varias, "Clotilde 'Ding' Castro Gould," *Guampedia*, accessed June 28, 2020, https://www.guampedia.com/clotilde-ding-castro-gould/.

92. Chris Perez Howard, *Edward: An American Tragedy* (Agana, Guam: Cyfred Ltd., 2006).

93. For a full list of his theatrical works, see Peter R. Onedera, "Theatrical Works of Peter Onedera," *Peter Robert Onedera* (blog), September 21, 2013, accessed June 12, 2020, http://peterrobertonedera.blogspot.com/2013/. Over forty of the plays have been produced on Guåhan at various theaters, schools, community centers, etc.

94. For a list of their publications, visit the University of Guam Press website: https://www.uog.edu/uogpress/.

95. Quoted from the University of Guam Press website: https://www.uog.edu/uogpress/publications/taiguini-books/ (accessed August 20, 2020).

96. Julius Sotomayor Cena, "Theater," *Guampedia*, last modified October 10, 2019, accessed March 10, 2021, https://www.guampedia.com/theater/.
97. See Cena, "Theater"; Peter R. Onedera, "Theater in a CHamoru Sense" (unpublished paper prepared for Art and Culture in Micronesia, Micronesian Studies Graduate Program, University of Guam, 1999); and Michael Lujan Bevacqua, "A Play Called Pagat," *Minagahet* (blog), April 24, 2014, accessed March 10, 2021, http://minagahet.blogspot.com/2014/04/a-play-called-pagat-michael-lujan.html.
98. See the website of Dakota Camacho, https://www.dakotacamacho.com.
99. See PC Muñoz's website: http://www.pcmunoz.com/about.html.
100. See Ami Mattison's Bandcamp page: https://amimattison.bandcamp.com.
101. See the group's website: http://ginenihila.blogspot.com.
102. Committee on Rules, Resolution No. 147–34 (June 14, 2017), Guam Legislature.
103. Tinaotao Humanities Guåhan (Guam Humanities Council), Ta Tuge' Mo'na, and Sinangån-ta are three examples of nonprofit organizations that have supported the literature of Guåhan.
104. On *Mariquita*: N. Sudo, "Colonial Mirror Images"; Paul Sharrad, "Filling in the Blanks: *Mariquita*, a Hybrid Biography from Guam," in "Islands Special," special issue, *New Literatures Review* (2011): 149–62; Valerie Woodward, "'I Guess They Didn't Want Us Asking Too Many Questions': Reading American Empire in Guam," *The Contemporary Pacific* 25, no. 1 (Spring 2013): 67–91. On Paula Quinene: Carolina Fernandez Rodriguez, "Chamorro WWII Romances: Combating Erasure with Survival and Vitality," *Journal of Popular Romance Studies* 8 (2019): 1–21.
105. Monique R. Carriveau Storie, "All Fifty Kathousand Cousins: Chamorro Teachers Responding to Contemporary Children's Literature Set in Guam" (PhD diss., University of Arizona, 2009); Sharleen J. Q. Santos-Bamba, "The Literate Lives of Chamorro Women in Modern Guam" (PhD diss., Indiana University of Pennsylvania, 2010). Storie has also published two essays related to her dissertation research: "The Emergence of 'Fantastic' in Chamorro Literature," Worlds of Words (website), The University of Arizona, November 21, 2011, https://wowlit.org/blog/2011/11/21/the-emergence-of-"fantastic"-chamorro-literature/; and "'That's So Chamorro': Representations of Culture in Chamorro Realistic Fiction," in *Diversity in Youth Literature: Opening Doors Through Reading*, ed. Jamie Campbell Naidoo and Sarah Park Dahlen (Chicago: American Library Association Editions, 2013), 83–93. It should be mentioned, although I do not include it since it does not focus on CHamoru literature, that CHamoru scholar Evelyn Flores wrote a dissertation, "Rewriting Paradise: Countering Desire, Denial and the Exotic in American Literary Representations of the Pacific" (PhD diss., University of Michigan, 2002).
106. Caitlin Yuri Yamamoto, "Emergent Voices of (Neo)colonial Resistance: The Contemporary Literatures, Cultures, and Histories of 'Micronesia'" (PhD diss., University of California, San Diego, 2016).

107. Michael Lujan Bevacqua and Isa Kelley Bowman, "Histories of Wonder, Futures of Wonder: Chamorro Activist Identity, Community, and Leadership in 'The Legend of Gadao' and 'The Women Who Saved Guåhan from a Giant Fish,'" *Marvels & Tales* 30, no. 1 (2016): https://digitalcommons.wayne.edu/marvels/vol30/iss1/6.

108. Leiana San Agustin Naholowa'a, "Beyond Matrifocality: A Literary Analysis of Mothering in Chamorro Narratives in Guam" (MA thesis, University of Guam, 2018); and Arielle Taitano Lowe, "Pakaka i Pachot-mu! Chamoru Yu'! A Mestiza Rhetoric Analysis of Guam's Chamaole Narratives" (MA thesis, University of Guam, 2020).

109. My essays include: "Signs of Being: Chamoru Poetry and the Work of C. T. Perez," *Jacket2*, April 2, 2011, http://jacket2.org/article/signs-being; "Singing Forwards and Backwards: Ancestral and Contemporary Chamorro Poetics," in *The Oxford Handbook of Indigenous American Literature*, ed. James H. Cox and Daniel Heath Justice (New York: Oxford University Press, 2014), 152–66; "From Organic Acts: Tsamorita, Rosaries, and the Poem of My Grandma's Life," *Life Writing Journal*, 2015, 45–67; "I Lina'la' Tataotao Ta'lo': The Rhetoric and Aesthetics of Militarism, Religiosity, and Commemoration," in *Huihui: Pacific Rhetoric and Aesthetics*, ed. Brandy Nālani McDougall, Georganne Nordstrom, and Jeff Carroll (Honolulu: University of Hawai'i Press, 2015), 50–71; "Native Chamorro Ecopoetry in the Work of Cecilia Perez," in *Ecopoetics and the Global Landscape: Critical Essays*, ed. Isabel Campos (New York: Rowman and Littlefield, 2019), 34–67; "'Thank God for the Maladjusted': The Transterritorial Turn Towards the Chamorro Poetry of Guåhan (Guam)," in *Oceanic Archives, Indigenous Epistemologies, and Transpacific American Studies*, ed. Otto Heim, Yuan Shu, and Kendall Johnson (Hong Kong: Hong Kong University Press, 2019), 45–76; "The Chamorro Creation Story, Guam Land Struggles, and Contemporary Poetry," *English Language Notes* 58, no. 1 (April 2020): 9–20.

110. Huan He, "On the Perpetual Motion of Search: The Transpacific Networked Poetics of Craig Santos Perez and Theresa H. K. Cha," *College Literature* 47, no. 1 (Winter 2020); Francisco Delgado, "Remade: Sovereign: Decolonizing Guam in the Age of Environmental Anxiety," *Memory Studies*, December 2019, 1–13; Bonnie Etherington, "Mapping Modernity in Guam: The Unincorporated Ecologies of Craig Santos Perez's Poetics," in *New Oceania: Modernisms and Modernities in the Pacific*, ed. Matthew Hayward and Maebh Long (New York: Routledge, 2019); Anne Mai Yee Jansen, "Writing *Toward* Action: Mapping an Affinity Poetics in Craig Santos Perez's *from unincorporated territory*," *Native American and Indigenous Studies Journal* 6, no. 2 (2019); Raymond D. Anderson, "Snakes, Swords, Blood and Sacrifice: Exploring Hybridity, Silence and Witnessing in the Emerging Narratives of Guahan," in *Narratives of Storytelling Across Cultures*, ed. Tony R. DeMars and Gabriel B. Tait (Lanham, Md.: Rowman & Littlefield, 2019); Paola Della Valle, "Diaspora, Memory and Chamorro Migration from Guam, in Craig Santos Perez's Poetry," *Semicerchio: Revista di*

Poesia Comparata 60 (2019): 43–50; Mary A. Knighton, "Guam, Un-Inc.; or Craig Santos Perez's Transterritorial Challenge to American Studies as Usual," in *The Routledge Companion to Transnational American Studies*, ed. Nina Morgan, Alfred Hornung, and Takayuki Tatsumi (New York: Routledge, 2019); Elizabeth DeLoughrey, "Toward a Critical Ocean Studies for the Anthropocene," *English Language Notes* 57, no. 1 (April 2019): 21–36; Otto Heim, "How (Not) to Globalize Oceania: Ecology and Politics in Contemporary Pacific Island Performance Arts," *Commonwealth Essays and Studies* 41, no. 1 (Autumn 2018): 131–46; J. Michael Martinez, "Tidal Poetics: The Poetry of Craig Santos Perez," in *American Poets in the 21st Century: Poetics of Social Engagement*, ed. Claudia Rankine and Michael Dowdy (Middletown, Conn.: Wesleyan University Press, 2018), 332–41; Collier Nogues, "'With [Our] Entire Breath': The US Military Buildup on Guåhan (Guam) and Craig Santos Perez's Literature of Resistance," *Shima Journal* 12, no. 1 (2018); Paloma Fresno-Calleja, "Fighting Gastrocolonialism in Indigenous Pacific Writing," *Interventions: International Journal of Postcolonial Studies*, 2017, 1041–55; John Carlos Rowe, "Shades of Paradise: Craig Santos Perez's Transpacific Voyages," in *Archipelagic American Studies*, ed. Brian Russell Roberts and Michelle Ann Stephens (Durham, N.C.: Duke University Press, 2017), 213–23; Jennifer K. Dick, "Craig Santos Perez and Myung Mi Kim: Voicing the Integral Divide; Transcending Suffering by Reshaping American History and Language," in *American Multiculturalism in Context: Views from at Home and Abroad*, ed. Sami Ludwig (Cambridge: Cambridge Scholars Publishing, 2017), 203–20; Katherine Baxter and Lytton Smith, "Writing in Translation: Robert Sullivan's *Star Waka* and Craig Santos Perez's *from unincorporated territory*," *Literary Geographies* 2, no. 2 (2016): 263–83; Robert J. Briggs, "There's No Place (Like Home): Craig Santos Perez's Poetry as Military Strategy," *Green Letters: Studies in Ecocriticism* 21, no. 1 (2016): 48–64; Jim Cocola, "Forget Your Pastoral: Haunani-Kay Trask and Craig Santos Perez," in *Places in the Making: Cultural Geography in American Poetry* (Iowa City: University of Iowa Press, 2016), 174–214; Otto Heim, "Locating Guam: The Cartography of the Pacific and Craig Santos Perez's Re-mapping of Unincorporated Territory," in *New Directions in Travel Writing Studies*, ed. Julia Kuehn and Paul Smethurst (London: Palgrave Macmillan, 2015), 180–98; Michael Lujan Bevacqua, "The Song Maps of Craig Santos Perez," *Transmotion* 1, no. 1 (2015); Cathy J. Schlund-Vials, "'Finding' Guam: Distant Epistemologies and Cartographic Pedagogies," *Asian American Literature: Discourses and Pedagogies* 5 (2014): 45–60; Valerie Woodward, "I Guess They Didn't Want Us Asking Too Many Questions: Reading American Empire in Guam," *The Contemporary Pacific* 25, no. 1 (Spring 2013): 67–91; Ryan Clark, "The Appositional Project: Craig Santos Perez's *from unincorporated territory [saina]*," *Spoon River Poetry Review*, November 10, 2013; Hsuan Hsu, "Guahan (Guam), Literary Emergence, and the American Pacific in *Homebase* and *from unincorporated territory*," *American Literary History* 24, no. 2 (Summer 2012): 281–307; Paul Lai, "Discontiguous States of America: The Paradox of Unincorporation in Craig Santos Perez's Poetics of Chamorro Guam," *The Journal of Transnational American Studies* 3, no. 2 (2011).

111. Robert Tenorio Torres, "Selected Marianas Folklore, Legend, Literature: A Critical Commentary" (MA thesis, San Diego State University, 1991); Robert Tenorio Torres, "Pre-Contact Marianas Folklore: A Critical Commentary," *Micronesian Journal of the Humanities and Social Sciences* 2, no. 1–2 (2003): 3–15; Robert Tenorio Torres, "Colonial and Conquest Lore of the Marianas: A Critical Commentary," *Micronesian Journal of the Humanities and Social Sciences* 2, no. 1–2 (2003): 23–30; Robert Tenorio Torres, "Post Colonial and Modern Literature of the Marianas: A Critical Commentary," *Micronesian Journal of the Humanities and Social Sciences* 3, no. 1–2 (2004): 26–44.
112. Torres, "Post Colonial and Modern Literature," 27.
113. Torres, 42.
114. For a survey of new Pacific literature, see Keown, *Pacific Islands Writing.*
115. Robert Lund, *Hour of Glory* (New York: John Day Company, 1950); Juan A. Sanchez, *History's Four Dark Days: A Memorial Ode to the Late John Fitzgerald Kennedy* (Saipan, Northern Mariana Islands: Trust Territory Printing Office, 1965); *Xanadu* and *Xanadu II* (Mangilao: University of Guam, 1966 and 1981–83); Louise Stout, *Kalou: A Legend of Saipan* (Saipan, Northern Mariana Islands: Trust Territory Printing Office, 1970); Peck, *I Speak the Beginning*; Chris Perez Howard, *Mariquita: A Tragedy of Guam* (Suva, Fiji: Institute of Pacific Studies, 1986); John Mazur, *Pacific War, Saipaniana, and Typhoons in Paradise* (Long Beach, Calif.: John Mazur, 1990).
116. Torres, "Colonial and Conquest Lore," 23.
117. Torres, 23.
118. See Torres, "Pre-Contact Marianas Folklore," 3; and Torres, "Post Colonial and Modern Literature," 42.
119. Torres, "Post Colonial and Modern Literature," 42.
120. Torres, 4.
121. Van Peenan, *Chamorro Legends,* 36–37.
122. Peck, *I Speak the Beginning,* i.
123. Peck, i.
124. Judy Flores, "Art and Identity in the Marianas Islands: The Reconstruction of 'Ancient' Chamorro Dance," in *Pacific Art: Persistence, Change and Meaning,* ed. Anita Herle, Nick Stanley, Karen Stevenson, and Robert L. Welsch (Honolulu: University of Hawai'i Press, 2002), 106–13. See also Judy Flores, "Art and Identity in the Mariana Islands: Issues of Reconstructing an Ancient Past" (PhD diss., University of East Anglia, 1999).
125. J. Flores, "Reconstruction of 'Ancient' Chamorro Dance," 106.
126. J. Flores, 108.
127. J. Flores, 109–110.
128. J. Flores, 110.

129. His full description reads: "Most Chamorro songs are composed in western styles introduced in the twentieth century. The common styles are country and western, cha-cha, *batsu* (waltz), polka, rock and roll, jitterbug, and pop ballads, though Chamorro music has been composed in virtually every style imaginable. Some of the songs are translations of popular American songs. Many others are adaptations of American songs, in which melodies are borrowed but songs are re-arranged or modified in various ways and original lyrics are completely discarded for new Chamorro ones." Clement Jr., "Kustumbre, Modernity, and Resistance," 5.
130. Clement Jr., "Kustumbre, Modernity, and Resistance," 5.
131. Clement Jr., 2.
132. Clement Jr., 107.
133. Clement Jr., 107.
134. Clement Jr., 287–88.
135. Storie, "All Fifty Kathousand Cousins," 12. See also Storie, "That's So Chamorro."
136. Storie, "All Fifty Kathousand Cousins," 331.
137. I first encountered "markers of authenticity" and "cultural identifiers" in Monnig, "Proving Chamorro," 42; and "summarizing symbols" in Dames, "Rethinking the Circle of Belonging," 135.
138. Storie, "All Fifty Kathousand Cousins," 385.
139. Vicente M. Diaz, "Voyaging for Anti-colonial Recovery: Austronesian Seafaring, Archipelagic Rethinking, and the Re-mapping of Indigeneity," *Pacific Asia Inquiry* 2, no. 1 (Fall 2011): 26.
140. Diaz, "Voyaging for Anti-colonial Recovery," 27.
141. While I focus on the figurative nature of etak and pookof, Diaz shows how islands *literally* move when their natural resources are extracted and exported around the world, when they have been obliterated by military weapons testing, or when they disappear under rising tides. Diaz, "Voyaging for Anti-colonial Recovery," 26–27.
142. See Greg Dening, *Beach Crossings: Voyaging Across Times, Cultures, and Self* (Philadelphia: University of Pennsylvania Press, 2004).
143. Will Kyselka, *The Hawaiian Sky* (Honolulu: Bess Press, 1989), 54.
144. Diaz, "Voyaging for Anti-colonial Recovery," 27.
145. Diaz, 21–22.
146. Michael Lujan Bevacqua, "The Song Maps of Craig Santos Perez," *Transmotion* 1, no. 1 (2015).
147. Diaz, "Voyaging for Anti-colonial Recovery," 22–27.
148. Diaz, 27.
149. Elizabeth DeLoughrey, *Routes and Roots: Navigating Caribbean and Pacific Island Literatures* (Honolulu: University of Hawai'i Press, 2007), 3.
150. DeLoughrey, *Routes and Roots*, 108, 129.
151. "Transoceanic imaginary" and "maritime narrative legacies" are from DeLoughrey, *Routes and Roots*, 96, 129. "Towards a new Oceania" is from Albert Wendt, "Towards a New Oceania," *Mana Review* 1, no. 1 (January 1976): 49–60.

152. Linda Tuhiwai Smith, *Decolonizing Methodologies: Research and Indigenous Peoples* (London: ZED Books, 1999), 142. Other texts about the importance of Indigenous methodologies include Robert Warrior, "The Native American Scholar: Toward a New Intellectual Agenda," *Wicazo Sa Review* 14, no. 2 (Fall 1999): 46–54; Inés Hernández-Ávila and Stefano Varese, "Indigenous Intellectual Sovereignties," *Wicazo Sa Review* 14, no. 2 (Fall 1999): 77–92; Jelana Porsanger, "An Essay About Indigenous Methodology," *NORDLIT* 15 (2004): 105–20; Linda Tuhiwai Smith, Yvonne S. Lincoln, and Norman K. Denzin, eds., *Handbook of Critical and Indigenous Methodologies* (Los Angeles: Sage Publications, 2008); and Shawn Wilson, *Research Is Ceremony: Indigenous Research Methods* (Nova Scotia: Fernwood Publishing Co., 2009).

153. A few key texts that discuss the importance of Pacific contexts in the analysis of Pacific literature include Sina Va'ai, *Literary Representations in Western Polynesia: Colonialism and Indigeneity* (Samoa: National University of Samoa, 1999); Haunani-Kay Trask, "Writing in Captivity: Poetry in a Time of Decolonization," in Hereniko and Wilson, *Inside Out*, 17–26; and Konai Helu Thaman, "Of Daffodils and Heilala: Understanding (Cultural) Context in Pacific Literature," in *Navigating Islands and Continents: Conversations and Contestations in and Around the Pacific*, ed. Cynthia Franklin, Ruth Hsu, and Suzanne Kosanke (Honolulu: University of Hawai'i Press, 2000), 40–50.

154. Essential sources include Paula Gunn Allen, *The Sacred Hoop: Recovering the Feminine Side in American Indian Traditions* (Boston: Beacon Press, 1986); and Simon Ortiz, "Towards a National Indian Literature: Cultural Authenticity in Nationalism," *MELUS* 8, no. 2 (Summer 1981): 12–20.

155. I first encountered this phrase in Va'ai, *Literary Representations in Western Polynesia*, 37. Other sources that address specific cultural antecedents and theories: Vilsoni Hereniko and Sig Schwarz, "Four Writers and One Critic," in Hereniko and Wilson, *Inside Out*, 62; Selina Tusitala Marsh, "Theory 'Versus' Pacific Islands Writing: Toward a Tama'ita'i Criticism in the Works of Three Pacific Islands Woman Poets," in Hereniko and Wilson, *Inside Out*, 339–47; and Steven Edmund Winduo, "Unwriting Oceania: The Repositioning of the Pacific Writer Scholars Within a Folk Narrative Space," *New Literary History* 31, no. 3 (Summer 2000): 605.

156. She writes: "Samoans relish the spoken word. The development of Samoan writing must be set against this tradition of language to be understood. The love of words, building up into logical argument and woven into intricate plots, allusion and innuendo, are all here. The development of an indigenous written literature has been slow, following a pattern evident in other developing countries moving from an oral to a written literacy." Peggy Fairbairn-Dunlop, "Samoan Writing: Searching for the Written Fagogo," *Pacific Islands Communication Journal* 14, no. 1 (1985): 41–42.

157. See ku'ualoha ho'omanawanui, "He Lei Ho'oheno no nā Kau a Kau: Language, Performance, and Form in Hawaiian Poetry," *The Contemporary Pacific* 17, no. 1 (2005): 29–81.

158. Epeli Hau'ofa, "Oral Traditions and Writing," *Landfall* 44, no. 4 (1990): 402–11.

159. Teresia Teaiwa, "What Remains to Be Seen: Reclaiming the Visual Roots of Pacific Literature," *PMLA* 125, no. 3 (2010): 730–36; Albert Wendt, "Tatauing the Post-colonial Body," *Span* 42–43 (April 1996): 26–27; ho'omanawanui, "He Lei Ho'oheno no nā Kau a Kau," 64; Robert Sullivan, "The English Moko: Exploring a Spiral," in *Figuring the Pacific: Aotearoa and Pacific Cultural Studies*, ed. Howard McNaughton and John Newton (Christchurch: University of Canterbury Press, 2005), 12–28.

160. See ho'omanawanui, "He Lei Ho'oheno no nā Kau a Kau."

161. Wendt, *Nuanua*, 3.

162. See Gerald Vizenor, *Narrative Chance: Postmodern Discourse on Native American Indian Literatures* (Albuquerque: University of New Mexico Press, 1989); Leslie Marmon Silko, *Yellow Woman and a Beauty of the Spirit: Essays on Native American Life Today* (New York: Simon & Schuster, 1997); Susan Berry Brill de Ramirez, *Contemporary American Indian Literatures and the Oral Tradition* (Tucson: University of Arizona Press, 1999); Daniel Heath Justice, *Our Fire Survives the Storm: A Cherokee Literary History* (Minneapolis: University of Minnesota Press, 2006); Penelope Myrtle Kelsey, *Tribal Theory in Native American Literature: Dakota and Haudenosaunee Writing and Indigenous Worldviews* (Lincoln: University of Nebraska Press, 2008); and James Cox, *Muting White Noise: Native American and European American Novel Traditions* (Norman: University of Oklahoma Press, 2009).

163. C. Allen, *Trans-Indigenous*, xxx.

164. Wendt, *Nuanua*, 3.

165. Wendt, 3.

166. Nearly every study of Pacific literature invokes the important role that literature has played in Pacific decolonial movements. A few prominent examples include Paul Sharrad, ed., *Readings in Pacific Literature* (Wollongong, Australia: University of Wollongong, 1993); Patrick Morrow, *Post-colonial Essays on South Pacific Literature* (Lewiston, N.Y.: Edwin Mellen Press, 1998); Hereniko and Wilson, *Inside Out*; Va'ai, *Literary Representations in Western Polynesia*; ku'ualoha ho'omanawanui, "Ha, Mana, Leo (Breath, Spirit, Voice): Kanaka Maoli Empowerment Through Literature," *American Indian Quarterly* 28, nos. 1/2 (Winter/Spring 2004): 86–91; Keown, *Pacific Islands Writing*; Michelle Keown, *Postcolonial Pacific Writing: Representations of the Body* (London: Routledge, 2009); and Susan Najita, *Decolonizing Cultures in the Pacific: Reading History and Trauma in Contemporary Fiction* (London: Routledge, 2008). Native American texts on literature and decolonization include: Elizabeth Cook-Lynn, "The American Indian Fiction Writers: Cosmopolitanism, Nationalism, the Third World, and First Nation Sovereignty," in *Why I Can't Read Wallace Stegner*, ed. Elizabeth Cook-Lynn (Madison: University of Wisconsin Press, 1996); Robert Allen Warrior, *Tribal Secrets: Recovering American Indian Intellectual Traditions* (Minneapolis: University of Minnesota Press, 1995); and Craig S.

Womack, *Red on Red: Native American Literary Separatism* (Minneapolis: University of Minnesota Press, 1999).

167. Maria Yatar, "Navigating Modernity" (presentation at the 16th annual Guam Association of Social Workers Conference, 1995), quoted in Lilli Perez, "An Ethnography of Reciprocity Among Chamorros in Guam" (PhD diss., Bryn Mawr, 1998), 36.

CHAPTER 1

1. The names of Fu'una and Puntan are also spelled Fo'na and Pontan.
2. Fu'a Rock is also known as Creation Point. The village of Umatac derives its name from the word *uma*, which refers to carrying something on the back or a heavy load on the shoulders. Leo Babauta, "Umatac (Humåtak)," *Guampedia*, accessed July 5, 2014, http://www.guampedia.com/umatac-humatak/.
3. Anne Perez Hattori, "Folktale: Puntan and Fu'una: Gods of Creation," *Guampedia*, accessed July 7, 2014, http://www.guampedia.com/puntan-and-fuuna-gods-of-creation. While the story I retell is the most common version of the creation story, there are slight variations that can be found in the collections of CHamoru "folklore" and "legends" mentioned in previous chapters, as well as among individual families or storytellers/chanters. One significant different version can be found in Celeste Perez, "Fu'una," *Guampedia*, accessed September 2, 2014, http://www.guampedia.com/fuuna/. That version of the creation story is told as a story of migration and settlement. The "infinite space" in which Puntan and Fu'una existed before creating the island represents "the journey through vast open sea without land or anything in sight." Their lack of parents "conveys the sentiment of starting anew in a land with none of their ancestors' remains." Symbolically, Fu'una is the first woman "to settle in the Mariana Islands and the mother of the Chamorro society." Puntan represents the first man and the "beginnings of the Chamorro people taking root in a new land." The story of Puntan and Fu'una is what I term a "first story" of Indigenous settlement because it tells the story of the first CHamorus to plant and harvest their crops, to build houses and care for the land, and to give birth and bury the dead—all of which create a genealogical belonging to the land.
4. Celeste Perez, "Fu'una."
5. Bevacqua, "Chamorro World View."
6. Elizabeth DeLoughrey and George B. Handley, "Introduction: Towards an Aesthetics of the Earth," in *Postcolonial Ecologies: Literatures of the Environment*, ed. Elizabeth DeLoughrey and George B. Handley (Oxford: Oxford University Press, 2011), 15.
7. Bevacqua, "Chamorro World View."
8. Bevacqua, "Chamorro World View."
9. Tolentino, "Ancient Chamorro Kinship and Land Tenure."
10. *Taotaomo'na* translates as "people of before," "people of before time," "people of early times," or "first people." Michael Lujan Bevacqua, "Taotaomo'na," *Gua-*

mpedia, accessed August 9, 2014, http://www.guampedia.com/taotaomona-taotaomona/.

11. Donald Soker, "The Taotaomona Stories of Guam," *Western Folklore* 31, no. 3 (July 1972): 156.
12. Bevacqua, "Taotaomo'na."
13. William Edwin Safford, *The Useful Plants of the Island of Guam [. . .]*, Contributions from the United States National Herbarium, vol. 9 (Washington, D.C.: Government Printing Office, 1905), 275.
14. One common petmisu is: "Guella yan Guello, dispensa ham låo Kåo siña ham manmaloffan yan manmanbisita gi tano miyu sa' yanggen un bisita i tano'må mi faloffan-ha' sin un famaisin." (Grandmother and Grandfather, excuse us. May we walk through and visit your land and when you come to our land we will welcome you to do the same.) Bevacqua, "Taotaomo'na."
15. Bevacqua, "Chamorro World View."
16. Celeste Perez, "Inafa'maolek," *Guampedia*, accessed September 1, 2014, http://www.guampedia.com/inafamaolek/.
17. Michael Phillips, "Land Ownership on Guam," *Guampedia*, accessed September 2, 2014, http://www.guampedia.com/landownershiponguam.
18. Kevin Lynch, in *The Image of the City*, describes the importance of wayfinding urban space by patterning a "generalized mental picture of the exterior physical world." This image, or mental map, is crafted from the "immediate sensation" of street names and numbers, architectural cues, and other directional markers, as well as the "memory of past experience." The image not only guides our action but also has "wide practical and emotional importance to the individual." Kevin Lynch, *The Image of the City* (Boston: Joint Center for Urban Studies, 1960), 2.
19. Kamau Brathwaite theorizes "tidalectics" as a methodology to interpret complex relationships between "sea and land, diaspora and indigeneity, and routes and roots," as Elizabeth DeLoughrey puts it in her introduction to *Routes and Roots: Navigating Caribbean and Pacific Island Literatures*, 2.
20. One prominent anthology that they have all appeared in is Evelyn Flores and Emelihter Kihleng, eds., *Indigenous Literatures from Micronesia* (Honolulu: University of Hawai'i Press, 2019).
21. Alfred W. Crosby, *Ecological Imperialism: The Biological Expansion of Europe, 900–1900* (Cambridge: Cambridge University Press, 2004).
22. See Édouard Glissant, *Poetics of Relation* (Ann Arbor: University of Michigan Press, 1997).
23. James (Sakej) Youngblood Henderson, "Ayukpachi: Empowering Aboriginal Thought," in *Protecting Indigenous Knowledge and Heritage: A Global Challenge*, ed. Marie Ann Battiste and James Youngblood Henderson (Saskatoon: Purich, 2000), 256.
24. See John Elder and Hertha D. Wong, eds., *Family of Earth and Sky: Indigenous Tales of Nature from Around the World* (Boston: Beacon Press, 1996); Donelle N. Dreese, *Ecocriticism: Creating Self and Place in Environmental and*

American Indian Literatures (New York: Peter Lang International Academic Publishers, 2002); Lee Schweninger, *Listening to the Land: Native American Literary Responses to the Landscape* (Athens, Ga.: University of Georgia Press, 2008); Robert Nelson, *Place and Vision: The Function of Landscape in Native American Fiction* (New York: Peter Lang, 1993); Joni Adamson, *American Indian Literature, Environmental Justice, and Ecocriticism: The Middle Place* (Tucson: University of Arizona Press, 2001); Chadwick Allen, *Blood Narrative: Indigenous Identity in American Indian and Maori Literary and Activist Texts* (Durham, N.C.: Duke University Press, 2002); J. McLaren, *New Pacific Literatures: Culture and Environment in the European Pacific* (New York: Garland Publishing Incorporated, 1993); Dennis Kawaharada, *Storied Landscapes: Hawaiian Literature and Place* (Honolulu: Kalamaku Press, 1999); hoʻomanawanui, "Ha, Mana, Leo"; kuʻualoha hoʻomanawanui, "'This Land Is Your Land, This Land Was My Land': Kanaka Maoli Versus Settler Representations of 'Aina in Contemporary Literature of Hawaiʻi," in *Asian Settler Colonialism: From Local Governance to the Habits of Everyday Life in Hawaiʻi*, ed. Candace Fujikane and Jonathan Y. Okamura (Honolulu: University of Hawaiʻi Press, 2008), 116–54.

25. DeLoughrey and Handley, introduction to *Postcolonial Ecologies*, 14.
26. DeLoughrey and Handley, 3.
27. Rob Wilson, "Oceania as Peril and Promise: Towards Theorizing a Worlded Vision of Trans-Pacific Ecopoetics" (paper presented at Oceania Archives and Transnational American Studies conference, Hong Kong University, June 4–6, 2012), 12.
28. R. Wilson, 5.
29. R. Wilson, 8.
30. Hsinya Huang, "Toward Transpacific Ecopoetics: Three Indigenous Texts," *Comparative Literature Studies* 50, no. 1 (2013): 122.
31. Huang, 144.
32. Huang, 123.
33. See, for example, Paul Sharrad, *Albert Wendt and Pacific Literature* (Auckland: Auckland University Press, 2003); Elizabeth DeLoughrey, *Allegories of the Anthropocene* (Durham, N.C.: Duke University Press, 2019); Teresa Shewry, *Hope at Sea: Possible Ecologies in Oceanic Literature* (Minneapolis: University of Minnesota Press, 2015); and Jessica Maufort, "The Postcolonial Ecopoetics of Patricia Grace's *Tu*: The Compost and the Labyrinth," *Ecozon@* 10, no. 1 (Spring 2019): 117–36.
34. C. T. Perez, "Signs of Being: A Chamorro Spiritual Journey" (MA thesis, University of Hawaiʻi, Mānoa). For the open-access version, see https://scholarspace.manoa.hawaii.edu/handle/10125/21197. This work is cited as "Signs" by page number in the running text.
35. Wiecko, "Jesuit Missionaries as Agents of Empire."
36. Phillips, "Land Ownership on Guam."

37. See Rogers, *Destiny's Landfall*; Hattori, *Colonial Dis-ease*; Underwood, "American Education"; DeLisle, "Navy Wives / Native Lives"; and Diaz, "Paved with Good Intentions."
38. Elyssa J. Santos, "'Practicing Economy': Chamorro Agency and U.S. Colonial Agricultural Projects, 1898–1941" (MA thesis, University of Hawai'i at Mānoa, 2018), vii.
39. Wakako Higuchi, "Japan's Industrial Development of a U.S. Territory: Guam, 1941–1944," *Pacific Studies* 31, no. 1 (March 2008): 58.
40. Higuchi, 60.
41. Higuchi, 70.
42. Higuchi, 70.
43. Nicholas Yamashita Quinata, "Kaiser Pre-Fab Homes," *Guampedia*, accessed May 30, 2013, http://guampedia.com/kaiser-pre-fab-homes/.
44. Nicholas Yamashita Quinata, "Hollow Block Cement Homes," *Guampedia*, accessed May 30, 2013, http://guampedia.com/hollow-block-cement-homes/.
45. See Larry Mayo, "Urbanization in the Pacific and Guam," *City and Society* 1, no. 2 (December 1987): 99–121. I also explore the urbanization of Guåhan in chapter 3.
46. The English translation is Perez's. It does not appear in the poem itself, but in a footnote to the poem.
47. Recent studies have shown that there is a connection between language diversity and ecological biodiversity. Tragically, this connection is also manifested in the fact that the decline of biodiversity and the extinction of species have been mirrored by the loss of Indigenous languages. See John Vidal, "As Forests Are Cleared and Species Vanish, There's One Other Loss: A World of Languages," *The Guardian*, June 7, 2014, accessed October 14, 2014, http://www.theguardian.com/environment/2014/jun/08/why-we-are-losing-a-world-of-languages. See also Asya Pereltsvaig, "Linguistic and Biological Diversity Overlap—But Why?," Languages of the World (website), May 17, 2012, accessed on October 14, 2014, http://languagesoftheworld.info/geolinguistics/linguistic-and-biological-diversity-overlap-but-why.html.
48. Martin B. Pray, "The Guam Visitors Bureau: An Analysis of Its Relationship to the Government of Guam" (MA thesis, University of Guam, 1978), 7.
49. Keith L. Camacho, "Enframing i Taotao Tano': Colonialism, Militarism, and Tourism in Twentieth Century Guam" (MA thesis, University of Hawai'i, Mānoa, 1998).
50. K. Camacho, "Enframing i Taotao Tano'," 166; Haunani-Kay Trask, *From a Native Daughter: Colonialism and Sovereignty in Hawai'i* (Monroe: Common Courage Press, 1993), 22.
51. K. Camacho, "Enframing i Taotao Tano'," 12.
52. Teresia Teaiwa, "Bikinis and Other S/Pacific N/Oceans," in *Voyaging Through the Contemporary Pacific*, ed. David Hanlon and Geoffrey White (Lanham, Md.: Rowman & Littlefield, 2000), 91–112.

53. K. Camacho, "Enframing i Taotao Tano'," 178.
54. K. Camacho, 165.
55. C. T. Perez, "Signs of Being," 45.
56. K. Camacho, "Enframing i Taotao Tano'," 163.
57. For versions of this legend, see "Folktale: The Young Maidens That Saved Guam," *Guampedia*, www.guampedia.com/how-the-young-maidens-saved-guam-folk tale/; Olympia Q. Camacho, *Legends of Guam* (Agana, Guam: Government of Guam, Department of Education, 1997); *Hemplon Nåna Siha: A Collection of Chamorro Legends and Stories* (Agana, Guam: Department of Chamorro Affairs, Division of Research, Publication and Training, 2001).
58. Kenneth Gofigan Kuper, "Na'la'la i Hila'-ta, Na'matatnga i Taotao-ta: Chamorro Language as Liberation from Colonization" (MA thesis, University of Hawai'i, Mānoa, 2014), 12.
59. The importance of grandparents in CHamoru culture is highlighted in Vicki Torsch, "Grandparenting Among the Chamorros of Guam," *Pacific Studies* 30, nos. 3/4 (December 2007): 81–101.
60. Kisha Borja-Kicho'cho' and Anghet Hoppe-Cruz, "I Kareran i Palåbran Måmi—The Journey of Our Words" (MA thesis, Center for Pacific Islands Studies, University of Hawai'i, Mānoa, 2010). For the open-access version, see https://scholarspace.manoa.hawaii.edu/handle/10125/24267. This work is cited as "Kareran" by page number in the running text.
61. The phrase "write the wrongs" is a possible reference to Anne Perez Hattori, "Righting Civil Wrongs: The Guam Congress Walkout of 1949," *ISLA: A Journal of Micronesian Studies* 3, no. 1 (Rainy Season 1995): 1–27.
62. The reader is able to decipher that the authors' poems alternate because the author of each poem is listed in the table of contents.
63. Kirk and Natividad, "Fortress Guam."
64. "Freedom of action" is "the ability of the U.S. to use bases and training facilities freely and without restriction at a particular locale, as well as affording the U.S. the ability to engage in rapid force posture movements and contingency response from those locations." Because Guåhan is a territory, the U.S. military does not face the same restrictions it might face in U.S. states (such as Hawai'i or Alaska) or sovereign countries (such as Japan or South Korea). See chapter 1 ("Purpose of and Need for Action") of United States Department of the Navy, *Environmental Impact Statement: Guam and CNMI Military Relocation*, vol. 2, *Marine Corps Relocation—Guam*, Guam and CNMI Military Relocation Supplemental Environmental Impact Statement (website), U.S. Department of the Navy, accessed March 18, 2015, http://www.guambuildupeis.us/documents/.
65. Daryl A. Haun, "Spanish Forts of Guam Overview," *Guampedia*, accessed October 17, 2014, http://www.guampedia.com/spanish-forts-of-guam-overview/. See also Yolanda Degadillo, Thomas B. McGrath, and Felicia Plaza, *Spanish Forts of Guam* (Mangilao, Guam: University of Guam Richard F. Taitano Micronesian Area Research Center, 1979).

66. See Tony Palomo, "WWII Rising Sun Dawns on Guam," *Guampedia*, accessed October 17, 2014, http://www.guampedia.com/wwii-rising-sun-dawns-on-guam/; and Peattie, *Nan'yō*.
67. Kirk and Natividad, "Fortress Guam."
68. For a deeper history of nuclear testing in the Marshall Islands, see Holly Barker, *Bravo for the Marshallese: Regaining Control in a Post-nuclear, Post-colonial World* (Belmont, Calif.: Wadsworth Publishing, 2004); Jack Niedenthal, *For the Good of Mankind: A History of the People of Bikini and Their Islands*, 2nd ed. (Majuro, Marshall Islands: BRAVO Publishing, 2013); Barbara Rose Johnston and Holly Barker, *Consequential Damages of Nuclear War: The Rongelap Report* (New York: Routledge, 2008); Giff Johnson, *Don't Ever Whisper: Darlene Keju—Pacific Health Pioneer, Champion for Nuclear Survivors* (Majuro, Marshall Islands: Giff Johnson, 2013); Monica Labriola et al., *Militarism and Nuclear Testing in the Pacific*, Teaching Oceania Series, vol. 1 (Honolulu: Center for Pacific Islands Studies, University of Hawai'i at Mānoa, 2019). For a poetic exploration of this topic, see Kathy Jetnil-Kijiner, *Iep Jaltok: Poems from a Marshallese Daughter* (Tucson: University of Arizona Press, 2017).
69. H.-K. Trask, *From a Native Daughter*; H.-K. Trask, "Writing in Captivity."
70. There are quite a few sources related to this topic. See Annie Isabel Fukushima and Gwyn Kirk, "Military Sexual Violence: From Frontline to Fenceline; The Root of the Sexual Assault Crisis Plaguing the Military Lies in Militarism Itself," *Foreign Policy in Focus*, June 17, 2013; Saundra Pollack et al., *Let the Good Times Roll: Prostitution and the U.S. Military* (New York: The New Press, 1992); Katherine Moon, *Sex Among Allies: Military Prostitution in U.S.-Korea Relations* (New York: Columbia University Press, 1997); Akemi Johnson, *Night in the American Village: Women in the Shadow of the U.S. Military Bases in Okinawa* (New York: The New Press, 2019); Donna M. Hughes, Katherine Y. Chon, and Derek P. Ellerman, "Modern-Day Comfort Women: The U.S. Military, Transnational Crime, and the Trafficking of Women," *Violence Against Women* 13, no. 9 (2007): 901–22; Beth Bailey and David Farber, *The First Strange Place: The Alchemy of Race and Sex in World War II Hawaii* (New York: The Free Press, 1992); and Sister Soledad Perpinan, "Militarism and the Sex Industry in the Philippines," in *Women and Violence*, ed. Miranda Davis (London: Zed Books, 1994). Additionally, scholars have examined gendered and sexual violence within the U.S. military. For example, see Rosemarie Skaine, *Sexual Assault in the U.S. Military: The Battle Within America's Armed Forces* (Santa Barbara, Calif.: Praeger Security International, 2015). David Vine also examines this topic in his book *Base Nation: How U.S. Military Bases Abroad Harm America and the World* (New York: Metropolitan Books, 2015).
71. Miyume Tanji, "Chamorro Warriors and Godmothers Meet Uncle Sam: Gender, Loyalty and Resistance to US Military Occupation in Postwar Guam," in *Gender, Power, and Military Occupations: Asia Pacific and the Middle East Since 1945*, ed. Christine De Matos and Rowena Ward (New York: Routledge, 2012), 98–117.

72. Ellen-Rae Cachola, Gwyn Kirk, Lisa Natividad, and Maria Reinat Pumarejo, "Women Working Across Borders for Peace and Genuine Security," *Peace Journal: A Journal of Social Justice* 22, no. 2 (2010): 168.
73. Sylvia Frain, "Women's Resistance in the Marianas Archipelago: A US Colonial Homefront and Militarized Frontline," *Feminist Formations* 29, no. 1 (Spring 2017): 97.
74. Camarin Meno and Nicole Allen, "Exploring Community Narratives of Violence Against Women Among Domestic Violence Responders in Guam," *American Journal of Community Psychology*, online publication ahead of print, November 2020.
75. For more on the different social classes in CHamoru society, see Dominica Tolentino, "Social Classes in Traditional CHamoru Society," *Guampedia*, last modified December 17, 2019, https://www.guampedia.com/social-classes-in-traditional-chamorro-society/.
76. Shannon J. Murphy, "Folktale: Puntan Dos Amantes," *Guampedia*, last modified October 14, 2019, https://www.guampedia.com/puntan-dos-amantes-folktale/.
77. Laura Marie Torres Souder, "Unveiling Herstory: Chamorro Women in Historical Perspective," in *Pacific History—Papers from the 8th Pacific History Association Conference*, ed. Donald H. Rubinstein (Mangilao, Guam: University of Guam Press and Micronesian Area Research Center, 1992), 143. Souder is also the author of perhaps the most important text on CHamoru women, *Daughters of the Island: Contemporary Chamorro Women Organizers on Guam* (1992).
78. For example, they mention Haunani-Kay Trask of Hawai'i, Grace Molisa of Vanuatu, Konai Helu Thaman of Tonga, Jully Makini of Solomon Islands, Nora Vagi Brash of Papua New Guinea, Ruth Saovana Spriggs of Bougainville, Momoe Malietoa Von Reiche and Makerita Va'ai of Sāmoa, Teresia Teaiwa of Kiribati, Emelihter Kihleng of Pohnpei, and Cecilia Perez and Anne Perez Hattori of Guåhan.
79. Souder, "Unveiling Herstory," 144.
80. Santos-Bamba, "Literate Lives of Chamorro Women." See also Sharleen Santos-Bamba, "The Languages of Three Generations of Chamorro Women," *Pacific Asia Inquiry* 4, no. 1 (Fall 2013): 84–93.
81. DeLisle, "Navy Wives / Native Lives"; Christine Taitano DeLisle, "Delivering the Body: Narratives of Family, Childbirth and Prewar Pattera" (MA thesis, University of Guam, 2001); Christine Taitano DeLisle, *Placental Politics: CHamoru Women, White Womanhood, and Indigeneity Under U.S. Colonialism in Guam* (Chapel Hill: University of North Carolina Press, 2020).
82. Naholowa'a, "Beyond Matrifocality."
83. Anne Perez Hattori, "Guardians of Our Soil: Indigenous Responses to Post–World War II Land Appropriation on Guam," in *Farms, Firms and Runways: Perspectives on U.S. Military Bases in the Western Pacific*, ed. L. Eve Armentrout (Chicago: Imprint Publications, 2001), 186–202.
84. Michael Perez, "Contested Sites: Pacific Resistance in Guam to U.S. Empire," *Amerasia Journal* 27, no. 1 (2001): 103.

85. Julian Aguon, "Update: Land Ownership on Guam," *Guampedia*, accessed October 23, 2014, http://www.guampedia.com/update-land-ownership-on-guam/.
86. Phillips, "Land Ownership on Guam."
87. Other important sources on CHamoru land activism include Michael Clement Jr., "The Sella Bay Ammunition Wharf Controversy: Economic Development, Indigenous Rights and Colonialism in Guam" (MA thesis, University of Guam, 2002); James Perez Viernes, "Fanhasso i Taotao Sumay: Displacement, Dispossession, and Survival in Guam" (MA thesis, University of Hawai'i, Mānoa, 2008); and Monnig, "Proving Chamorro," ch. 5 ("The Land Describes You"). For a broader history of land tenure and struggle in the Pacific, see Ronald Crocombe, ed., *Customary Land Tenure and Sustainable Development* (Suva: Institute of Pacific Studies, 1995); Ronald Crocombe and Malama Maleisea, eds., *Land Issues in the Pacific* (Suva: Institute of Pacific Studies, 1994); and Ronald Crocombe, *Land Tenure in Oceania*, 3rd ed. (Suva: Institute of Pacific Studies, 1987).
88. Michael Lujan Bevacqua, "Pågat," *Minagahet* (blog), May 16, 2010, accessed October 25, 2014, http://minagahet.blogspot.com/2010/05/pagat.html.
89. Protest signs often read "Save Pågat" and included drawings of the endangered Mariana eight-spot butterfly. Bevacqua, "Pågat."
90. Greta Nilsson, *Endangered Species Handbook*, Animal Welfare Institute (website), 2005, accessed October 21, 2014, http://www.endangeredspecieshandbook.org/chapters.php.
91. University of Washington, "Brown Tree Snake Could Mean Guam Will Lose More Than Its Birds," *Science Daily*, August 10, 2008, accessed October 23, 2014, www.sciencedaily.com/releases/2008/08/080808090313.htm.
92. The Stream Team, "Residents of Mariana Islands Protest US Military Live-Fire Training Plans," *The Stream Blog, Al Jazeera America*, accessed October 25, 2014, http://america.aljazeera.com/watch/shows/the-stream/the-stream-officialblog/2013/11/11/residents-of-marianaislandsprotestusmilitarylivefiretrainingplan.html.
93. Bernard Punzalan, "Lukao Fuha yan i Pina'ok Tumaiguini," Chamorro Roots Genealogy Project (website), accessed October 24, 2014, http://chamorroroots.com/v3/index.php?option=com_content&view=article&id=219:lukao-fuha&catid=34:history&Itemid=1.

CHAPTER 2

1. Lawrence J. Cunningham, "Latte Structures," *Guampedia*, accessed September 6, 2012, http://guampedia.com/latte-structures/.
2. However, at least two examples exist of circular arrangements.
3. Rosalind L. Hunter-Anderson, "Latte," *Guampedia*, accessed September 8, 2012, http://guampedia.com/latte/. Scholars have also argued that latte architecture could have deeper historical origins in Austronesia. See R. Waterson, "Houses and the Built Environment in Island South-East Asia: Tracing Some

Shared Themes in the Uses of Space," in *Inside Austronesian Houses*, ed. J. Fox (Canberra: ANU E-Press, 1993), 227–42; and R. Waterson, *The Living House: An Anthropology of Architecture in South-East Asia* (Oxford: Oxford University Press, 1997).

4. Michael W. Graves, "Organization and Differentiation Within Late Prehistoric Ranked Social Units, Mariana Islands, Western Pacific," *Journal of Field Archaeology* 13 (1986): 144.
5. Fred Rodriguez, "Latte's Significance," *Guampedia*, accessed September 8, 2012, http://guampedia.com/lattes-significance/.
6. Juliana Flinn, "Private Houses, Public Sharing: Pollapese Migrants Coping with Change," in *Home in the Islands: Housing and Social Change in the Pacific*, ed. Jan Rensel and Margaret Rodman (Honolulu: University of Hawai'i Press, 1997), 132.
7. Flinn, "Private Houses," 137.
8. Jan Rensel, "Introduction," in Rensel and Rodman, *Home in the Islands*, 12. See also Paul Oliver, *Dwellings: The House Across the World* (Oxford: Phaidon Press, 1987); and Colia Duly, *The Houses of Mankind* (London: Thames and Hudson, 1979).
9. Graves, "Organization and Differentiation," 146.
10. F. Rodriguez, "Latte's Significance."
11. F. Rodriguez, "Latte's Significance."
12. F. Rodriguez, "Latte's Significance."
13. See Jean-Paul Bourdier and Nezar AlSayyad, eds., *Dwellings, Settlements and Tradition: Cross-Cultural Perspectives* (Lanham, Md.: University Press of America, 1989).
14. Flinn, "Private Houses," 132.
15. For a full list of his theatrical works, see Onedera, "Theatrical Works of Peter Onedera."
16. For a brief discussion of theater in Guåhan and Onedera's playwriting, see Diana Looser, *Remaking Pacific Pasts: History, Memory, and Identity in Contemporary Theater from Oceania* (Honolulu: University of Hawai'i Press, 2014), 53. For Onedera's own discussion of CHamoru theater, see his "Theater in a Chamoru Sense."
17. See the group's website here: https://ginenihila.blogspot.com.
18. Tanya M. Champaco Mendiola, "Peter Onedera," *Guampedia*, accessed June 11, 2020, https://www.guampedia.com/peter-onedera-2/.
19. Robert A. Underwood, "At the Edge of Chamoru and English," *Pacific Daily News*, October 13, 2017, accessed June 12, 2020, https://www.guampdn.com/story/opinion/columnists/2017/10/13/chamoru-and-english/760395001/. See also Clarisa G. Quan, "From 'Esteemed Colleagues' to 'Steamed Collix': Language Use and Accent Awareness in Guam's Colloquial Chamorro English," *Micronesian Educator* 14 (2010): 5–20; and Dave Santos, Ric Castro, and Chris Mahilum, *English the Chamoru Way!* (Agana, Guam: Images Publishing, 1992).

Onedera uses the phrase in his autobiography *Gi i Tilu Gradu (In the Third Grade)*, when he describes how students were taught English on Guåhan: "Each grade level gathered in one large classroom chosen for their grade level. Teachers from third grade classes maneuvered their students into a single line around the room and took their places in the center where chairs were placed in neat rows, side by side, for students who misspelled a word and thereby would be eliminated. The pronouncer and moderator was a volunteer from the community invited because of his or her expertise in pronouncing English words in the English way and not English the Chamoru way." Peter R. Onedera, *Gi i Tilu Gradu (In the Third Grade)* (Pittsburgh: Rosedog Press, 2009), 55.

20. Fanai Castro, "Sinajana (Sinahånña)," *Guampedia*, accessed June 11, 2020, https://www.guampedia.com/sinajana/.
21. All quotations from this poem are found in Peter R. Onedera, *Visions of a Chamoru* (Agana, Guam: self-published, 1995), 8. The poem is subsequently cited in the running text as "I Walked."
22. Rensel, "Introduction."
23. Lawrence J. Cunningham, "Pole and Thatched Homes," *Guampedia*, accessed May 30, 2013, http://guampedia.com/pole-and-thatched-homes/.
24. Lawrence J. Cunningham, "De Silleria," *Guampedia*, accessed May 30, 2013, http://guampedia.com/de-silleria/.
25. Lawrence J. Cunningham, "Mampostería," *Guampedia*, accessed May 30, 2013, http://guampedia.com/mamposteria/.
26. Flinn, "Private Houses," 140.
27. Flinn, 140.
28. Flinn, 142.
29. Nicholas Yamashita Quinata, "Wood and Tin Houses," *Guampedia*, accessed May 30, 2013, http://guampedia.com/wood-and-tin-houses/.
30. Rensel, "Introduction."
31. See Larry Mayo, "Occupations and Chamorro Social Status: A Study of Urbanization in Guam" (PhD diss., University of California, Berkeley, 1984).
32. The word *quonset* originates from the Algonquian, meaning "small, long place," commenting on the resemblance between Native American longhouses and what would be known as Quonset huts. With this in mind, it is ironic that CHamorus would become confined, to some extent, by a colonial replication of a Native American housing structure.
33. Nicholas Yamashita Quinata, "Quonset Huts," *Guampedia*, accessed May 30, 2013, http://guampedia.com/quonset-huts/.
34. Wendt, "Towards a New Oceania," 80.
35. Wendt, 81. Wendt explores Sāmoan and colonial architecture and housing in several of his works, most prominently in his novel *Leaves of the Banyan Tree* (Longman Paul, 1979).
36. Faye Untalan Muñoz, "Chamorro Migration to the US," *Guampedia*, accessed July 3, 2014, http://www.guampedia.com/chamorro-migration-to-the-u-s/.

See also Faye Untalan Muñoz, "An Exploratory Study of Island Migrations: Chamorros of Guam" (PhD diss., University of Southern California, 1984).

37. Setha M. Low, "Indigenous Architecture and the Spanish American Plaza in Mesoamerica and the Caribbean," *American Anthropologist New Series* 97, no. 4 (Dec. 1995): 748.
38. Rensel, "Introduction." For a further discussion of how colonialism has impacted Indigenous housing, see John B. Hertz, "Authenticity, Colonialism, and the Struggle with Modernity," *Journal of Architectural Education* 55, no. 4 (May 2002): 220–27; Ali Djerbi and Abdelwahab Safi, "Teaching the History of Architecture in Algeria, Tunisia, and Morocco: Colonialism, Independence, and Globalization," *Journal of the Society of Architectural Historians* 62, no. 1 (Mar. 2003): 102–9; and Andrew Reid et al., "Tswana Architecture and Responses to Colonialism," *World Archaeology* 28, no. 3 (Feb. 1997): 370–92.
39. Philippe Godard, *Latte: The Mysterious Megaliths of the Marianas* (Perth: Arolhos Publishing, 1995), 32.
40. Wakako Higuchi, "A History of Pre-war Japanese Residents of Guam," in *Guam History: Perspectives*, vol. 1, ed. Lee D. Carter, William L. Wuerch, and Rosa Roberto Carter (Mangilao: Micronesian Area Research Center, University of Guam), 144.
41. K. Camacho, *Cultures of Commemoration*, 46.
42. Rogers, *Destiny's Landfall*, 181.
43. While most CHamoru survivors note the violence of Japanese soldiers, a few examples exist of moments of compassion and sympathy. For example, Joaquin Cruz remembered an unknown Japanese soldier who befriended his family and provided them with food; in return, Cruz taught the soldier how to make coconut oil. Another survivor, Maria Cruz, remembered a Japanese man who helped her family avoid harm during the U.S. bombing and invasion. K. Camacho, *Cultures of Commemoration*, 50.
44. K. Camacho, *Cultures of Commemoration*, 68.
45. For a historical and political study of the postwar United States war crimes tribunals that tried those who worked for Japan's military government during the war, see Keith L. Camacho, *Sacred Men: Law, Torture, and Retribution in Guam* (Durham, N.C.: Duke University Press, 2019).
46. K. Camacho, *Cultures of Commemoration*, 67.
47. K. Camacho, "Enframing i Taotao Tano'," 179.
48. K. Camacho, *Cultures of Commemoration*, 98.
49. K. Camacho, 98.
50. K. Camacho, 99.
51. Guam Nikkei Association website, accessed September 3, 2020, http://guamnikkeiassociation.blogspot.com/2013/02/history-of-guam-nikkei-association.html.
52. For a discussion of food in Pacific literature, see Paloma Fresno-Calleja, "Fighting Gastrocolonialism in Indigenous Pacific Writing," *Interventions: International Journal of Postcolonial Studies* 19, no. 7 (2017): 2–15.

53. Rensel, "Introduction," 7.
54. Rensel, 7.
55. Quoted in Tihu Lujan, "'The Chorus of Our Lives': Onedera's CHamoru Poetry Book for Future Generations of Guam," *The Guam Daily Post*, November 11, 2018, accessed June 25, 2020, https://www.postguam.com/news/local/the-chorus-of-our-lives/article_7a885056-e3ec-11e8-9fbe-e3e04d677e07.html.
56. The CHamoru version appears in Peter R. Onedera, *Taimanu na Ini* (Mangilao: University of Guam Press, 2018), 53. This translated, bilingual version was obtained via personal communication, June 25, 2020, and maintains Onedera's formatting.
57. Patricia Grace, *Potiki* (1986; repr., Honolulu: University of Hawai'i Press, 1995).
58. Christine Prentice, "Storytelling in Alice Munro's *Lives of Girls and Women* and Patricia Grace's *Potiki*," *Australian-Canadian Studies: A Journal for the Humanities and Social Sciences* 8, no. 2 (1991): 34.
59. Bridget Orr, "The Maori House of Fiction," in *Cultural Institutions of the Novel*, ed. Deidre Lynch and William B. Warner (Durham, N.C.: Duke University Press, 1996), 91.
60. Patricia Grace, "Influences on Writing," in Hereniko and Wilson, *Inside Out*, 72.
61. Grace, *Potiki*, 104.
62. Elizabeth DeLoughrey, "The Spiral Temporality of Patricia Grace's *Potiki*," *Ariel* 30, no. 1 (Jan 1999): 60.
63. Grace, *Potiki*, 104.
64. Other scholarship on *Potiki* includes Eva Rask Knudsen, *The Circle and the Spiral: A Study of Australian Aboriginal and New Zealand Maori Literature* (Amsterdam: Rodopi, 2004); 'Umi Perkins, "Pono and the *Koru*: Toward Indigenous Theory in Pacific Island Literature," *Hūlili* 4, no. 1 (2007): 59–89; and Linda Michelle Rodenburg, "Spiral Reading Strategies: Re/citing Māori and Aboriginal Stories in Relation to the Nation" (PhD diss., University of Otago, Dunedin, 2011). Other important sources on the whare whakairo include Michelle Keown, "The Whare Whakairo as Symbol of Maori Identity," *SPAN* 47 (1998): 39–56; Hirini Melbourne, "Whare Whakairo: Maori 'Literary' Traditions," in *Dirty Silence: Aspects of Language and Literature in New Zealand*, ed. Graham McGregor and Mark Williams (Auckland: Oxford University Press, 1991), 129–41; and Ranginui Walker, "Marae: A Place to Stand," in *Te Ao Hurihuri: Aspects of Maoritanga*, ed. Michael King (Auckland: Reed, 1992), 15–27.
65. Laura Thompson, "The Function of Latte in the Marianas," *Journal of the Polynesian Society* 49, no. 3 (1940): 447.
66. Andrew Laguana et al., "Estorian i Latte: A Story of Latte," *Micronesica* 42, no. 1/2 (2012): 116.
67. Godard, *Latte*, 32.
68. Three well-known examples are line drawings by William Morgan, Noel Quitugua, and Noe Pegarido. Descriptions of these different renderings can be

found in Laguana et al., "Estorian i Latte," 89–92. These line drawings appear in Cunningham, *Ancient Chamorro Society*; W. Morgan, *Prehistoric Architecture in Micronesia* (Austin: University of Texas Press, 1988); and S. Russell, *Tiempon i Manmofo'na: Ancient Chamorro Culture and History of the Northern Mariana Islands* (Saipan: Commonwealth of the Northern Mariana Islands Division of Historic Preservation, 1998).

69. Laguana et al., "Estorian i Latte," 92. I discuss the canoe *Saina* and the significance of canoeing and navigation in CHamoru culture and identity in chapter 3.
70. University of Guam, "UOG Students Learn Ancient Art of Carving Latte Stones," news release, January 5, 2018, accessed November 8, 2020, https://www.uog.edu/news-announcements-migrated/uog-students-learn-ancient-art-of-carving-latte-stones.php.
71. Laguana et al., "Estorian i Latte," 114.
72. Rensel, "Introduction," 7–8.

CHAPTER 3

1. Rogers, *Destiny's Landfall*, 6.
2. Rogers, 31.
3. Lawrence J. Cunningham, Ward Kranz, and Manny Sikau, "Restoring Traditional Seafaring and Navigation in Guam," *Micronesian Journal of the Humanities and Social Sciences* 5, no. 1–2 (November 2006): 314.
4. David Lewis, *The Voyaging Stars: Secrets of the Pacific Island Navigators* (New York: W. W. Norton, 1978), 55.
5. Lewis, *Voyaging Stars*, 54.
6. Diaz, "Voyaging for Anti-colonial Recovery," 26.
7. See A. C. Haddon and James Hornell, *Canoes of Oceania* (Honolulu: Bishop Museum Press, 1975); and Richard J. Shell, *Proas in the Marianas, 1668–1742* (Mangilao, Guam: University of Guam Richard F. Taitano Micronesian Area Research Center, 1992).
8. See Andrew Diaz Artero, "Canoe Building," *Guampedia*, accessed May 13, 2014, http://guampedia.com/canoe-building-2/; and Michael Lujan Bevacqua, "Agad'na: Canoe Builders," *Guampedia*, accessed May 13, 2014, http://guampedia.com/agadna-canoe-builders/.
9. Judy Flores, "Ancient Chamorro Concepts of Beauty," *Guampedia*, accessed June 13, 2014, http://guampedia.com/concepts-of-beauty-in-ancient-chamorro-society/.
10. Diaz, "Voyaging for Anti-colonial Recovery," 26. See also David Lewis, *We, the Navigators: The Ancient Art of Landfinding in the Pacific* (Canberra: Australian National University Press, 1972); and Vicente M. Diaz, "Sniffing Oceania's Behind," *The Contemporary Pacific* 24, no. 2 (2012): 323–44.
11. Diaz, "Voyaging for Anti-colonial Recovery," 22, 27.
12. Diaz, 25.
13. Wiecko, "Jesuit Missionaries as Agents of Empire."

14. DeLoughrey, *Routes and Roots*, 109. See also Paul D'Arcy, *The People of the Sea: Environment, Identity, and History in Oceania* (Honolulu: University of Hawai'i Press, 2006); and Richard Feinberg, ed., *Seafaring in the Contemporary Pacific Islands* (DeKalb: Northern Illinois University Press, 1995).
15. Judith R. Amesbury, "Pelagic Fishing in the Mariana Archipelago: From the Prehistoric Period to the Present," *Terra Australis*, no. 39 (2008): 46.
16. For scholarship on the themes of migration and diaspora in Pacific literature, see Erin Suzuki, "Sacred Travelers: Diasporic Narratives of Pacific Literature" (PhD diss., University of California, Los Angeles, 2010); Michelle Keown, "Globalization and Pacific Diaspora Culture," in Keown, *Pacific Islands Writing*, 185–195; Alice Te Punga Somerville, *Once Were Pacific: Maori Connections to Oceania* (Minneapolis: University of Minnesota Press, 2012); and DeLoughrey, *Routes and Roots*.
17. DeLoughrey, *Routes and Roots*, 129.
18. DeLoughrey, 129.
19. Lehua Taitano, *A Bell Made of Stones* (Kane'ohe, Hawai'i: Tinfish Press, 2013). This work is cited as *Bell* by page number in the running text.
20. Paul Spickard, "Introduction: Pacific Diaspora?," in *Pacific Diaspora: Island Peoples in the United States and Across the Pacific*, ed. Paul Spickard, Joanne L. Rondilla, and Debbie Hippolite Wright (Honolulu: University of Hawai'i Press, 2002), 2–3.
21. Epeli Hau'ofa, "Our Sea of Islands," in *We Are the Ocean: Selected Works* (Honolulu: University of Hawai'i Press, 2008), 32–33.
22. Hau'ofa, "Our Sea of Islands," 45.
23. See Ian C. Campbell, *A History of the Pacific Islands* (Berkeley: University of California Press, 1989); K. R. Rowe, *Where the Waves Fall: A New South Sea Islands History from First Settlement to Colonial Rule* (Honolulu: University of Hawai'i Press, 1984); Donald Denoon et al., eds., *The Cambridge History of the Pacific Islanders* (Cambridge: Cambridge University Press, 1997); Buschmann, Slack Jr., and Tueller, *Navigating the Spanish Lake*; and Francis X. Hezel, *First Taint of Civilization: A History of the Caroline and Marshall Islands in Colonial Days, 1521–1885* (Honolulu: University of Hawai'i Press, 2000).
24. Spickard describes these pathways and routes as "the sinews of empire." Spickard, "Introduction."
25. See J. Kēhaulani Kauanui, "Diasporic Deracination and 'Off-Island' Hawaiians," *The Contemporary Pacific* 19, no. 1 (2007): 137–60. See also Jean Barmann, "New Land, New Lives: Hawaiian Settlement in British Columbia," *Hawaiian Journal of History* 29 (1995): 1–32; David Chappell, *Double Ghosts: Oceanian Voyagers on Euroamerican Ships* (New York: M. E. Sharpe, 1997); Janice Duncan, *Minority Without a Champion: Kanakas on the Pacific Coast, 1788–1850* (Portland: Oregon Historical Society, 1972); Tom Koppel, *Kanaka: The Untold Story of Hawaiian Pioneers in British Columbia and the Pacific Northwest* (Vancouver: Whitecap Books, 1995); and David Chang, *The World and All the Things*

upon It: Native Hawaiian Geographies of Exploration (Minneapolis: University of Minnesota Press, 2016).

26. See H. E. Maude, *Slavers in Paradise: The Peruvian Slave Trade in Polynesia, 1862–1864* (Canberra: Australian National University Press, 1981); and Gerald Horne, *The White Pacific: U.S. Imperialism and Black Slavery in the South Seas After the Civil War* (Honolulu: University of Hawai'i Press, 2007).
27. Spickard, "Introduction."
28. Climate change is causing the newest wave of Pacific migration. See John R. Campbell, "Climate-Change Migration in the Pacific," *The Contemporary Pacific* 26, no. 1 (2014): 1–28; Bruce Burson, ed., *Climate Change and Migration in the South Pacific Region: Policy Perspectives* (Wellington: Institute of Policy Studies, 2010); and Elaine Stratford, Carol Farbotko, and Heather Lazrus, "Tuvalu, Sovereignty and Climate Change: Considering Fenua, the Archipelago and Emigration," *Islands Studies Journal* 8, no. 1 (2013): 67–83.
29. John Connell, "Paradise Left? Pacific Island Voyagers in the Modern World," in Spickard, Rondilla, and Wright, *Pacific Diaspora*, 69.
30. Connell, "Paradise Left?," 86.
31. The scholarship on Pacific migration and diaspora is vast. Some critical works include: Murray Chapman, ed., "Mobility and Identity in the Island Pacific," special issue, *Pacific Viewpoint* 26, no. 1 (1985); Graham Harvey and Charles D. Thompson Jr., eds., *Indigenous Diasporas and Dislocations* (Burlington, Vt.: Ashgate Publishing Limited, 2005); Ken'ichi Sudo and Shuji Yoshida, eds., *Contemporary Migration in Oceania: Diaspora and Network* (Osaka: Japan Center for Area Studies, 1997); Cluny Macpherson, Paul Spoonley, and Melani Anae, eds., *Tangata O Te Moana Nui: The Evolving Identities of Pacific Peoples in Aotearoa / New Zealand* (Palmerston North, New Zealand: Dunmore Press, 2001); Spickard, Rondilla, and Wright, *Pacific Diaspora*; Victoria S. Lockwood, ed., *Globalization and Culture Change in the Pacific Islands* (Upper Saddle River, N.J.: Prentice Hall, 2004); John Connell, ed., *Migration and Development in the South Pacific* (Canberra: Australian National University, 1989); and Grant McCall and John Connell, eds., *A World Perspective on Pacific Islander Migration: Australia, New Zealand and the USA* (Sydney: Centre for Pacific Studies, University of New South Wales, 1993).
32. See Kalissa Alexeveff, "Love Food: Exchange and Sustenance in the Cook Islands Diaspora," *Australian Journal of Anthropology* 15, no. 1 (2002): 68–80; Christine Ward Gailey, "A Good Man Is Hard to Find: Overseas Migration and the Decentered Family in the Tongan Islands," *Critique of Anthropology* 12, no. 1 (1992): 47–74; Judith Barker, "Home Alone: The Effects of Out-Migration on Niuean Elders' Living Arrangements and Social Supports," *Pacific Studies* 17, no. 3 (1994): 41–81; Kerry James, "Reading the Leaves: The Role of Tongan Women's Traditional Wealth and Other Contraflows in the Processes of Modern Migration and Remittance," *Pacific Studies* 20, no. 1 (1997): 1–27.
33. See Ilana Gershon, "Viewing Diasporas from the Pacific: What Pacific Ethnographies Offer Pacific Diaspora Studies," *The Contemporary Pacific* 19, no. 2 (Fall

2007): 474–502; Barbara Burns McGrath, "Seattle Fa'a Sāmoa," *The Contemporary Pacific* 14 (2002): 307–40; Craig Janes, *Migration, Social Change, and Health: A Samoan Community in Urban California* (Stanford: Stanford University Press, 1990); Helen Lee, *Tongan Overseas: Between Two Shores* (Honolulu: University of Hawai'i Press, 2003); Cathy Small, *Voyages: From Tongan Villages to American Suburbs* (Ithaca, N.Y.: Cornell University Press, 1997); Dennis A. Ahlburg and Michael J. Levin, *The Northeast Passage: A Study of Pacific Islander Migration to American Samoa and the United States* (Canberra: National Centre for Development Studies, Australian National University, 1990); and Halualani, *In the Name of Hawaiians.*

34. See Robert C. Kiste, *The Bikinians: A Study in Forced Migration* (Menlo Park, Calif.: Cummings, 1974); Francis X. Hezel and Michael J. Levin, "Micronesian Emigration: The Brain Drain in Palau, Marshalls, and the Federated States," *Journal of the Pacific Society* 29 (1987): 16–34; Francis X. Hezel and Thomas B. McGrath, "The Great Flight Northward: FSM Migration to Guam and the Northern Mariana Islands," *Pacific Studies* 13, no. 1 (1989): 57–64; Karen L. Nero and Faustina K. Rehuher, "Pursuing the Dream: Historical Perspectives on Micronesian Movement Patterns," in McCall and Connell, *Pacific Islander Migration*, 239–55; Donald H. Rubinstein, "Movements in Micronesia: Post-Compact (1987) Micronesian Migrants to Guam and Saipan," in McCall and Connell, *Pacific Islander Migration*, 259–63; L. J. Gorenflo and Michael J. Levin, "Changing Migration Patterns in the Federated States of Micronesia," *ISLA: A Journal of Micronesian Studies* 3 (1995): 29–71; Francis X. Hezel and Michael J. Levin, "New Trends in Micronesian Migration: FSM Migration to Guam and the Marianas, 1990–1993," *Pacific Studies* 19, no. 1 (1996): 91–114; and Francis X. Hezel and J. Dobbin, "Micronesian Migration Since World War II," *The Micronesian Counselor* 19 (1996): accessed March 17, 2015, http://www.micsem.org/pubs/counselor/frames/micmigfr.html.

35. See Faustina Rehuher, "Daughters for the Return Home: Palauan Women in Transition in Hawaii Colleges and Universities" (MA thesis, University of Hawai'i, Mānoa, 1989); Richard D. Sherman, "Ethnic Institutions and Identity: Palauan Migrants on Guam," *Micronesica* 17, no. 1–2 (1981); Donald H. Rubinstein and Michael J. Levin, "Micronesian Migration to Guam: Social and Economic Characteristics," *Asian and Pacific Migration Journal* 1, no. 2 (1992): 350–85; Linda Allen, "Enid 'Atoll': A Marshallese Migrant Community in the Midwestern United States" (PhD diss., University of Iowa, 1997); K. D. Smith, *A Survey of Micronesian Immigrants to Guam: Predictors of Coping and Access to Life Essentials* (Mangilao: Micronesian Language Institute, University of Guam, 1994); Joakim Peter, "Chuukese Travelers and the Idea of Horizon," *Asia Pacific Viewpoint* 41, no. 3 (December 2000): 253–67; Isebong Asang, "Remaking Footprints: Palauan Migrants in Hawai'i," *The Contemporary Pacific* 12 (2000): 371–84; Jim Hess, Karen L. Nero, and Michael L. Burton, "Creating Options: Forming a Marshallese Community in Orange County, California,"

The Contemporary Pacific 13 (2001): 89–121; Elizabeth Grieco, *The Remittance Behavior of Immigrant Households: Micronesians in Hawai'i and Guam* (New York: LFB Scholarly Publishing, 2003); Mac Marshall, *Namoluk, Beyond the Reef: The Transformation of a Micronesian Community* (Boulder, Colo.: Westview Press, 2004); Francis X. Hezel and E. Samuel, "Micronesians Abroad," *Micronesian Counselor* 64 (2006): accessed March 17, 2015, http://micsem.org/pubs/counselor/frames/microsabroadfr.htm; and Lola Quan Bautista, *Steadfast Movement Around Micronesia: Satowan Enlargements Beyond Migration* (Lanham, Md.: Lexington Books, 2010).

36. Robert A. Underwood, "Excursions into Inauthenticity: The Chamorros of Guam," *Pacific Viewpoint* 26 (1985): 162.
37. Underwood, 164.
38. Underwood, 167.
39. See Underwood, "Excursions into Inauthenticity"; Muñoz, "Chamorro Migration to the US"; and Muñoz, "Exploratory Study of Island Migrations."
40. United States Census Bureau, *2010 Census: Chamorros in the United States*, May 2012, accessed July 2, 2014, http://bsp.guam.gov/Chamorros%20in%20the%20United%20States_2011.1.pdf. See also United States Census Bureau, *The Native Hawaiian and Other Pacific Islander Population: 2010*, 2010 Census Briefs, C2010BR-12, May 2012, accessed July 2, 2014, http://www.census.gov/prod/cen2010/briefs/c2010br-12.pdf.
41. United States Census Bureau, *2010 Census: Chamorros in the United States*.
42. Muñoz, "Chamorro Migration to the US."
43. Underwood, "Excursions into Inauthenticity," 173; italics mine.
44. Underwood, 167.
45. Jesi Lujan Bennett, "Apmam Tiempo Ti Uli'e Hit (Long Time No See): Chamorro Diaspora and the Transpacific Home" (MA thesis, University of Hawai'i, Mānoa, 2013), 4.
46. Bennett, "Apmam Tiempo Ti Uli'e Hit," 28.
47. Michael Perez, "Pacific Identities Beyond US Racial Formations: The Case of Chamorro Ambivalence and Flux," *Social Identities* 8, no. 3 (2002): 465.
48. M. Perez, 468–69.
49. M. Perez, 469.
50. Muñoz, "Chamorro Migration to the US."
51. Underwood, "Excursions into Inauthenticity," 171.
52. Albert Wendt, "Inside Us the Dead," in Wendt, *Lali*, 284.
53. Epeli Hau'ofa, "The Ocean in Us," *The Contemporary Pacific* 10, no. 2 (Fall 1998): 409.
54. M. Perez, "Pacific Identities," 473.
55. For an interesting take on diasporic interactions in cyberspace, see Alan Howard, "Pacific-Based Virtual Communities: Rotuma on the World Wide Web," *The Contemporary Pacific* 11, no. 1 (Spring 1999): 139–85. For the potential

pedagogical use of the Internet in Pacific studies, see Terence Wesley-Smith, "Net Gains? Pacific Studies in Cyberspace," *The Contemporary Pacific* 15, no. 1 (Spring 2003): 117–36.

56. C. Allen, *Trans-Indigenous*, 196.
57. C. Allen, 229.
58. C. Allen, 197.
59. C. Allen, 230.
60. There exists some scholarship on Micronesian children, including K. A. Paul, "Is There a Problem Here? The History of Micronesian Immigration and Its Effect on the Experience of Micronesian Children in Hawai'i's Schools" (MA thesis, University of Hawai'i, Mānoa, 2003); and D. J. Watts, "Factors Affecting Marshallese Student Achievement in an Elementary School: A Case Study" (PhD diss., University of Arkansas, 2011).
61. Wendt, "Tatauing the Post-colonial Body," 402.
62. Bo Flood, *Marianas Island Legends: Myth and Magic* (Honolulu: Bess Press, 2001).
63. Underwood, "Excursions into Inauthenticity," 179.
64. See Thomas Gladwin, *East Is a Big Bird: Navigation and Logic on Puluwat Atoll* (Cambridge, Mass.: Harvard University Press, 1970); and Ben R. Finney, ed., *Pacific Navigation and Voyaging* (Wellington: Polynesian Society, 1976).
65. Lewis, *Voyaging Stars*, 185.
66. Lewis, 201.
67. Cunningham, Kranz, and Sikau, "Restoring Traditional Seafaring," 317.
68. *Ayuyu* is the name of the coconut crab, and Hurao is the name of a well-known CHamoru chief who fought and died during the Chamorro-Spanish wars. See James Fee, "Proa: Speed and Lightness over the Waves," *Guam Pacific Daily News*, August 27, 2009, accessed June 10, 2014, http://www.guampdn.com/guampublishing/navigator/data/EkVEFVllypYkXdAtNj.htm; Katrina Palanca, "Guam Cultural Group Constructs 2 Traditional Canoes," *Guam Pacific Daily News*, July 20, 2012, accessed June 10, 2014, http://pidp.eastwestcenter.org/pireport/2012/July/07-20-15.htm; and Shaina Marie Santos, "Flying Proa: A Pacific Marvel," *Guam Stripes*, September 12, 2013, accessed June 10, 2014, http://guam.stripes.com/travel/flying-proa-pacific-marvel.
69. Mario Borja, "Our Sakman Story: One Sentence in History," in *One Archipelago, Many Stories: Integrating Our Narratives (2nd Marianas History Conference: Art, Culture, and Science)*, vol. 2 (Mangilao, Guam: Guampedia Foundation), 93–118.
70. Borja, "Our Sakman Story," 111.
71. Bennett, "Apmam Tiempo Ti Uli'e Hit," 27–28.
72. Bennett, 30.
73. Bennett, 63.
74. See https://www.facebook.com/chamorrodiaspora/.

75. Diaz, "Voyaging for Anti-colonial Recovery," 27.
76. M. Perez, "Pacific Identities," 476.

CHAPTER 4

1. Clement Jr., "Kustumbre, Modernity and Resistance," 49–51. See also Kasperbauer, "Chamorro Culture."
2. K. Aguon, "Guam Dilemma," 92.
3. K. Camacho, "Chamorro Literature," 520.
4. Other forms of related Chamorro orature include mari (poetic debate song) and lalai (general chants). Michael Clement Sr. explores the history of and multiple names for the kåntan chamorrita, including *tsamorita, chamorita,* and *chamorrita,* in "The Ancient Origins of Chamorro Music" (MA thesis, University of Guam, 2001).
5. J. Flores, "Kantan Chamorrita Revisited," 20.
6. Kim Bailey, "Chamorrita Songs: A Surviving Legacy of the Mexican Verso?" (paper presented at the 26th annual meeting of the Society for Ethnomusicology, Honolulu, Hawai'i, Oct. 16, 1981), 1–2.
7. Bailey, "Chamorrita Songs," 2.
8. J. Flores, "Kantan Chamorrita Revisited," 22 (first quotation); Peck, *I Speak the Beginning,* i (second quotation). Clement Sr. points to the "secret language and use of nonsense syllables" in ancient Chamorro love songs known as fino gualafon (language of the moon). Clement Sr., "Ancient Origins of Chamorro Music," 65. A discussion of "hidden meaning" in Hawaiian literature is explored in Brandy Nālani McDougall, *Finding Meaning: Kaona and Contemporary Hawaiian Literature* (Tucson: University of Arizona Press, 2016).
9. J. Flores, "Kantan Chamorrita Revisited," 22.
10. Carmen I. Santos, "Guam's Folklore," in *Umatac by the Sea: A Village in Transition,* ed. Rebecca Stephenson and Hiro Kurashina (Mangilao, Guam: Micronesian Area Research Center, 1982), 130.
11. Laura Marie Torres Souder, "Kantan Chamorrita: Traditional Chamorro Poetry, Past and Future," *Mānoa* 5, no. 1 (1993): 189.
12. Michael R. Clement Sr., "Micronesia: IV. Mariana Islands. 2. Guam," in *The New Grove Dictionary of Music and Musicians,* 2nd ed., vol. 16 (London: Macmillan, 2001), 613.
13. Clement Sr., "Ancient Origins of Chamorro Music," 34–35.
14. Clement Sr., 36.
15. Clement Sr., 34.
16. J. Flores, "Kantan Chamorrita Revisited," 21.
17. Souder, "Kantan Chamorrita," 190.
18. Clement Sr., "Tsamorita Singing," *Chamorroweb,* accessed February 7, 2009, http://chamorroweb.com/tsamorita-singing.asp.
19. Diego, "Reclaiming Identity," 93–94.
20. Kuper, "Na'la'la i Hila'-ta," 18–19.

21. Anthony Apuron, "The Role the Church Played in Helping to Preserve the Chamorro Language and Culture" (paper presented at the Marianas Ballroom, Hilton Hotel, Tumon, Guam, April 1, 1996).
22. Clement Sr., "Ancient Origins of Chamorro Music," 97.
23. Clement Sr., 96.
24. Kuper, "Na'la'la i Hila'-ta," 21.
25. For a focus on the American education system, see Underwood, "American Education"; and Pilar Lujan, "Role of Education in the Preservation of Guam's Indigenous Language," in *Kinalamten Pulitikåt: Siñenten i Chamorro: Issues in Guam's Political Development: The Chamorro Perspective* (Agana, Guam: Political Status Education Coordinating Commission, 1996), 17–25.
26. Hattori, "Colonialism, Capitalism and Nationalism."
27. Kuper, "Na'la'la i Hila'-ta," 45.
28. Robert A. Underwood, "English and Chamorro on Guam," *World Englishes* 8, no. 1 (1989): 79.
29. Kuper, "Na'la'la i Hila'-ta," 27.
30. Clement Jr., "Kustumbre, Modernity and Resistance," 135.
31. Kuper, "Na'la'la i Hila'-ta," 28. "Fino' Chamorro" translates as "Chamorro language."
32. Clement Jr., "Kustumbre, Modernity and Resistance," 126.
33. Clement Jr., 117–18. For more on the impact of colonial media, see Underwood, "Role of Mass Media."
34. J. Flores, "Kantan Chamorrita Revisited," 25.
35. Robert A. Underwood, "Language Survival, the Ideology of English and Education in Guam," *Educational Research Quarterly* 20, no. 4 (1984).
36. Diego, "Reclaiming Identity," 257.
37. Census data cited in Kuper, "Na'la'la i Hila'-ta," 3.
38. Donald Topping, Pedro M. Ogo, and Bernadita C. Dungca, *Chamorro-English Dictionary* (Honolulu: University of Hawai'i Press, 1975), x.
39. Souder, "Kantan Chamorrita," 191.
40. Jessica Ann Unpingco Solis, "Traditions and Transitions: Explorations of Chamorro Culture Through the Rosary Practice" (MA thesis, University of California, Los Angeles, 2014), 2.
41. Solis, "Traditions and Transitions," 19.
42. Solis, 3.
43. Judy Flores, "Chant," *Guampedia*, accessed March 18, 2012, http://guampedia.com/chant/.
44. L. Thompson, *Guam and Its People*, 157.
45. J. Flores, "Kantan Chamorrita Revisited," 24.
46. Clement Jr., "Kustumbre, Modernity and Resistance," 287–88.
47. J. Flores, "Kantan Chamorrita Revisited," 27.
48. Clement Sr., "Tsamorita Singing."
49. J. Flores, "Kantan Chamorrita Revisited," 25.
50. Borja-Kicho'cho' and Hoppe-Cruz, "I Kareran i Palåbran Måmi," 11–40.

51. Souder, "Kantan Chamorrita," 190.
52. Souder, "Unveiling Herstory," 143.
53. Nathalie N. Perez, "Melvin Won Pat-Borja," *Guampedia*, accessed December 4, 2014, www.guampedia.com/melvin-won-pat-borja/.
54. Fanai Castro, "Poetry/Spoken Word," *Guampedia*, accessed December 4, 2014, www.guampedia.com/poetryspoken-word/.
55. For my writing on Jay Baza Pascua, see Craig Santos Perez, "The Chamorro Creation Story, Guam Land Struggles, and Contemporary Poetry," *English Language Notes* 58, no. 1 (April 2020): 9–20.
56. Castro, "Poetry/Spoken Word."
57. Castro, "Poetry/Spoken Word."
58. Castro, "Poetry/Spoken Word."
59. J. Flores, "Kantan Chamorrita Revisited," 21.
60. Ryan Leon Guerrero and Walla Wai, "Brave New Voices 2011 Team Guahan," performance at Brave New Voices Competition, video, 5:24, posted by Erica Benton, July 24, 2011, https://www.youtube.com/watch?v=cvjxqy1dHU4.
61. The print version of the poem can be found here: Ryan Leon Guerrero and Walla Wai, "Self-Guamination (Sneak Peek) Spoken Word Poetry," Kinahulo' Linahyan: The Awakening of the Masses (website), accessed December 12, 2014, http://kinahulo.bandcamp.com/track/willa-wai-ryan-leon-guerrero-self-guamination-sneak-peek-spoken-word-poetry. All quotations of the poem come from this print version and the above-cited video: R. Leon Guerrero and Wai, "Brave New Voices 2011 Team Guahan."
62. Personal communication with Ryan Leon Guerrero and Walla Wai, November 11, 2020.
63. United States Census Bureau, *2010 Census of Population and Housing: Guam*, May 2012, www.census.gov/prod/cen2010/island/GUAMprofile.pdf.
64. See Clarisa G. Quan, "Filipinos on Guam," *Guampedia*, last modified October 8, 2020, https://www.guampedia.com/filipinos-on-guam/; Bruce L. Campbell, "The Filipino Community of Guam, 1945–1975" (MA thesis, University of Hawai'i, 1987); and Alfred P. Flores, "'No Walk in the Park': US Empire and the Racialization of Civilian Military Labor in Guam, 1944–1962," *American Quarterly* 67, no. 3 (2015): 813–35.
65. Vicente Diaz, "To 'P' or Not to 'P'? Marking the Territory Between Pacific Islander and Asian American Studies," *Journal of Asian American Studies* 7, no. 3 (2004): 194. See also Vicente Diaz, "Bye Bye Ms. American Pie: The Historical Relations Between Chamorros and Filipinos and the American Dream," *ISLA: A Journal of Micronesian Studies* 3, no. 1 (1995): 147–60.
66. Tabitha Caser Espina, "Unsettling the Rhetorics of the Politics of Filipinos on Guåhan" (PhD diss., Washington State University, 2020); Josephine Faith Ong, "The Colonial Boundaries of Exilic Discourse: Contextualizing Mabini's Incarceration in Guåhan" (MA thesis, University of California, Los Angeles, 2019). Scholars and activists Vivian Dames, Tressa Diaz, and Jamela Santos have also

been active in forming CHamoru and Filipino solidarity. There is related scholarship about "Asian settler colonialism" and decolonial Asian and Pacific Islander solidarity in Hawai'i in the work of Candace Fujikane, Dean Saranillio, Kim Compoc, Katherine Achacoso, Demiliza Saramosing, Aiko Yamashiro, Ellen-Rae Cachola, Darlene Rodrigues, Reyna Aiko Leah Lani Ramolete Hayashi, Vernadette Gonzalez, Grace Alvaro Caligtan, Christine Lipat, Melisa Casumbal-Salazar, Maiana Minahal, and Shannon Cristobal, to name a few.

67. Paul Lyons, "Wayne Kaumualii Westlake, Richard Hamasaki, and the Afterlives of (Native/Non-Native) Collaboration Against Empire in Hawai'i," *Anglistica* 15, no. 2 (2011).

68. Diaz, "Bye Bye Ms. American Pie," 159.

69. During the nineteenth and twentieth centuries, ethnologists and folklorists collected, translated, transcribed, archived, published, and interpreted Indigenous oral tales, songs, and chants. Some texts include: Dennis Tedlock, "On the Translation of Style in Oral Narratives," *JAFL* 84 (1971): 114–37; Mary Austin, *The American Rhythm: Studies and Reexpressions of Amerindian Songs* (1923; repr., New York: Cooper Square Publishers, 1970); Nellie Barnes, ed., *American Indian Love Lyrics and Other Verse: From the Songs of the North American Indians* (New York: The Macmillan Company, 1925); Arthur Grove Day, ed., *The Sky Clears: Poetry of the American Indians* (Lincoln: University of Nebraska Press, 1951); William R. Trask's two-volume *The Unwritten Song: Poetry of the Primitive and Traditional Peoples of the World* (New York: Macmillan, 1966); William Brandon, *The Magic World: American Indian Songs and Poems* (Athens, Ohio: Ohio University Press, 1971); John Bierhorst, ed., *In The Trail of the Wind* (New York: Farrar, Straus and Giroux, 1971); John Bierhorst, ed., *The Red Swan: Myths and Tales of the American Indians* (New York: Farrar, Straus and Giroux, 1976); John Bierhorst, ed., *Four Masterworks of American Indian Literature: Quetzalcoatl / The Ritual of Condolence / Cuceb / The Night Chant* (New York: Farrar, Straus and Giroux, 1974); Jerome Rothenberg, ed., *Technicians of the Sacred: A Range of Poetries from Africa, America, Asia, and Oceania* (New York: Anchor Books, 1969); Jerome Rothenberg, "Total Translation: An Experiment in the Presentation of American Indian Poetry," in *Literature of the American Indians*, ed. Abraham Chapman (New York: New American Library, 1975); Dennis Tedlock, *Finding the Center: Narrative Poetry of the Zuni Indians; From Performances in the Zuni by Andrew Peynetsa and Walter Sanchez* (New York: The Dial Press, 1972); and Dell Hymes, *"In Vain I Tried to Tell You": Essays in Native American Ethnopoetics*, Studies in Native American Literature 1 (Philadelphia: University of Pennsylvania Press, 1981).

70. Kenneth Rosen, ed., *Voices of the Rainbow: Contemporary Poetry by American Indians* (New York: Arcade Publishing, 1975), xx.

71. See Kenneth Lincoln, *Native American Renaissance* (Berkeley: University of California Press, 1983); Andrew Wiget, *Native American Literature* (Boston: Twayne Publishers, 1985); Arnold Krupat, ed., *New Voices in Native American*

Literary Criticism (Washington, D.C.: Smithsonian, 1993); Norma Wilson, *The Nature of Native American Poetry* (Albuquerque: University of New Mexico Press, 2001); and Blanca Schorcht, *Storied Voices in Native American Texts: Harry Robinson, Thomas King, James Welch and Leslie Marmon Silko* (New York: Routledge, 2003).

72. Brill de Ramirez, *Contemporary American Indian Literatures.*
73. Kimberly Blaeser, *Gerald Vizenor: Writing in the Oral Tradition* (Norman: University of Oklahoma Press, 1996).
74. Helen May Dennis, *Native American Literature: Towards a Spatialized Reading* (New York: Routledge, 2007), 4–5.
75. Subramani, *South Pacific Literature: From Myth to Fabulation* (Suva: Institute of Pacific Studies, 1992), 5.
76. In several essays, critic and writer Subramani attempted to draw links between the oral and written traditions. See his "Oceania: From Oral Tradition to Literature in English," *Span*, no. 6 (April 1978): 31–35; "Oral Literature and the Beginning of Prose Fiction in Tonga," *Faikava: A Tongan Literary Journal* 6 (1980): 35–39; "Oral Forms in Wendt's Fiction," *Echos du Commonwealth* 8 (1981): 56–67; and "Artists in a Changing South Pacific: The Oral Poet and the Writers," in *Language and Literature in Multicultural Contexts*, ed. Stendra Nandan (Suva, Fiji: University of the South Pacific / Association for Commonwealth Language and Literature Studies, 1983), 317–25.
77. Fairbairn-Dunlop, "Samoan Writing," 41–42.
78. Fairbairn-Dunlop, 54.
79. Epeli Hau'ofa, "The Writer as an Outsider," *World Englishes* 9, no. 2 (1990): 245.
80. Hau'ofa, "Oral Traditions and Writing," 402.
81. Other examples include Miriam Fuchs, "Reading Towards the Indigenous Pacific: Patricia Grace's *Potiki*: A Case Study," *SPAN* 36, no. 2 (1993): 566–83; Michelle Keown, "Orality, Textuality, and Memory: The Language of Pacific Literatures," in Keown, *Pacific Islands Writing*, 147–84; and ku'ualoha ho'omanawanui, *voices of fire: reweaving the literary lei of pele and hi'iaka* (Minneapolis: University of Minnesota Press, 2014).
82. All citations of this poem are from Anne Perez Hattori, "Thieves," *Storyboard: A Journal of Pacific Imagery*, no. 5 (1995): 46. The poem is cited in the running text as "Thieves."
83. See Rogers, *Destiny's Landfall*, 7.
84. An interesting connection to this discourse of impurity and blood can be found in Hawaiian studies; in particular, see J. Kēhaulani Kauanui, *Hawaiian Blood: Colonialism and the Politics of Sovereignty and Indigeneity* (Durham, N.C.: Duke University Press, 2008).
85. Michael Lujan Bevacqua, "My Island Is One Big American Footnote," in *The Space Between: Negotiating Culture, Place, and Identity in the Pacific*, ed. Marata Tamaira (Honolulu: Center for Pacific Islands Studies, 2009), 120–22. The poem is cited by page number in the running text.

86. Bevacqua, "Thieves," *Minagahet* (blog), January 22, 2014, accessed December 5, 2014, http://minagahet.blogspot.com/2014/01/thieves.html. In this blog post, Bevacqua remarks how Perez Hattori's poem "Thieves" influenced the development of his political and decolonial consciousness.
87. See K. Camacho, "Enframing i Taotao Tano'."
88. Bevacqua, "Chamorros, Ghosts, Non-voting Delegates," 2.
89. Michael Lujan Bevacqua, "Guam: Where America's Empire Begins," *Minagahet* (blog), February 18, 2008, accessed May 15, 2014, http://minagahet.blogspot.com/2008/02/guam-where-americas-military-empire.html.
90. See P. Lujan, "Role of Education."
91. See the organization's website: https://www.huraoacademy.com.
92. Laura Marie Torres Souder, "A Significant Step in CHamoru Revitalization Efforts," *Guam Daily Post*, April 28, 2019, accessed October 31, 2020, https://www.postguam.com/forum/featured_columnists/a-significant-step-in-chamoru-revitalization-efforts/article_288a89bc-673c-11e9-975f-034809785dd4.html.
93. J. Flores, "Chant."
94. For a deeper analysis of CHamoru dance, see Judy Flores, "The Re-creation of Chamorro Dance as Observed Through the Festival of Pacific Arts," *Pacific Arts*, no. 25 (December 2002): 47–63.
95. J. Flores, "Re-creation of Chamorro Dance," 50.
96. See his website: https://www.dakotacamacho.com.
97. Allan M. Nazareno, "A Study on the Effect of Spanish Culture on the Traditional Music and Dances of Guam" (MA thesis, California State University Dominguez Hills, 2005), 64.
98. Souder, "Kantan Chamorrita," 191. See also J. Flores, "Kantan Chamorrita Revisited," 24.
99. Nazareno, "Study on the Effect of Spanish Culture," 64.
100. Nazareno, 64.
101. Souder, "Kantan Chamorrita," 192.
102. While I did not originally include capitalism in my analysis, one peer reviewer of this manuscript provided the insightful and compelling suggestion that "mobilizing the forms of kåntan chamorrita reads as a refusal to accept the enclosure of the commons. Themes and lyrics seen as a communal resource to be used freely and respectfully by all, not enclosed by restrictive copyrights."

CONCLUSION

1. Storie, "All Fifty Kathousand Cousins," 75.
2. Guam Executive Order 86–14 (August 4, 1986).
3. Frederick B. Quinene, *An Islander's Voice* (Mangilao: University of Guam Press, 2020).
4. Victoria-Lola Leon Guerrero, introduction to Quinene, *Islander's Voice*, vii.
5. Frank Quimby, "Guam Commonwealth Act," *Guampedia*, accessed June 21, 2020, https://www.guampedia.com/guam-commonwealth-act/.

6. Quimby, "Guam Commonwealth Act."
7. For a deeper reading of Guåhan's quest for commonwealth, see *Kinalamten Pulitikåt: Siñenten i Chamorro / Issues in Guam's Political Development: The Chamorro Perspective* (Agana, Guam: Political Status Education Coordinating Commission, 1996); Dames, "Rethinking the Circle of Belonging"; and Howard Willens and Dirk A. Ballendorf, *The Secret Guam Study: How President Ford's Approval of the Commonwealth Was Blocked by Federal Officials* (Mangilao: University of Guam Press, 2004).
8. "The Quest for a Commonwealth" and "What Am I" are included in *An Islander's Voice*, but I am quoting directly from the congressional hearing record. For both poems, see *Hearing Before the Subcommittee on Insular and International Affairs of the Committee on Interior and Insular Affairs, House of Representatives, One Hundred and First Congress, First Session, on H.R. 98, Guam Commonwealth Act* (December 12, 1989), 108–9. Quotations are cited in the running text as "Quest" and "What Am I."
9. *Hearing Before the Committee on Resources, House of Representatives, One Hundred and Fifth Congress, First Session, on H.R. 100, Guam Commonwealth Act* (October 29, 1997), 303.
10. Quimby, "Guam Commonwealth Act."
11. Kirk and Natividad, "Fortress Guam."
12. Kirk and Natividad, "Fortress Guam."
13. The draft of the environmental impact statement was released for download at www.guambuildupeis.us and in printed form at the University of Guam Robert F. Kennedy Memorial Library and the Nieves M. Flores Memorial Library on Guam, as well as at the mayor's offices in several villages of Guåhan, including Dededo, Yigo, Agat, Mangilao, and Barrigada. See United States Department of the Navy, "Draft Environmental Impact Statement for Guam and CNMI Military Relocation Available for Public Review," Guam and CNMI Military Relocation Supplemental Environmental Impact Statement (website), U.S. Department of the Navy, accessed March 20, 2015, http://guambuildupeis.us/.
14. Kirk and Natividad, "Fortress Guam."
15. The comment period lasted from November 20, 2009, to February 17, 2010. Comments were accepted online or by mail; additionally, the public could submit oral and/or written comments during the four public hearings on Guåhan, which were held between January 7 and January 12, 2010, at two public high schools, the University of Guam Field House, and the Yigo Gymnasium. See United States Department of the Navy, "Draft Environmental Impact Statement."
16. Leo Babauta, "Santa Rita," *Guampedia*, accessed March 20, 2015, http://www.guampedia.com/santa-rita/. For a history of Sumay, see Viernes, "Fanhasso i Taotao Sumay."
17. Nathalie Pereda, "Melvin Won Pat-Borja," *Guampedia*, last modified October 13, 2019, accessed March 19, 2021, https://www.guampedia.com/melvin-won-pat-borja/.

18. We Are Guåhan, "About," We Are Guåhan (website), accessed March 20, 2015, http://www.weareguahan.com/about-weareguahan/. Emphasis added.
19. It should be noted that Camacho-Dungca's father was a kåntan chamorrita poet. See the interview with Bernadita Camacho-Dungca quoted in Michael R. Clement Sr., "Traditional Chamorro Dialog Song of the Mariana Islands," Chamorroweb, accessed January 20, 2012, http://chamorroweb.com/tsamorita-singing.asp.
20. *Guam Daily Post* News Staff, "Chamorro Language Advocate Bernadita Dungca Dies," *Guam Daily Post*, February 18, 2016.
21. Bernadita Camacho-Dungca, "Inifresi," quoted in Guam Executive Order No. 98–28: "Relative to Adopting Inifresi, the Chamoru 'Pledge of Allegiance'" (Oct 29, 1998), accessed February 6, 2012, http://documents.guam.gov/sites/default/files/E.O.-98-28-Relative-to-Adopting-Inifresi-the-Chamorro-P.pdf.
22. Several translations and versions of "Inifresi" exist. One translation is provided in "Guam Pledge: Inifresi," *Guampedia*, https://www.guampedia.com/guam-pledge-chamorro-inefresi/:

    From the highest of my thoughts,
    from the deepest of my heart,
    and with the utmost of my strength,
    I offer myself to protect
    and to defend the beliefs,
    the culture,
    the language,
    the air,
    the water and the land of the Chamorro,
    which are our inherent God-given rights.
    This I will affirm by the holy words and our banner,
    the flag of Guåhan!

23. See Diaz, *Repositioning the Missionary*.
24. For a history and analysis of the Guam flag, see DeLisle, "Navy Wives / Native Lives."
25. Guam Executive Order No. 98–28: "Inifresi."
26. Melvin Won Pat-Borja, "No Deal," video, 4:45, posted by We Are Guahan, January 8, 2010, accessed February 23, 2012, http://www.youtube.com/watch?v=YzmXU6u5CTE.
27. Won Pat-Borja, "No Deal." Quotations of this spoken-word poem come from the written version provided through personal communication, and they are subsequently cited in the running text by title alone.
28. Bevacqua, "Exceptional Life and Death of a Chamorro Soldier," 35.
29. Kirk and Natividad, "Fortress Guam."
30. Matthew D. LaPlante, "U.S. Territories: A Recruiter's Paradise," *Salt Lake Tribune*, August 5, 2007.

31. K. Camacho, *Cultures of Commemoration*, 86.
32. K. Camacho, 89.
33. K. Camacho, 109.
34. Diaz, "Deliberating 'Liberation Day,'" 162.
35. Bevacqua, "Exceptional Life and Death of a Chamorro Soldier," 36.
36. Bevacqua, 48.
37. I write about Borja-Kicho'cho' performing her poem "Re-occupation Day (aka 'Liberation Day')" in my essay "'Thank God for the Maladjusted': The Transterritorial Turn Towards the Chamorro Poetry of Guahan," in *Oceanic Archives, Indigenous Epistemologies, and Transpacific American Studies*, ed. Otto Heim, Yuan Shu, and Kendall Johnson (Hong Kong: Hong Kong University Press, 2019).
38. For an examination of the activism to protect Pågat, see Tiara R. Na'puti and Michael Lujan Bevacqua, "Militarization and Resistance from Guåhan: Protecting and Defending Pågat," *American Quarterly* 67, no. 3 (September 2015): 837–58.
39. CHamorus have been traveling to the United Nations to testify on Guåhan's colonial status for decades. For a study of these testimonies, see Tiara R. Na'puti, "Speaking the Language of Peace: Resistance and Rhetoric in Guåhan Self-Determination Movement," *Anthropologica* 56, no. 2 (2014): 301–13.
40. For an examination of the activism to protect Litekyan (Ritidian), see Tiara R. Na'puti, "Archipelagic Rhetoric: Remapping the Marianas and Challenging Militarization from 'A Stirring Place,'" *Communication and Critical/Cultural Studies* 16, no. 1 (2019): 4–25.
41. Julian Aguon, "No Country for Eight-Spot Butterflies," *Progressive International*, June 11, 2020, accessed June 15, 2020, https://progressive.international/wire/2020-06-12-julian-aguon-no-country-for-eight-spot-butterflies/en.
42. H.-K. Trask, "Writing in Captivity," 12.
43. Laura Marie Torres Souder and Robert A. Underwood, "Preface," in Souder and Underwood, *Chamorro Self-Determination*, viii.
44. To illustrate this point, the editors include several poems in the anthology that speak to the issue of CHamoru self-determination.
45. K. Camacho, "Chamorro Literature," 520.
46. Skinner, "Contemporary Micronesian Literature," 3.

SELECTED BIBLIOGRAPHY

AUDIOVISUAL SOURCES

Borja-Kicho'cho', Kisha. "Re-occupation Day (aka Liberation Day)." Speech at public hearing, January 2010. Video, 3:07. Accessed February 24, 2012. http://www.youtube.com/watch?v=Fi5yN9ehtZI.

Leon Guerrero, Ryan, and Walla Wai. "Brave New Voices 2011 Team Guahan." Performance at Brave New Voices Competition, 2011. Video, 5:24. Posted by Erica Benton, July 24, 2011. https://www.youtube.com/watch?v=cvjxqy1dHU4.

Leon Guerrero, Ryan, and Walla Wai. "Self-Guamination (Sneak Peek) Spoken Word Poetry." Audio recording of poem. Kinahulo' Linahyan: The Awakening of the Masses (website). Accessed December 12, 2014. http://kinahulo.bandcamp.com/track/willa-wai-ryan-leon-guerrero-self-guamination-sneak-peek-spoken-word-poetry.

Won Pat-Borja, Melvin. "No Deal." Video, 4:45. Posted by We Are Guahan, January 8, 2010. Accessed February 23, 2012. http://www.youtube.com/watch?v=YzmXU6u5CTE.

GOVERNMENT DOCUMENTS

Guam Executive Order No. 86–14 (August 4, 1986).

Guam Executive Order No. 98–28: "Relative to Adopting Inifresi, the Chamoru 'Pledge of Allegiance'" (October 29, 1998). Accessed February 6, 2012. http://documents.guam.gov/sites/default/files/E.O.-98-28-Relative-to-Adopting-Inifresi-the-Chamorro-P.pdf.

Guam Executive Order No. 2010–06 (2010). Accessed February 20, 2015. http://documents.guam.gov/sites/default/files/EO-2010-06.pdf.

Martínez Cobo, José R. *Study of the Problem of Discrimination Against Indigenous Populations.* United Nations Subcommission on Prevention of Discrimination and Protection of Minorities, E/CN.4/Sub.2/1986/7 and Add.4 (1987).

United Nations. "United Nations and Decolonization." United Nations (website). Accessed December 14, 2014. http://www.un.org/en/decolonization/nonselfgov territories.shtml.

United States Census Bureau. *2010 Census: Chamorros in the United States.* May 2012. Accessed July 2, 2014. http://bsp.guam.gov/Chamorros%20in%20the%20 United%20States_2011.1.pdf.

United States Census Bureau. *2010 Census: Native Hawaiian.* May 2012. Accessed July 2, 2014. http://www.census.gov/newsroom/releases/archives/native_hawaiian /cb12-83.html.

United States Census Bureau. *2010 Census of Population and Housing: Guam.* May 2012. www.census.gov/prod/cen2010/island/GUAMprofile.pdf.

United States Census Bureau. *The Native Hawaiian and Other Pacific Islander Population: 2010.* 2010 Census Briefs, C2010BR-12, May 2012. Accessed July 2, 2014. http://www.census.gov/prod/cen2010/briefs/c2010br-12.pdf.

United States Department of the Navy. "Draft Environmental Impact Statement for Guam and CNMI Military Relocation Available for Public Review." Guam and CNMI Military Relocation Supplemental Environmental Impact Statement (website), U.S. Department of the Navy. Accessed March 20, 2015. http://guam buildupeis.us/.

United States Department of the Navy. *Environmental Impact Statement: Guam and CNMI Military Relocation.* Vol. 2, *Marine Corps Relocation—Guam.* Guam and CNMI Military Relocation Supplemental Environmental Impact Statement (website), U.S. Department of the Navy. Accessed March 18, 2015. http://www.guam buildupeis.us/documents/.

JOURNALS

Storyboard: A Journal of Pacific Imagery. Mangilao: University of Guam, 1991–2001, 2006, 2009–present.

Xanadu and *Xanadu II.* Mangilao: University of Guam, 1966, 1981–1983.

OTHER SOURCES

Adamson, Joni. *American Indian Literature, Environmental Justice, and Ecocriticism: The Middle Place.* Tucson: University of Arizona Press, 2001.

Aguon, Julian. "No Country for Eight-Spot Butterflies." *Progressive International,* June 11, 2020. Accessed June 15, 2020. https://progressive.international/wire/2020 -06-12-julian-aguon-no-country-for-eight-spot-butterflies/en.

Aguon, Julian. "Update: Land Ownership on Guam." *Guampedia.* Accessed October 23, 2014. http://www.guampedia.com/update-land-ownership-on-guam/.

Aguon, Katherine B. "The Guam Dilemma: The Need for a Pacific Island Education Perspective." In *Kinalamten Pulitikåt: Siñenten i Chamorro / Issues in Guam's*

Political Development: The Chamorro Perspective, 92. Agana, Guam: Political Status Education Coordinating Commission, 1996.

Ahlburg, Dennis A., and Michael J. Levin. *The Northeast Passage: A Study of Pacific Islander Migration to American Samoa and the United States*. Canberra: National Centre for Development Studies, Australian National University, 1990.

Alexeveff, Kalissa. "Love Food: Exchange and Sustenance in the Cook Islands Diaspora." *Australian Journal of Anthropology* 15, no. 1 (2002): 68–80.

Allen, Chadwick. *Blood Narrative: Indigenous Identity in American Indian and Maori Literary and Activist Texts*. Durham, N.C.: Duke University Press, 2002.

Allen, Chadwick. *Trans-Indigenous: Methodologies for Global Native Literary Studies*. Minneapolis: University of Minnesota Press, 2012.

Allen, Linda. "Enid 'Atoll': A Marshallese Migrant Community in the Midwestern United States." PhD diss., University of Iowa, Iowa City, 1997.

Allen, Paula Gunn. *The Sacred Hoop: Recovering the Feminine Side in American Indian Traditions*. Boston: Beacon Press, 1986.

Amesbury, Judith R. "Pelagic Fishing in the Mariana Archipelago: From the Prehistoric Period to the Present." *Terra Australis*, no. 39 (2008): 33–57.

Anaya, S. J. *Indigenous Peoples in International Law*. New York: Oxford University Press, 2004.

Anson, George. *A Voyage Round the World, in the Years MDCCXL, I, II, III, IV: Compiled from Papers and Other Materials of the Right Honourable George Lord Anson, and Published Under His Direction by Richard Walter, Chaplain of His Majesty's Ship the Centurion*. 1748. Reprint, Cambridge: Cambridge University Press, 2015.

Apuron, Anthony. "The Role the Church Played in Helping to Preserve the Chamorro Language and Culture." Paper presented at the Marianas Ballroom, Hilton Hotel, Tumon, Guam, April 1, 1996.

Arago, Jacques. *Narrative of a Voyage Round the World, in the Uranie and Physicienne Corvettes, Commanded by M. de Freycinet During the Years 1817, 1818, 1819, and 1820*. London: Treuttel and Wurtz, 1823.

Artero, Andrew Diaz. "Canoe Building." *Guampedia*. Accessed May 13, 2014. http://guampedia.com/canoe-building-2/.

Asang, Isebong. "Remaking Footprints: Palauan Migrants in Hawai'i." *The Contemporary Pacific* 12 (2000): 371–84.

Atienza, David. "CHamoru 'Adaptive Resistance' During the Spanish Conquest and Colonization in the Mariana Islands." Paper presented at the 4th Marianas History Conference, Guam, 2020.

Austin, Mary. *The American Rhythm: Studies and Reexpressions of Amerindian Songs*. 1923. Reprint, New York: Cooper Square Publishers, 1970.

Babauta, Leo. "Santa Rita." *Guampedia*. Accessed March 20, 2015. http://www.guampedia.com/santa-rita/.

Babauta, Leo. "Umatac (Humåtak)." *Guampedia*. Accessed July 5, 2014. http://www.guampedia.com/umatac-humatak/.

Babauta, Leo. "War Atrocities: Manenggon Concentration Camp." *Guampedia*. Accessed September 27, 2014. http://www.guampedia.com/war-atrocities-manenggon-concentration-camp/.

Bailey, Kim. "Chamorrita Songs: A Surviving Legacy of the Mexican Verso?" Paper presented at the 26th annual meeting of the Society for Ethnomusicology, Honolulu, Hawai'i, October 16, 1981.

Barker, Judith. "Home Alone: The Effects of Out-Migration on Niuean Elders' Living Arrangements and Social Supports." *Pacific Studies* 17, no. 3 (1994): 41–81.

Barmann, Jean. "New Land, New Lives: Hawaiian Settlement in British Columbia." *Hawaiian Journal of History* 29 (1995): 1–32.

Barnes, Nellie, ed. *American Indian Love Lyrics and Other Verse: From the Songs of the North American Indians*. New York: The Macmillan Company, 1925.

Bautista, Lola Quan. *Steadfast Movement Around Micronesia: Satowan Enlargements Beyond Migration*. Lanham, Md.: Lexington Books, 2010.

Bennett, Jesi Lujan. "Apmam Tiempo Ti Uli'e Hit (Long Time No See): Chamorro Diaspora and the Transpacific Home." MA thesis, University of Hawai'i, Mānoa, 2013.

Bevacqua, Michael Lujan. "Agad'na: Canoe Builders." *Guampedia*. Accessed May 13, 2014. http://guampedia.com/agadna-canoe-builders/.

Bevacqua, Michael Lujan. "Chamorros, Ghosts, Non-voting Delegates: GUAM! Where the Production of America's Sovereignty Begins." PhD diss., University of California, San Diego, 2010.

Bevacqua, Michael Lujan. "CHamoru World View." *Guampedia*. Accessed July 7, 2014. http://www.guampedia.com/chamorroworldview.

Bevacqua, Michael Lujan. "The Exceptional Life and Death of a Chamorro Soldier: Tracing the Militarization of Desire in Guam, ~~USA~~." In *Militarized Currents: Toward a Decolonized Future in Asia and the Pacific*, edited by Setsu Shigematsu and Keith L. Camacho, 33–62. Minneapolis: University of Minnesota Press, 2010.

Bevacqua, Michael Lujan. "Guam: Where America's Empire Begins." *Minagahet* (blog), February 18, 2008. Accessed May 15, 2014. http://minagahet.blogspot.com/2008/02/guam-where-americas-military-empire.html.

Bevacqua, Michael Lujan. "My Island Is One Big American Footnote." In *The Space Between: Negotiating Culture, Place, and Identity in the Pacific*, edited by Marata Tamaira, 120–22. Honolulu: Center for Pacific Islands Studies, 2009.

Bevacqua, Michael Lujan. "Pågat." *Minagahet* (blog), May 16, 2010. Accessed October 25, 2014. http://minagahet.blogspot.com/2010/05/pagat.html.

Bevacqua, Michael Lujan. "Pågat Protest Today." *Minagahet* (blog), July 23, 2010. Accessed October 25, 2014. http://minagahet.blogspot.com/2010/07/pagat-protest-today.html.

Bevacqua, Michael Lujan. "A Play Called Pagat." *Minagahet* (blog), April 24, 2014. Accessed March 10, 2021. http://minagahet.blogspot.com/2014/04/a-play-called-pagat-michael-lujan.html.

Bevacqua, Michael Lujan. "The Song Maps of Craig Santos Perez." *Transmotion* 1, no. 1 (2015).

Bevacqua, Michael Lujan. "Taotaomo'na." *Guampedia*. Accessed August 9, 2014. http://www.guampedia.com/taotaomona-taotaomona/.

Bevacqua, Michael Lujan. "Thieves." *Minagahet* (blog), January 22, 2014. Accessed December 5, 2014. http://minagahet.blogspot.com/2014/01/thieves.html.

Bevacqua, Michael Lujan, and Isa Kelley Bowman. "Histories of Wonder, Futures of Wonder: Chamorro Activist Identity, Community, and Leadership in 'The Legend of Gadao' and 'The Women Who Saved Guåhan from a Giant Fish.'" *Marvels & Tales* 30, no. 1 (2016). https://digitalcommons.wayne.edu/marvels/vol30/iss1/6.

Bierhorst, John, ed. *Four Masterworks of American Indian Literature: Quetzalcoatl / The Ritual of Condolence / Cuceb / The Night Chant*. New York: Farrar, Straus and Giroux, 1974.

Bierhorst, John, ed. *In the Trail of the Wind: American Indian Poems and Ritual Orations*. New York: Farrar, Straus and Giroux, 1971.

Bierhorst, John, ed. *The Red Swan: Myths and Tales of the American Indians*. New York: Farrar, Straus and Giroux, 1976.

Blaeser, Kimberly. *Gerald Vizenor: Writing in the Oral Tradition*. Norman: University of Oklahoma Press, 1996.

Borja, Mario. "Our Sakman Story: One Sentence in History." In *One Archipelago, Many Stories: Integrating Our Narratives (2nd Marianas History Conference: Art, Culture, and Science)*, vol. 2, 93–118. Mangilao, Guam: Guampedia Foundation, 2013.

Borja-Kicho'cho', Kisha, and Anghet Hoppe-Cruz, "I Kareran i Palåbran Måmi—The Journey of Our Words." MA thesis, University of Hawai'i, Mānoa, 2010.

Bourdier, Jean-Paul, and Nezar AlSayyad, eds. *Dwellings, Settlements and Tradition: Cross-Cultural Perspectives*. Lanham, Md.: University Press of America, 1989.

Brandon, William. *The Magic World: American Indian Songs and Poems*. Athens, Ohio: Ohio University Press, 1971.

Brill de Ramirez, Susan Berry. *Contemporary American Indian Literatures and the Oral Tradition*. Tucson: University of Arizona Press, 1999.

Brinton, Daniel G. *Brinton's Library of Aboriginal American Literature, Number 1: The Maya Chronicles*. Philadelphia: D. G. Brinton, 1882. www.archive.org/details/libraryofaborigi01brinuoft.

Burson, Bruce, ed. *Climate Change and Migration in the South Pacific Region: Policy Perspectives*. Wellington: Institute of Policy Studies, 2010.

Buschmann, Rainer F., Edward R. Slack Jr., and James B. Tueller, eds. *Navigating the Spanish Lake: The Pacific in the Iberian World 1521–1898*. Honolulu: University of Hawai'i Press, 2014.

Cachola, Ellen-Rae, Gwyn Kirk, Lisa Natividad, and Maria Reinat Pumarejo. "Women Working Across Borders for Peace and Genuine Security." *Peace Journal: A Journal of Social Justice*, 22, no. 2 (2010): 164–70.

Camacho, Keith L. "Chamorro Literature." In *The Pacific Islands: An Encyclopedia*, edited by Brij V. Lal and Kate Fortune, 520. Honolulu: University of Hawai'i Press, 2000.

Camacho, Keith L. *Cultures of Commemoration: The Politics of War, Memory, and History in the Mariana Islands*. Honolulu: University of Hawai'i Press, 2011.

Camacho, Keith L. "Enframing i Taotao Tano': Colonialism, Militarism, and Tourism in Twentieth Century Guam." MA thesis, University of Hawai'i, Mānoa, 1998.

Camacho, Keith L. *Sacred Men: Law, Torture, and Retribution in Guam*. Durham, N.C.: Duke University Press, 2019.

Camacho, Keith L., and Laurel A. Monnig. "Uncomfortable Fatigues: Chamorro Soldiers, Gendered Identities, and the Question of Decolonization in Guam." In *Militarized Currents: Toward a Decolonized Future in Asia and the Pacific*, edited by Setsu Shigematsu and Keith L. Camacho, 147–79. Minneapolis: University of Minnesota Press, 2010.

Camacho, Olympia Q. *Legends of Guam*. Agana, Guam: Government of Guam, Department of Education, 1997.

Camacho-Dungca, Bernadita. "Inifresi." In Guam Executive Order No. 98–28: "Relative to Adopting Inifresi, the Chamoru 'Pledge of Allegiance'" (October 29, 1998). Accessed February 6, 2012. http://documents.guam.gov/sites/default/files/E.O.-98-28-Relative-to-Adopting-Inifresi-the-Chamorro-P.pdf.

Campbell, Bruce L. "The Filipino Community of Guam, 1945–1975." MA thesis, University of Hawai'i, 1987.

Campbell, Ian C. *A History of the Pacific Islands*. Berkeley: University of California Press, 1989.

Campbell, John R. "Climate-Change Migration in the Pacific." *The Contemporary Pacific* 26, no. 1 (2014): 1–28.

Castro, Fanai. "Poetry/Spoken Word." *Guampedia*. Accessed December 4, 2014. www.guampedia.com/poetryspoken-word/.

Castro, Fanai. "Sinajana (Sinahånña)." *Guampedia*. Accessed June 11, 2020. https://www.guampedia.com/sinajana/.

Cena, Julius Sotomayor. "Theater." *Guampedia*. Last modified October 10, 2019. Accessed March 10, 2021. https://www.guampedia.com/theater/.

Chapman, Murray, ed. "Mobility and Identity in the Island Pacific." Special issue, *Pacific Viewpoint* 26, no. 1 (1985).

Chappell, David. *Double Ghosts: Oceanian Voyagers on Euroamerican Ships*. New York: M. E. Sharpe, 1997.

Clark, Ryan. "The Appositional Project: Craig Santos Perez's *from unincorporated territory [saina]*." *Spoon River Poetry Review*, November 10, 2013. http://www.srpr.org/blog/the-appositional-project-craig-santos-perezs-from-unincorporated-territory-saina/.

Clement, Michael, Jr. "Kustumbre, Modernity and Resistance: The Subaltern Narrative in Chamorro Language Music." PhD diss., University of Hawai'i, Mānoa, 2011.

Clement, Michael, Jr. "The Sella Bay Ammunition Wharf Controversy: Economic Development, Indigenous Rights and Colonialism in Guam." MA thesis, University of Guam, 2002.

Clement, Michael R., Sr. "The Ancient Origins of Chamorro Music." MA thesis, University of Guam, 2001.

Clement, Michael R., Sr. "Micronesia: IV. Mariana Islands. 2. Guam." In *The New Grove Dictionary of Music and Musicians*, 2nd ed., vol. 16, 613. London: Macmillan, 2001.

Clement, Michael R., Sr. "Traditional Chamorro Dialog Song of the Mariana Islands." Chamorroweb. Accessed January 20, 2012. http://chamorroweb.com/tsamorita-singing.asp.

Clement, Michael R., Sr. "Tsamorita Singing." Chamorroweb. Accessed February 7, 2009. http://chamorroweb.com/tsamorita-singing.asp.

Clifford, James. "Indigenous Articulations." *The Contemporary Pacific* 13, no. 2 (Fall 2001): 468–90.

Coates, K. S. *A Global History of Indigenous Peoples: Struggle and Survival*. New York: Palgrave Macmillan, 2004.

Connell, John, ed. *Migration and Development in the South Pacific*. Canberra: Australian National University, 1989.

Connell, John. "Paradise Left? Pacific Island Voyagers in the Modern World." In Spickard, Rondilla, and Wright, *Pacific Diaspora*, 69–86. Honolulu: University of Hawai'i Press, 2002.

Cook-Lynn, Elizabeth. "The American Indian Fiction Writers: Cosmopolitanism, Nationalism, the Third World, and First Nation Sovereignty." In *Why I Can't Read Wallace Stegner*, edited by Elizabeth Cook-Lynn, 78–96. Madison: University of Wisconsin Press, 1996.

Cox, James. *Muting White Noise: Native American and European American Novel Traditions*. Norman: University of Oklahoma Press, 2009.

Crocombe, Ronald, ed. *Customary Land Tenure and Sustainable Development*. Suva: Institute of Pacific Studies, 1995.

Crocombe, Ronald. *Land Tenure in Oceania*. 3rd ed. Suva: Institute of Pacific Studies, 1987.

Crocombe, Ronald, and Malama Maleisea, eds. *Land Issues in the Pacific*. Suva: Institute of Pacific Studies, 1994.

Crosby, Alfred W. *Ecological Imperialism: The Biological Expansion of Europe, 900–1900*. Cambridge: Cambridge University Press, 2004.

Cruz, Mary Therese. "(Re)Searching Identity: Being Chamorro in an American Colony." PhD diss., University of Hawai'i, Mānoa, 2012.

Cunningham, Lawrence. *Ancient Chamorro Kinship Organization*. Agat, Guam: L. Joseph Press, 1984.

Cunningham, Lawrence. *Ancient Chamorro Society*. Honolulu: Bess Press, 1992.

Cunningham, Lawrence. "De Silleria." *Guampedia*. Accessed May 30, 2013. http://guampedia.com/de-silleria/.

Cunningham, Lawrence. "Latte Structures." *Guampedia*. Accessed September 6, 2012. http://guampedia.com/latte-structures/.

Cunningham, Lawrence. "Mampostería." *Guampedia*. Accessed May 30, 2013. http://guampedia.com/mamposteria/.

Cunningham, Lawrence. "Pole and Thatched Homes." *Guampedia*. Accessed May 30, 2013. http://guampedia.com/pole-and-thatched-homes/.

Cunningham, Lawrence J., Ward Kranz, and Manny Sikau. "Restoring Traditional Seafaring and Navigation in Guam." *Micronesian Journal of the Humanities and Social Sciences* 5, no. 1–2 (November 2006): 314–19.

Dames, Vivian. "Rethinking the Circle of Belonging: American Citizenship and the Chamorros of Guam." PhD diss., University of Michigan, 2000.

D'Arcy, Paul. *The People of the Sea: Environment, Identity, and History in Oceania*. Honolulu: University of Hawai'i Press, 2006.

Day, Arthur Grove, ed. *The Sky Clears: Poetry of the American Indians*. Lincoln: University of Nebraska Press, 1951.

Degadillo, Yolanda, Thomas B. McGrath, and Felicia Plaza. *Spanish Forts of Guam*. Micronesia Area Research Center Publication Series 7. Mangilao: University of Guam Richard F. Taitano Micronesian Area Research Center, 1979.

DeLisle, Christine Taitano. "Delivering the Body: Narratives of Family, Childbirth and Prewar Pattera." MA thesis, University of Guam, 2001.

DeLisle, Christine Taitano. "Navy Wives / Native Lives: The Cultural and Historical Relations Between Naval Wives and Chamorro Women in Guam, 1898–1945." PhD diss., University of Michigan, 2008.

DeLisle, Christine Taitano. *Placental Politics: CHamoru Women, White Womanhood, and Indigeneity under U.S. Colonialism in Guam*. Chapel Hill: University of North Carolina Press, 2020.

DeLoughrey, Elizabeth. *Routes and Roots: Navigating Caribbean and Pacific Island Literatures*. Honolulu: University of Hawai'i Press, 2007.

DeLoughrey, Elizabeth. "The Spiral Temporality of Patricia Grace's *Potiki*." *Ariel* 30, no. 1 (Jan 1999): 59–83.

DeLoughrey, Elizabeth, and George B. Handley, eds. *Postcolonial Ecologies: Literatures of the Environment*. Oxford: Oxford University Press, 2011.

Dening, Greg. *Beach Crossings: Voyaging Across Times, Cultures, and Self*. Philadelphia: University of Pennsylvania Press, 2004.

Dennis, Helen May. *Native American Literature: Towards a Spatialized Reading*. New York: Routledge, 2007.

Denoon, Donald, Malama Meleisea, Stewart Firth, Jocelyn Linnekin, and Karen Nero, eds. *The Cambridge History of the Pacific Islanders*. Cambridge: Cambridge University Press, 1997.

Department of Chamorro Affairs. *Chamorro Heritage: A Sense of Place—Guidelines, Procedures, and Recommendations for Authenticating Chamorro Heritage*. Hale'-ta series. Agana, Guam: Department of Chamorro Affairs, Research, Publication and Training Division, 2003.

Diaz, Vicente M. "Bye Bye Ms. American Pie: The Historical Relations Between Chamorros and Filipinos and the American Dream." *ISLA: A Journal of Micronesian Studies* 3, no. 1 (1995): 147–60.

Diaz, Vicente M. "Deliberating 'Liberation Day': Identity, History, Memory, and War in Guam." In *Perilous Memories: The Asia-Pacific War(s)*, edited by T. Fujitani, Geoffrey M. White, and Lisa Yoneyama, 155–89. Durham, N.C.: Duke University Press, 2001.

Diaz, Vicente M. "Paved with Good Intentions . . . Roads, Citizenship and a Century of American Colonialism in Guam." Paper presented at the Centennial of the Spanish-American War Summer Seminar, Obermann Center for Advanced Study, University of Iowa, 1998.

Diaz, Vicente M. *Repositioning the Missionary: Rewriting the Histories of Colonialism, Native Catholicism, and Indigeneity in Guam*. Honolulu: University of Hawaiʻi Press, 2010.

Diaz, Vicente M. "Simply Chamorro: Telling Tales of Demise and Survival in Guam." *The Contemporary Pacific* 6, no. 1 (Spring 1994): 29–58.

Diaz, Vicente M. "Sniffing Oceania's Behind." *The Contemporary Pacific* 24, no. 2 (2012): 323–44.

Diaz, Vicente M. "To 'P' or Not to 'P'? Marking the Territory Between Pacific Islander and Asian American Studies." *Journal of Asian American Studies* 7, no. 3 (2004): 183–208.

Diaz, Vicente M. "Voyaging for Anti-colonial Recovery: Austronesian Seafaring, Archipelagic Rethinking, and the Re-mapping of Indigeneity." *Pacific Asia Inquiry* 2, no. 1 (Fall 2011): 21–32.

Diaz, Vicente M., and J. Kēhaulani Kauanui. "Native Pacific Cultural Studies on the Edge." *The Contemporary Pacific* 13, no. 2 (2001): 315–42.

Diego, Elizabeth A. Paulino. "Reclaiming Identity in Articulating What It Means to Be Chamorro: A Phenomenological Study of the Indigenous Peoples of Guam." PhD diss., Gonzaga University, 2010.

Djerbi, Ali, and Abdelwahab Safi. "Teaching the History of Architecture in Algeria, Tunisia, and Morocco: Colonialism, Independence, and Globalization." *Journal of the Society of Architectural Historians* 62, no. 1 (Mar. 2003): 102–9.

Dreese, Donelle N. *Ecocriticism: Creating Self and Place in Environmental and American Indian Literatures*. New York: Peter Lang International Academic Publishers, 2002.

Duncan, Janice. *Minority Without a Champion: Kanakas on the Pacific Coast, 1788–1850*. Portland: Oregon Historical Society, 1972.

Elder, John, and Hertha D. Wong, eds. *Family of Earth and Sky: Indigenous Tales of Nature from Around the World*. Boston: Beacon Press, 1996.

Fairbairn-Dunlop, Peggy. "Samoan Writing: Searching for the Written Fagogo." *Pacific Islands Communication Journal* 14, no. 1 (1985): 41–69.

Farrell, Don A. "The Partition of the Marianas: A Diplomatic History, 1898–1919." *ISLA: A Journal of Micronesian Studies* 2, no. 2 (Dry Season 1994): 273–301.

Fee, James. "Proa: Speed and Lightness over the Waves." *Guam Pacific Daily News*, August 27, 2009. Accessed June 10, 2014. http://www.guampdn.com/guampublishing/navigator/data/EkVEFVllypYkXdAtNj.htm.

Feinberg, Richard, ed. *Seafaring in the Contemporary Pacific Islands*. DeKalb: Northern Illinois University Press, 1995.

Finney, Ben R., ed. *Pacific Navigation and Voyaging*. Wellington: Polynesian Society, 1976.

Firth, Stewart. "Decolonization." In *Remembrance of Pacific Pasts: An Invitation to Remake History*, edited by Robert Borofsky, 314–32. Honolulu: University of Hawai'i Press, 2000.

Flinn, Juliana. "Private Houses, Public Sharing: Pollapese Migrants Coping with Change." In Rensel and Rodman, *Home in the Islands*, 132–50.

Flood, Bo. *Marianas Island Legends: Myth and Magic*. Honolulu: Bess Press, 2001.

Flores, Alfred. "'No Walk in the Park': U.S. Empire and the Racialization of Civilian Military Labor in Guam, 1944–1962." In *American Quarterly* 67, no. 3 (2015): 813–35.

Flores, Evelyn. "Rewriting Paradise: Countering Desire, Denial and the Exotic in American Literary Representations of the Pacific." PhD diss., University of Michigan, 2002.

Flores, Evelyn, and Emelihter Kihleng, eds. *Indigenous Literatures from Micronesia*. Honolulu: University of Hawai'i Press, 2019.

Flores, Judy. "Ancient Chamorro Concepts of Beauty." *Guampedia*. Accessed June 13, 2014. http://guampedia.com/concepts-of-beauty-in-ancient-chamorro-society/.

Flores, Judy. "Art and Identity in the Mariana Islands: Issues of Reconstructing an Ancient Past." PhD diss., University of East Anglia, 1999.

Flores, Judy. "Art and Identity in the Marianas Islands: The Reconstruction of 'Ancient' Chamorro Dance." In *Pacific Art: Persistence, Change and Meaning*, edited by Anita Herle, Nick Stanley, Karen Stevenson, and Robert L. Welsch, 106–13. Honolulu: University of Hawai'i Press, 2002.

Flores, Judy. "Chant." *Guampedia*. Accessed March 18, 2012. http://guampedia.com/chant/.

Flores, Judy. "Kantan Chamorrita Revisited in the New Millennium." In *Transnationalism and Modernity in the Music and Dance of Oceania: Essays in Honour of Barbara B. Smith*, edited by H. Lawrence, 19–31. Sydney: University of Sydney, 2001.

Flores, Judy. "The Re-creation of Chamorro Dance as Observed Through the Festival of Pacific Arts." *Pacific Arts*, no. 25 (December 2002): 47–63.

Frain, Sylvia. "Women's Resistance in the Marianas Archipelago: A US Colonial Homefront and Militarized Frontline." *Feminist Formations* 29, no. 1 (Spring 2017): 97–135.

Fuchs, Miriam. "Reading Towards the Indigenous Pacific: Patricia Grace's *Potiki*, a Case Study." *SPAN* 36, no. 2 (1993): 566–83.

Gailey, Christine Ward. "A Good Man Is Hard to Find: Overseas Migration and the Decentered Family in the Tongan Islands." *Critique of Anthropology* 12, no. 1 (1992): 47–74.

García, F. *Life and Martyrdom of the Venerable Father Diego Luis de San Vitores of the Society of Jesus*. 1683. Reprint, Madrid: Ivan García Infanzen, 1994.

Garroutte, Eva Marie. *Real Indians: Identity and the Survival of Native America*. Berkeley: University of California Press, 2003.

Gershon, Ilana. "Viewing Diasporas from the Pacific: What Pacific Ethnographies Offer Pacific Diaspora Studies." *The Contemporary Pacific* 19, no. 2 (Fall 2007): 474–502.

Gladwin, Thomas. *East Is a Big Bird: Navigation and Logic on Puluwat Atoll*. Cambridge, Mass.: Harvard University Press, 1970.

Glissant, Édouard. *Poetics of Relation*. Ann Arbor: University of Michigan Press, 1997.

Godard, Philippe. *Latte: The Mysterious Megaliths of the Marianas*. Perth: Arolhos Publishing, 1995.

Gorenflo, L. J., and Michael J. Levin. "Changing Migration Patterns in the Federated States of Micronesia." *ISLA: A Journal of Micronesian Studies* 3 (1995): 29–71.

Grace, Patricia. "Influences on Writing." In Hereniko and Wilson, *Inside Out*, 75–84.

Grace, Patricia. *Potiki*. 1986. Reprint, Honolulu: University of Hawai'i Press, 1995.

Graves, Michael W. "Organization and Differentiation Within Late Prehistoric Ranked Social Units, Mariana Islands, Western Pacific." *Journal of Field Archaeology* 13 (1986): 139–54.

Grey, Eve. *Legends of Micronesia*. Saipan, Northern Mariana Islands: Trust Territory Literature Production Center, 1951.

Grieco, Elizabeth. *The Remittance Behavior of Immigrant Households: Micronesians in Hawai'i and Guam*. New York: LFB Scholarly Publishing, 2003.

Guam Daily Post News Staff. "Chamorro Language Advocate Bernadita Dungca Dies." *Guam Daily Post*, February 18, 2016.

Guam Department of Education. *Legends of Guam*. Agana: Guam Department of Education, 1981.

"Guam's Seven Historical Eras." *Guampedia*, October 10, 2019. Accessed August 26, 2020. https://www.guampedia.com/guams-seven-historical-eras/.

Haddon, A. C., and James Hornell. *Canoes of Oceania*. Honolulu: Bishop Museum Press, 1975.

Halualani, Rona Tamiko. *In the Name of Hawaiians: Native Identities and Cultural Politics*. Minneapolis: University of Minnesota Press, 2002.

Hanlon, David. *Remaking Micronesia: Discourses over Development in a Pacific Territory, 1944–1982*. Honolulu: University of Hawai'i Press, 1998.

Hanlon, David. "The 'Sea of Little Lands': Examining Micronesia's Place in 'Our Sea of Islands.'" *The Contemporary Pacific* 21, no. 1 (2009): 91–110.

Harvey, Graham, and Charles D. Thompson Jr., eds. *Indigenous Diasporas and Dislocations*. Burlington, Vt.: Ashgate Publishing Limited, 2005.

Hattori, Anne Perez. *Colonial Dis-ease: US Navy Health Policies and the Chamorros of Guam, 1898–1941*. Honolulu: University of Hawai'i Press, 2004.

Hattori, Anne Perez. "Colonialism, Capitalism and Nationalism in the US Navy's Expulsion of Guam's Spanish Catholic Priests, 1898–1900." *The Journal of Pacific History* 44, no. 2 (2009): 281–302.

Hattori, Anne Perez. "Folktale: Puntan and Fu'una: Gods of Creation." *Guampedia*. Accessed July 7, 2014. http://www.guampedia.com/puntan-and-fuuna-gods-of-creation.

Hattori, Anne Perez. "Guardians of Our Soil: Indigenous Responses to Post–World War II Land Appropriation on Guam." In *Farms, Firms and Runways: Perspectives on U.S. Military Bases in the Western Pacific*, edited by L. Eve Armentrout, 186–202. Chicago: Imprint Publications, 2001.

Hattori, Anne Perez. "Navy Blues: US Naval Rule on Guam and the Rough Road to Assimilation, 1898–1941." *Pacific Asia Inquiry* 5, no. 1 (Fall 2014): 13–30.

Hattori, Anne Perez. "Righting Civil Wrongs: The Guam Congress Walkout of 1949." *ISLA: A Journal of Micronesian Studies* 3, no. 1 (Rainy Season 1995): 1–27.

Hattori, Anne Perez. "Thieves." *Storyboard: A Journal of Pacific Imagery*, no. 5 (1995): 46.

Haun, Daryl A. "Spanish Forts of Guam Overview." *Guampedia*. Accessed October 17, 2014. http://www.guampedia.com/spanish-forts-of-guam-overview/.

Hau'ofa, Epeli. "The Ocean in Us." *The Contemporary Pacific* 10, no. 2 (Fall 1998): 391–410.

Hau'ofa, Epeli. "Oral Traditions and Writing." *Landfall* 44, no. 4 (1990): 402–11.

Hau'ofa, Epeli. *We Are the Ocean: Selected Works*. Honolulu: University of Hawai'i Press, 2008.

Hau'ofa, Epeli. "The Writer as an Outsider." *World Englishes* 9, no. 2 (1990): 245–53.

Heim, Otto. "Locating Guam: The Cartography of the Pacific and Craig Santos Perez's Remapping of Unincorporated Territory." In *New Directions in Travel Writing Studies*, edited by Julia Kuehn and Paul Smethurst. New York: Palgrave Macmillan, 2015.

Hemplon Nåna Siha: A Collection of Chamorro Legends and Stories. Agana, Guam: Department of Chamorro Affairs, Division of Research, Publication and Training, 2001.

Henderson, James (Sakej) Youngblood. "Ayukpachi: Empowering Aboriginal Thought." In *Protecting Indigenous Knowledge and Heritage: A Global Challenge*, edited by Marie Ann Battiste and James Youngblood Henderson, 248–78. Saskatoon: Purich, 2000.

Hereniko, Vilsoni, and Rob Wilson, eds. *Inside Out: Literature, Cultural Politics, and Identity in the New Pacific*. Lanham, Md.: Rowman & Littlefield, 1999.

Hernández-Ávila, Inés, and Stefano Varese. "Indigenous Intellectual Sovereignties." *Wicazo Sa Review* 14, no. 2 (Fall 1999): 77–92.

Hertz, John B. "Authenticity, Colonialism, and the Struggle with Modernity." *Journal of Architectural Education* 55, no. 4 (May 2002): 220–27.

Hess, Jim, Karen L. Nero, and Michael L. Burton. "Creating Options: Forming a Marshallese Community in Orange County, California." *The Contemporary Pacific* 13 (2001): 89–121.

Hezel, Francis X. *First Taint of Civilization: A History of the Caroline and Marshall Islands in Colonial Days, 1521–1885*. Honolulu: University of Hawai'i Press, 2000.

Hezel, Francis X. "From Conquest to Colonization: Spain in the Marianas, 1690–1740." *Journal of Pacific History* 23 (1988): 137–55.

Hezel, Francis X. "From Conversion to Conquest: The Early Spanish Mission in the Marianas." *Journal of Pacific History* 17 (1982): 115–20.

Hezel, Francis X., and J. Dobbin. "Micronesian Migration Since World War II." *The Micronesian Counselor* 19 (1996). Accessed March 17, 2015. http://www.micsem.org/pubs/counselor/frames/micmigfr.html.

Hezel, Francis X., and Michael J. Levin. "Micronesian Emigration: The Brain Drain in Palau, Marshalls, and the Federated States." *Journal of the Pacific Society* 29 (1987): 16–34.

Hezel, Francis X., and Michael J. Levin. "New Trends in Micronesian Migration: FSM Migration to Guam and the Marianas, 1990–1993." *Pacific Studies* 19, no. 1 (1996): 91–114.

Hezel, Francis X., and Thomas B. McGrath. "The Great Flight Northward: FSM Migration to Guam and the Northern Mariana Islands." *Pacific Studies* 13, no. 1 (1989): 57–64.

Hezel, Francis X., and E. Samuel. "Micronesians Abroad." *Micronesian Counselor* 64 (2006). Accessed March 17, 2015. http://micsem.org/pubs/counselor/frames/microsabroadfr.htm.

Higuchi, Wakako. "A History of Pre-war Japanese Residents of Guam." In *Guam History: Perspectives*, vol. 1, edited by Lee D. Carter, William L. Wuerch, and Rosa Roberto Carter, 141–80. Mangilao: Micronesian Area Research Center, University of Guam, 1997.

Higuchi, Wakako. "Japanisation Policy for the Chamorros of Guam, 1941–1944." *The Journal of Pacific History* 36, no. 1 (2001): 19–35.

Higuchi, Wakako. "Japan's Industrial Development of a U.S. Territory: Guam, 1941–1944." *Pacific Studies* 31, no. 1 (March 2008): 55–104.

Hofschneider, Penelope Bordallo. *A Campaign for Political Rights on the Island of Guam, 1899–1950*. Saipan: CNMI Division of Historic Preservation, 2001.

ho'omanawanui, ku'ualoha. "Ha, Mana, Leo (Breath, Spirit, Voice): Kanaka Maoli Empowerment Through Literature." *American Indian Quarterly* 28, nos. 1–2 (Winter/Spring 2004): 86–91.

ho'omanawanui, ku'ualoha. "He Lei Ho'oheno no nā Kau a Kau: Language, Performance, and Form in Hawaiian Poetry." *The Contemporary Pacific* 17, no. 1 (2005): 29–81.

ho'omanawanui, ku'ualoha. "'This Land Is Your Land, This Land Was My Land': Kanaka Maoli Versus Settler Representations of 'Aina in Contemporary Literature of Hawai'i." In *Asian Settler Colonialism: From Local Governance to the Habits of Everyday Life in Hawai'i*, edited by Candace Fujikane and Jonathan Y. Okamura, 116–54. Honolulu: University of Hawai'i Press, 2008.

ho'omanawanui, ku'ualoha. *voices of fire: reweaving the literary lei of pele and hi'iaka*. Minneapolis: University of Minnesota Press, 2014.

Horne, Gerald. *The White Pacific: U.S. Imperialism and Black Slavery in the South Seas After the Civil War*. Honolulu: University of Hawai'i Press, 2007.

Howard, Alan. "Pacific-Based Virtual Communities: Rotuma on the World Wide Web." *The Contemporary Pacific* 11, no. 1 (Spring 1999): 139–85.

Howard, Chris Perez. *Edward: An American Tragedy*. Agana, Guam: Cyfred, Ltd., 2006.

Howard, Chris Perez. *Mariquita: A Tragedy of Guam*. Suva, Fiji: Institute of Pacific Studies, 1986.

Howard, Chris Perez. "Thoughts and Confessions of a Chamorro Advocate." In Souder and Underwood, *Chamorro Self-Determination*, 125–26.

Hsu, Hsuan. "Circa 1898: Overseas Empire and Transnational American Studies." *The Journal of Transnational American Studies* 3, no. 2 (2011).

Hsu, Hsuan. "Guahan (Guam), Literary Emergence, and the American Pacific in *Homebase* and *from unincorporated territory*." *American Literary History* 24, no. 2 (Summer 2012): 281–307.

Huang, Hsinya. "Toward Transpacific Ecopoetics: Three Indigenous Texts." *Comparative Literature Studies* 50, no. 1 (2013): 120–47.

Huggan, Graham, and Helen Tiffin, eds. *Postcolonial Ecocriticism*. New York: Routledge, 2010.

Hughes, Lotte. *The No-Nonsense Guide to Indigenous Peoples*. London: New Internationalist / Verso Books, 2003.

Hunter-Anderson, Rosalind L. "Latte." *Guampedia*. Accessed September 8, 2012. http://guampedia.com/latte/.

Hymes, Dell. *In Vain I Tried to Tell You: Essays in Native American Ethnopoetics*. Studies in Native American Literature 1. Philadelphia: University of Pennsylvania Press, 1981.

Iyechad, Lilli Perez. *An Historical Perspective of Helping Practices Associated with Birth, Marriage, and Death Among Chamorros in Guam*. New York: Edwin Mellen Press, 2001.

James, Kerry. "Reading the Leaves: The Role of Tongan Women's Traditional Wealth and Other Contraflows in the Processes of Modern Migration and Remittance." *Pacific Studies* 20, no. 1 (1997): 1–27.

Janes, Craig. *Migration, Social Change, and Health: A Samoan Community in Urban California*. Stanford: Stanford University Press, 1990.

Justice, Daniel Heath. *Our Fire Survives the Storm: A Cherokee Literary History*. Minneapolis: University of Minnesota Press, 2006.

Kaplan, Amy. *The Anarchy of Empire in the Making of U.S. Culture*. Cambridge, Mass.: Harvard University Press, 2005.

Kasperbauer, Carmen Artero. "The Chamorro Culture." In *Kinalamten Pulitikåt: Siñenten i Chamorro / Issues in Guam's Political Development: The Chamorro Perspective*, 26–38. Agana, Guam: Political Status Education Coordinating Commission, 1996.

Kauanui, J. Kēhaulani. "Diasporic Deracination and 'Off-Island' Hawaiians." *The Contemporary Pacific* 19, no. 1 (2007): 137–60.

Kawaharada, Dennis. *Storied Landscapes: Hawaiian Literature and Place*. Honolulu: Kalamaku Press, 1999.

Kelsey, Penelope Myrtle. *Tribal Theory in Native American Literature: Dakota and Haudenosaunee Writing and Indigenous Worldviews*. Lincoln: University of Nebraska Press, 2008.

Keown, Michelle. *Pacific Islands Writing: The Postcolonial Literatures of Aotearoa / New Zealand and Oceania*. Oxford: Oxford University Press, 2007.

Keown, Michelle. *Postcolonial Pacific Writing: Representations of the Body*. London: Routledge, 2009.

Kinalamten Pulitikåt: Siñenten i Chamorro / Issues in Guam's Political Development: The Chamorro Perspective. Agana, Guam: Political Status Education Coordinating Commission, 1996.

Kirk, Gwen, and Lisa Natividad. "Fortress Guam: Resistance to U.S. Military Mega-Buildup." *The Asia-Pacific Journal* 8, issue 19, no. 1 (May 10, 2010). Accessed April 15, 2014. http://japanfocus.org/-Gwyn-Kirk/3356.

Kiste, Robert C. *The Bikinians: A Study in Forced Migration*. Menlo Park, Calif.: Cummings, 1974.

Knudsen, Eva Rask. *The Circle and the Spiral: A Study of Australian Aboriginal and New Zealand Maori Literature*. Amsterdam: Rodopi, 2004.

Koppel, Tom. *Kanaka: The Untold Story of Hawaiian Pioneers in British Columbia and the Pacific Northwest*. Vancouver: Whitecap Books, 1995.

Krupat, Arnold, ed. *New Voices in Native American Literary Criticism*. Washington, D.C.: Smithsonian, 1993.

Kumision i Fino' CHamoru yan Fina'nå'guen i Historia yan Lina'la' i Taotao Tåno' (Commission on CHamoru Language and the Teaching of the History and Culture of the Indigenous People of Guam). "Utugrafihan CHamoru, Guåhan (Guam CHamoru Orthography)." Commission on Chamoru Language (website). Revised and updated April 2019. Accessed June 12, 2020. https://kumisionchamoru.guam.gov/wp-content/uploads/2019/04/Orthography-as-of-April-9-2019.pdf.

Kuper, Kenneth Gofigan. "Na'la'la i Hila'-ta, Na'matatnga i Taotao-ta: Chamorro Language as Liberation from Colonization." MA thesis, University of Hawai'i, Mānoa, 2014.

Kyselka, Will. *The Hawaiian Sky*. Honolulu: Bess Press, 1989.

Laguana, Andrew, et al. "Estorian i Latte: A Story of Latte." *Micronesica* 42, no. 1/2 (2012): 80–120.

Lai, Paul. "Discontiguous States of America: The Paradox of Unincorporation in Craig Santos Perez's Poetics of Chamorro Guam." *The Journal of Transnational American Studies* 3, no. 2 (2011).

LaPlante, Matthew D. "U.S. Territories: A Recruiter's Paradise." *Salt Lake Tribune*, August 5, 2007.

Lee, Helen. *Tongan Overseas: Between Two Shores*. Honolulu: University of Hawai'i Press, 2003.

Leibowitz, Arnold H. *Defining Status: A Comprehensive Analysis of United States Territorial Relations*. Boston: Martinus Nijhoff, 1989.

Leon Guerrero, Victoria-Lola. "The War Reparations Saga: Why Guam's Survivors Still Await Justice." Guam War Survivor Story (website). Accessed March 10, 2015. http://guamwarsurvivorstory.com/index.php/latest-news/40-the-war-reparations-saga-why-guam-s-survivors-still-await-justice.

Lewis, David. *The Voyaging Stars: Secrets of the Pacific Island Navigators*. New York: W. W. Norton, 1978.

Lewis, David. *We, the Navigators: The Ancient Art of Landfinding in the Pacific*. Canberra: Australian National University Press, 1972.

Lincoln, Kenneth. *Native American Renaissance*. Berkeley: University of California Press, 1983.

Lockwood, Victoria S., ed. *Globalization and Culture Change in the Pacific Islands*. Upper Saddle River, N.J.: Prentice Hall, 2004.

Looser, Diana. *Remaking Pacific Pasts: History, Memory, and Identity in Contemporary Theater from Oceania*. Honolulu: University of Hawai'i Press, 2014.

Low, Setha M. "Indigenous Architecture and the Spanish American Plaza in Mesoamerica and the Caribbean." *American Anthropologist*, n.s., 97, no. 4 (Dec. 1995): 748–62.

Lowe, Arielle Taitano. "Pakaka i Pachot-mu! Chamoru Yu'! A Mestiza Rhetoric Analysis of Guam's Chamaole Narratives." MA thesis, University of Guam, 2020.

Lujan, Pilar. "Role of Education in the Preservation of Guam's Indigenous Language." In *Kinalamten Pulitikåt: Siñenten i Chamorro / Issues in Guam's Political Development: The Chamorro Perspective*, 17–25. Agana, Guam: Political Status Education Coordinating Commission, 1996.

Lujan, Tihu. "'The Chorus of Our Lives': Onedera's CHamoru Poetry Book for Future Generations of Guam." *Guam Daily Post*, November 11, 2018. Accessed June 25, 2020. https://www.postguam.com/news/local/the-chorus-of-our-lives/article_7a885056-e3ec-11e8-9fbe-e3e04d677e07.html.

Lund, Robert. *Hour of Glory*. New York: John Day Company, 1950.

Lutz, Catherine. "US Military Bases on Guam in Global Perspective." *The Asia-Pacific Journal* 8, no. 30 (July 26, 2010). Accessed April 15 2014. http://www.japanfocus.org/-catherine-lutz/3389.

Lynch, Kevin. *The Image of the City*. Boston: Joint Center for Urban Studies, 1960.

Lyons, Paul. "Wayne Kaumualii Westlake, Richard Hamasaki, and the Afterlives of (Native/Non-Native) Collaboration Against Empire in Hawai'i." *Anglistica* 15, no. 2 (2011).

Macpherson, Cluny, Paul Spoonley, and Melani Anae, eds. *Tangata O Te Moana Nui: The Evolving Identities of Pacific Peoples in Aotearoa / New Zealand*. Palmerston North, New Zealand: Dunmore Press, 2001.

Marsh, Selina Tusitala. "Theory 'Versus' Pacific Islands Writing: Toward a Tama'ita'i Criticism in the Works of Three Pacific Islands Woman Poets." In Hereniko and Wilson, *Inside Out*, 339–47.

Marshall, Mac. *Namoluk, Beyond the Reef: The Transformation of a Micronesian Community*. Boulder: Westview Press, 2004.

Maude, H. E. *Slavers in Paradise: The Peruvian Slave Trade in Polynesia, 1862–1864.* Canberra: Australian National University Press, 1981.

Maybury-Lewis, D. *Indigenous Peoples, Ethnic Groups, and the State.* 2nd ed. Boston: Allyn & Bacon, 2002.

Mayo, Larry. "Occupations and Chamorro Social Status: A Study of Urbanization in Guam." PhD diss., University of California, Berkeley, 1984.

Mayo, Larry. "Urbanization in the Pacific and Guam." *City and Society* 1, no. 2 (December 1987): 99–121.

McCall, Grant, and John Connell, eds. *A World Perspective on Pacific Islander Migration: Australia, New Zealand and the USA.* Sydney: Centre for Pacific Studies, University of New South Wales, 1993.

McDougall, Brandy Nālani. *Finding Meaning: Kaona and Contemporary Hawaiian Literature.* Tucson: University of Arizona Press, 2016.

McDougall, Brandy Nālani. "'O Ka Lipo O Ka Lā, 'O Ka Lipo O Ka Pō: Cosmogonic Kaona in Contemporary Kanaka Maoli Literature." PhD diss., University of Hawai'i, Mānoa, 2011.

McGrath, Barbara Burns. "Seattle Fa'a Sāmoa." *The Contemporary Pacific* 14 (2002): 307–40.

McLaren, John D. *New Pacific Literatures: Culture and Environment in the European Pacific.* New York: Garland Publishing Incorporated, 1993.

Mendiola, Tanya M. Champaco. "Peter Onedera." *Guampedia.* Accessed June 11, 2020. https://www.guampedia.com/peter-onedera-2/.

Meno, Camarin, and Nicole Allen. "Exploring Community Narratives of Violence Against Women Among Domestic Violence Responders in Guam." *American Journal of Community Psychology*, online publication ahead of print, November 2020.

Miller, Bonnie M. *From Liberation to Conquest: The Visual and Popular Cultures of the Spanish-American War of 1898.* Amherst: University of Massachusetts Press, 2011.

Minde, H., ed. *Indigenous Peoples: Self-Determination, Knowledge, Indigeneity.* Utrecht: Eburon Delft, 2008.

Monnig, Laurel Anne. "'Proving Chamorro': Indigenous Narratives of Race, Identity, and Decolonization on Guam." PhD diss., University of Illinois at Urbana-Champaign, 2007.

Moorehead, Alan. *The Fatal Impact: An Account of the Invasion of the South Pacific 1769–1840.* London: Harper Collins, 1966.

Morgan, W. *Prehistoric Architecture in Micronesia.* Austin: University of Texas Press, 1988.

Morrow, Patrick. *Post-colonial Essays on South Pacific Literature.* Lewiston, N.Y.: Edwin Mellen Press, 1998.

Muñoz, Faye Untalan. "Chamorro Migration to the US." *Guampedia.* Accessed July 3, 2014. http://www.guampedia.com/chamorro-migration-to-the-u-s/.

Muñoz, Faye Untalan. "An Exploratory Study of Island Migrations: Chamorros of Guam." PhD diss., University of Southern California, 1984.

Murphy, Shannon J. "Folktale: Puntan Dos Amantes." *Guampedia*. Last modified October 14, 2019. https://www.guampedia.com/puntan-dos-amantes-folktale/.

Naholowa'a, Leiana San Agustin. "Beyond Matrifocality: A Literary Analysis of Mothering in Chamorro Narratives in Guam." MA thesis, University of Guam, 2018.

Najita, Susan. *Decolonizing Cultures in the Pacific: Reading History and Trauma in Contemporary Fiction*. London: Routledge, 2008.

Na'puti, Tiara R. "Archipelagic Rhetoric: Remapping the Marianas and Challenging Militarization from 'A Stirring Place.'" *Communication and Critical/Cultural Studies* 16, no. 1 (2019): 4–25.

Na'puti, Tiara R. "Speaking the Language of Peace: Resistance and Rhetoric in Guåhan Self-Determination Movement." *Anthropologica* 56, no. 2 (2014): 301–13.

Na'puti, Tiara R., and Michael Lujan Bevacqua. "Militarization and Resistance from Guåhan: Protecting and Defending Pågat." *American Quarterly* 67, no. 3 (September 2015): 837–58.

Nazareno, Allan M. "A Study on the Effect of Spanish Culture on the Traditional Music and Dances of Guam." MA thesis, California State University Dominguez Hills, 2005.

Nelson, Robert. *Place and Vision: The Function of Landscape in Native American Fiction*. New York: Peter Lang, 1993.

Nero, Karen L. "Missed Opportunities: American Anthropological Studies of Micronesian Arts." In *American Anthropology in Micronesia: An Assessment*, edited by R. Kiste and M. Marshall, 255–99. Honolulu: University of Hawai'i Press, 1999.

Nero, Karen L., and Faustina K. Rehuher. "Pursuing the Dream: Historical Perspectives on Micronesian Movement Patterns." In McCall and Connell, *Pacific Islander Migration*, 239–55.

Nieves M. Flores Memorial Library Staff. *Legends of Guam*. Agana: Guam Museum, 1971.

Niezen, Ronald. *The Origins of Indigenism: Human Rights and the Politics of Identity*. Berkeley: University of California Press, 2003.

Nilsson, Greta. *Endangered Species Handbook*. Animal Welfare Institute (website), 2005. Accessed October 21, 2014. http://www.endangeredspecieshandbook.org/chapters.php.

Onedera, Peter R. "About." Guam Nikkei Association (website). Accessed September 3, 2020. http://guamnikkeiassociation.blogspot.com/2013/02/history-of-guam-nikkei-association.html.

Onedera, Peter R. *Gi i Tilu Gradu (In the Third Grade)*. Pittsburgh: Rosedog Press, 2009.

Onedera, Peter R. *Taimanu na Ini*. Mangilao: University of Guam Press, 2018.

Onedera, Peter R. "Theater in a Chamoru Sense." Unpublished paper prepared for Art and Culture in Micronesia, Micronesian Studies Graduate Program, University of Guam, 1999.

Onedera, Peter R. "Theatrical Works of Peter Onedera." *Peter Robert Onedera* (blog), September 21, 2013. Accessed June 12, 2020. http://peterrobertonedera.blogspot.com/2013/.

Onedera, Peter R. *Visions of a Chamoru*. Agana, Guam: self-published, 1995.

Orr, Bridget. "The Maori House of Fiction." In *Cultural Institutions of the Novel*, edited by Deidre Lynch and William B. Warner, 73–95. Durham, N.C.: Duke University Press, 1996.

Ortiz, Simon. "Towards a National Indian Literature: Cultural Authenticity in Nationalism." *MELUS: The Journal of the Society for the Study of Multi-Ethnic Literature of the United States* 8, no. 2 (Summer 1981): 7–12.

Owens, Louis. *Other Destinies: Understanding the American Indian Novel*. Norman: University of Oklahoma Press, 1992.

Palanca, Katrina. "Guam Cultural Group Constructs 2 Traditional Canoes." *Guam Pacific Daily News*, July 20, 2012.

Palomo, Tony. "WWII Rising Sun Dawns on Guam." *Guampedia*. Accessed October 17, 2014. http://www.guampedia.com/wwii-rising-sun-dawns-on-guam/.

Paul, K. A. "Is There a Problem Here? The History of Micronesian Immigration and Its Effect on the Experience of Micronesian Children in Hawai'i's Schools." MA thesis, University of Hawai'i, Mānoa, 2003.

Peattie, Mark R. *Nan'yō: The Rise and Fall of the Japanese in Micronesia, 1885–1945*. Honolulu: University of Hawai'i Press, 1988.

Peck, William. *I Speak the Beginning: Anthology of Surviving Poetry of the Northern Mariana Islands*. Saipan, Northern Mariana Islands: Commonwealth Arts Council, 1982.

Pereda, Nathalie. "Melvin Won Pat-Borja." *Guampedia*. Last modified October 13, 2019. Accessed March 19, 2021. https://www.guampedia.com/melvin-won-pat-borja/.

Pereltsvaig, Asya. "Linguistic and Biological Diversity Overlap—But Why?" Languages of the World (website), May 17, 2012. Accessed October 14, 2014. http://languagesoftheworld.info/geolinguistics/linguistic-and-biological-diversity-overlap-but-why.html.

Perez, C. T. "A Chamorro Retelling of Liberation." In *Kinalamten Pulitikåt: Siñenten i Chamorro / Issues in Guam's Political Development: The Chamorro Perspective*. Agana, Guam: Political Status Education Coordination Commission, 1996.

Perez, C. T. "De-liberating Liberation: A Discussion of the Expression of Chamorro Identity Through Symbols of American Patriotism." Unpublished paper, 1994.

Perez, C. T. "Signs of Being: A Chamorro Spiritual Journey." MA thesis, University of Hawai'i, Mānoa, 1997.

Perez, Celeste. "Fu'una." *Guampedia*. Accessed September 2, 2014. http://www.guampedia.com/fuuna/.

Perez, Celeste. "Inafa'maolek." *Guampedia*. Accessed September 1, 2014. http://www.guampedia.com/inafamaolek/.

Perez, Craig Santos. *from unincorporated territory [guma']*. Richmond, Calif.: Omnidawn Publishing, 2014.

Perez, Craig Santos. *from unincorporated territory [hacha]*. Kane'ohe, Hawai'i: Tinfish Press, 2008. Reprint, Richmond, Calif.: Omnidawn Publishing, 2017.

Perez, Craig Santos. *from unincorporated territory [lukao]*. Richmond, Calif.: Omnidawn Publishing, 2017.

Perez, Craig Santos. *from unincorporated territory [saina]*. Richmond, Calif.: Omnidawn Publishing, 2010.

Perez, Craig Santos. "Signs of Being: Chamoru Poetry and the Work of Cecilia C. T. Perez." *Jacket2*, 2011. http://jacket2.org/article/signs-being.

Perez, Helen. "Bittersweet Memories." In *Chamorro Childhood*, edited by Michael Lujan Bevacqua, Victoria Leon Guerrero, and Craig Santos Perez, 27–33. Berkeley: Achiote Press, 2008.

Perez, Lilli. "An Ethnography of Reciprocity Among Chamorros in Guam." PhD diss., Bryn Mawr, 1998.

Perez, Louis A., Jr. *The War of 1898: The United States and Cuba in History and Historiography*. Chapel Hill, N.C.: University of North Carolina Press, 1998.

Perez, Michael. "Contested Sites: Pacific Resistance in Guam to U.S. Empire." *Amerasia Journal* 27, no. 1 (2001): 97–115.

Perez, Michael. "The Dialectic of Indigenous Identity in the Wake of Colonialism: The Case of Chamorros of Guam." PhD diss., University of California, Riverside, 1997.

Perez, Michael. "Pacific Identities Beyond US Racial Formations: The Case of Chamorro Ambivalence and Flux." *Social Identities* 8, no. 3 (2002): 457–79.

Perez, Nathalie N. "Melvin Won Pat-Borja." *Guampedia*. Accessed December 4, 2014. www.guampedia.com/melvin-won-pat-borja/.

Perkins, 'Umi. "Pono and the *Koru*: Toward Indigenous Theory in Pacific Island Literature." *Hūlili* 4, no. 1 (2007): 59–89.

Perry, R. J. *From Time Immemorial: Indigenous Peoples and State Systems*. Austin: University of Texas Press, 1996.

Peter, Joakim. "Chuukese Travellers and the Idea of Horizon." *Asia Pacific Viewpoint* 41, no. 3 (December 2000): 253–67.

Phillips, Michael F. "Land." In *Kinalamten Pulitikåt: Siñenten i Chamorro / Issues in Guam's Political Development: The Chamorro Perspective*, 3–10. Agana, Guam: Political Status Education Coordinating Commission, 1996.

Phillips, Michael F. "Land Ownership on Guam." *Guampedia*. Accessed September 2, 2014. http://www.guampedia.com/landownershiponguam.

Pier, Patricia Taimanglo. "An Exploratory Study of Community Trauma and Culturally Responsive Counseling with Chamorro Clients." PhD diss., University of Massachusetts, Amherst, 1998.

Pigafetta, Antonio. *Magellan's Voyage: A Narrative Account of the First Circumnavigation*. Translated and edited by R. A. Skelton. New Haven: Yale University Press, 1969.

Porsanger, Jelana. "An Essay About Indigenous Methodology." *NORDLIT* 15 (2004): 105–20.

Pray, Martin B. "The Guam Visitors Bureau: An Analysis of Its Relationship to the Government of Guam." MA thesis, University of Guam, 1978.

Prentice, Christine. "Storytelling in Alice Munro's *Lives of Girls and Women* and Patricia Grace's *Potiki*." *Australian-Canadian Studies: A Journal for the Humanities and Social Sciences* 8, no. 2 (1991): 27–40.

Punzalan, Bernard. "Guam World War II War Claims: A Legislative History." *Guampedia*. Accessed March 10, 2015. http://www.guampedia.com/guam-world-war-ii-war-claims-legislative-history/.

Punzalan, Bernard. "Lukao Fuha yan i Pina'ok Tumaiguini." Chamorro Roots Genealogy Project (website), February 5, 2014. Accessed October 24, 2014. http://chamorroroots.com/v3/index.php?option=com_content&view=article&id=219:lukao-fuha&catid=34:history&Itemid=1.

Quan, Clarisa G. "Filipinos on Guam." *Guampedia*. Last modified October 8, 2020. https://www.guampedia.com/filipinos-on-guam/.

Quimby, Frank. "Guam Commonwealth Act." *Guampedia*. Accessed June 21, 2020. https://www.guampedia.com/guam-commonwealth-act/.

Quimby, Frank. "The Hierro Commerce: Culture Contact, Appropriation and Colonial Entanglement in the Marianas, 1521–1668." *The Journal of Pacific History* 46, no. 1 (June 2011).

Quimby, Frank. "The Matao Iron Trade Part 1: Contact and Commerce." *Guampedia*. Updated September 27, 2020. Accessed November 5, 2020. https://www.guampedia.com/the-matao-iron-trade-part-i-contact-and-commerce/.

Quinata, Nicholas Yamashita. "Hollow Block Cement Homes." *Guampedia*. Accessed May 30, 2013. http://guampedia.com/hollow-block-cement-homes/.

Quinata, Nicholas Yamashita. "Kaiser Pre-Fab Homes." *Guampedia*. Accessed May 30, 2013. http://guampedia.com/kaiser-pre-fab-homes/.

Quinata, Nicholas Yamashita. "Quonset Huts," *Guampedia*. Accessed May 30, 2013. http://guampedia.com/quonset-huts/.

Quinata, Nicholas Yamashita. "Wood and Tin Houses." *Guampedia*. Accessed May 30, 2013. http://guampedia.com/wood-and-tin-houses/.

Quinene, Frederick B. *An Islander's Voice*. Mangilao: University of Guam Press, 2020.

Raustiala, Kal. *Does the Constitution Follow the Flag? The Evolution of Territoriality in American Law*. New York: Oxford University Press, 2009.

Rehuher, Faustina. "Daughters for the Return Home: Palauan Women in Transition in Hawaii Colleges and Universities." MA thesis, University of Hawai'i, Mānoa, 1989.

Reid, Andrew, Paul Lane, Alinah Segobye, Lowe Borjeson, Nonofo Mathibidi, and Princess Sekgarametso. "Tswana Architecture and Responses to Colonialism." *World Archaeology* 28, no. 3 (Feb. 1997): 370–92.

Rensel, Jan. "Introduction." In Rensel and Rodman, *Home in the Islands*, 7–26.

Rensel, Jan, and Margaret Rodman, eds. *Home in the Islands: Housing and Social Change in the Pacific*. Honolulu: University of Hawai'i Press, 1997.

Rodenburg, Linda Michelle. "Spiral Reading Strategies: Re/citing Māori and Aboriginal Stories in Relation to the Nation." PhD diss., University of Otago, Dunedin, 2011.

Rodriguez, Carolina Fernandez. "Chamorro WWII Romances: Combating Erasure with Survival and Vitality." *Journal of Popular Romance Studies* 8 (2019): 1–21.

Rodriguez, Fred. "Latte's Significance." *Guampedia*. Accessed September 8, 2012. http://guampedia.com/lattes-significance/.

Rodriguez-Pinero, L. *Indigenous Peoples, Postcolonialism, and International Law: The ILO Regime (1919–1989)*. New York: Oxford University Press, 2005.

Rogers, Robert F. *Destiny's Landfall: A History of Guam*. Honolulu: University of Hawai'i Press, 1995.

Rosen, Kenneth, ed. *Voices of the Rainbow: Contemporary Poetry by American Indians*. New York: Arcade Publishing, 1975.

Rothenberg, Jerome, ed. *Technicians of the Sacred: A Range of Poetries from Africa, America, Asia, and Oceania*. New York: Anchor Books, 1969.

Rothenberg, Jerome. "Total Translation: An Experiment in the Presentation of American Indian Poetry." In *Literature of the American Indians*, edited by Abraham Chapman, 292–307. New York: New American Library, 1975.

Rowe, K. R. *Where the Waves Fall: A New South Sea Islands History from First Settlement to Colonial Rule*. Honolulu: University of Hawai'i Press, 1984.

Rubinstein, Donald H. "Movements in Micronesia: Post-compact (1987) Micronesian Migrants to Guam and Saipan." In McCall and Connell, *Pacific Islander Migration*, 259–63.

Rubinstein, Donald H., and Michael J. Levin. "Micronesian Migration to Guam: Social and Economic Characteristics." *Asian and Pacific Migration Journal* 1, no. 2 (1992): 350–85.

Russell, S. *Tiempon i Manmofo'na: Ancient Chamorro Culture and History of the Northern Mariana Islands*. Saipan: Commonwealth of the Northern Mariana Islands Division of Historic Preservation, 1998.

Safford, William Edwin. *The Useful Plants of the Island of Guam: With an Introductory Account of the Physical Features and Natural History of the Island, of the Character and History of Its People, and of Their Agriculture*. Contributions from the United States National Herbarium, vol. 9. Washington, D.C.: Government Printing Office, 1905.

Sanchez, Juan A. *History's Four Dark Days: A Memorial Ode to the Late John Fitzgerald Kennedy*. Saipan, Northern Mariana Islands: Trust Territory Printing Office, 1965.

Santos, Carmen I. "Guam's Folklore." In *Umatac by the Sea: A Village in Transition*, edited by Rebecca Stephenson and Hiro Kurashina, 87–113. Mangilao, Guam: Micronesian Area Research Center, 1982.

Santos, Dave, Ric Castro, and Chris Mahilum. *English the Chamoru Way!* Agana, Guam: Images Publishing, 1992.

Santos, Elyssa J. "'Practicing Economy': Chamorro Agency and U.S. Colonial Agricultural Projects, 1898–1941." MA thesis, Center for Pacific Islands, University of Hawai'i, Mānoa, 2018.

Santos, Shaina Marie. "Flying Proa: A Pacific Marvel." *Guam Stripes*, September 12, 2013.

Santos-Bamba, Sharleen J. Q. "The Languages of Three Generations of Chamorro Women." *Pacific Asia Inquiry* 4, no. 1 (Fall 2013): 84–93.

Santos-Bamba, Sharleen J. Q. "The Literate Lives of Chamorro Women in Modern Guam." PhD diss., Indiana University of Pennsylvania, 2010.

Schlund-Vials, Cathy J. "'Finding' Guam: Distant Epistemologies and Cartographic Pedagogies." *Asian American Literature: Discourses and Pedagogies* 5 (2014): 45–60.

Schorcht, Blanca. *Storied Voices in Native American Texts: Harry Robinson, Thomas King, James Welch and Leslie Marmon Silko*. New York: Routledge, 2003.

Schweninger, Lee. *Listening to the Land: Native American Literary Responses to the Landscape*. Athens, Ga.: University of Georgia Press, 2008.

Sharrad, Paul. "Filling in the Blanks: *Mariquita*, a Hybrid Biography from Guam." In "Islands Special," special issue, *New Literatures Review* 47–48 (2011): 149–62.

Sharrad, Paul, ed. *Readings in Pacific Literature*. Wollongong, Australia: New Literature Research Centre, University of Wollongong, 1993.

Shell, Richard J. *Proas in the Marianas, 1668–1742*. Mangilao: University of Guam Richard F. Taitano Micronesian Area Research Center, 1992.

Sherman, Richard D. "Ethnic Institutions and Identity: Palauan Migrants on Guam." *Micronesica* 17, no. 1–2 (1981): 29–46.

Silko, Leslie Marmon. *Yellow Woman and a Beauty of the Spirit: Essays on Native American Life Today*. New York: Simon and Schuster, 1997.

Simms, Norman Toby. *Silence and Invisibility: A Study of the Literatures of the Pacific, Australia, and New Zealand*. Washington, D.C.: Three Continents Press, 1986.

Sissons, Jeffrey. *First Peoples: Indigenous Cultures and Their Futures*. London: Reaktion Books, 2005.

Skinner, Mark E. "Contemporary Micronesian Literature: A Preliminary Bibliography." MA thesis, University of Hawai'i, Mānoa, 1990.

Small, Cathy. *Voyages: From Tongan Villages to American Suburbs*. Ithaca, N.Y.: Cornell University Press, 1997.

Smith, K. D. *A Survey of Micronesian Immigrants to Guam: Predictors of Coping and Access to Life Essentials*. Mangilao: Micronesian Language Institute, University of Guam, 1994.

Smith, Linda Tuhiwai. *Decolonizing Methodologies: Research and Indigenous Peoples*. London: ZED Books, 1999.

Smith, Linda Tuhiwai, Yvonne S. Lincoln, and Norman K. Denzin, eds. *Handbook of Critical and Indigenous Methodologies*. Los Angeles: Sage Publications, 2008.

Soker, Donald. "The Taotaomona Stories of Guam." *Western Folklore* 31, no. 3 (July 1972): 153–67.

Solis, Jessica Ann Unpingco. "Traditions and Transitions: Explorations of Chamorro Culture Through the Rosary Practice." MA thesis, University of California, Los Angeles, 2014.

Souder, Laura Marie Torres. *Daughters of the Island: Contemporary Chamorro Women Organizers on Guam*. Lanham, Md.: University Press of America, 1992.

Souder, Laura Marie Torres. "Kantan Chamorrita: Traditional Chamorro Poetry, Past and Future." *Mānoa* 5, no. 1 (1993): 189–92.

Souder, Laura Marie Torres. "A Significant Step in CHamoru Revitalization Efforts." *Guam Daily Post*, April 28, 2019. Accessed October 31, 2020. https://www.postguam.com/forum/featured_columnists/a-significant-step-in-chamoru-revitalization-efforts/article_288a89bc-673c-11e9-975f-034809785dd4.html.

Souder, Laura Marie Torres. "Unveiling Herstory: Chamorro Women in Historical Perspective." In *Pacific History—Papers from the 8th Pacific History Association Conference*, edited by Donald H. Rubinstein, 143–61. Mangilao: University of Guam Press and Micronesian Area Research Center, 1992.

Souder, Laura Marie Torres, and Robert A. Underwood, eds. *Chamorro Self-Determination: The Right of a People / I Derechon i Taotao*. Mangilao: Chamorro Studies Association and Micronesian Area Research Center, University of Guam, 1987.

Spickard, Paul. "Introduction: Pacific Diaspora?" In Spickard, Rondilla, and Wright, *Pacific Diaspora*, 1–27.

Spickard, Paul, Joanne Rondilla, and Debbie Hippolite Wright, eds. *Pacific Diaspora: Island Peoples in the United States and Across the Pacific*. Honolulu: University of Hawai'i Press, 2002.

Storie, Monique R. Carriveau. "All Fifty Kathousand Cousins: Chamorro Teachers Responding to Contemporary Children's Literature Set in Guam." PhD diss., University of Arizona, 2009.

Storie, Monique R. Carriveau. "The Emergence of 'Fantastic' in Chamorro Literature." Worlds of Words (website), The University of Arizona, November 21, 2011. https://wowlit.org/blog/2011/11/21/the-emergence-of-"fantastic"-chamorro-literature/.

Storie, Monique R. Carriveau. "'That's So Chamorro': Representations of Culture in Chamorro Realistic Fiction." In *Diversity in Youth Literature: Opening Doors Through Reading*, edited by Jamie Campbell Naidoo and Sarah Park Dahlen, 83–93. Chicago: American Library Association Editions, 2013.

Stout, Louise. *Kalou: A Legend of Saipan*. Saipan, Northern Mariana Islands: Trust Territory Printing Office, 1970.

Stratford, Elaine, Carol Farbotko, and Heather Lazrus. "Tuvalu, Sovereignty and Climate Change: Considering Fenua, the Archipelago and Emigration." *Islands Studies Journal* 8, no. 1 (2013): 67–83.

The Stream Team. "Residents of Mariana Islands Protest US Military Live-Fire Training Plans." *The Stream Blog, Al Jazeera America*, November 11, 2015. Accessed October 25, 2014. http://america.aljazeera.com/watch/shows/the-stream/the-stream-officialblog/2013/11/11/residents-of-marianaislandsprotestusmilitarylivefiretrainingplan.html.

Subramani. "Artists in a Changing South Pacific: The Oral Poet and the Writers." In *Language and Literature in Multicultural Contexts*, edited by Stendra Nandan, 317–25. Suva, Fiji: University of the South Pacific / Association for Commonwealth Language and Literature Studies, 1983.

Subramani. "Oceania: From Oral Tradition to Literature in English." *Span*, no. 6 (April 1978): 31–35.

Subramani. "Oral Forms in Wendt's Fiction." *Echos du Commonwealth* 8 (1981): 56–67.

Subramani. "Oral Literature and the Beginning of Prose Fiction in Tonga." *Faikava: A Tongan Literary Journal* 6 (1980): 35–39.

Subramani. *South Pacific Literature: From Myth to Fabulation*. Suva, Fiji: Institute of Pacific Studies, 1992.

Sudo, Ken'ichi, and Shuji Yoshida, eds. *Contemporary Migration in Oceania: Diaspora and Network*. Osaka: Japan Center for Area Studies, 1997.

Sudo, Naoto. "Colonial Mirror Images of Micronesia and Japan: Beyond the Tug of War Between 'Americanization' and 'Japanization.'" *Postcolonial Text* 1, no. 1 (2004).

Sullivan, Robert. "The English Moko: Exploring a Spiral." In *Figuring the Pacific: Aotearoa and Pacific Cultural Studies*, edited by Howard McNaughton and John Newton, 12–28. Christchurch: University of Canterbury Press, 2005.

Suzuki, Erin. "Sacred Travelers: Diasporic Narratives of Pacific Literature." PhD diss., University of California, Los Angeles, 2010.

Taitano, Gina E. "Chamorro vs. Chamoru." *Guampedia*. Accessed January 30, 2015. http://guampedia.com/chamorro-vs-chamoru.

Taitano, Lehua. *A Bell Made of Stones*. Kane'ohe, Hawai'i: Tinfish Press, 2013.

Talley, Jeannine E. "Editor's Comments." *Storyboard: A Journal of Pacific Imagery*, no. 4 (1996): 5–6.

Tanji, Miyume. "Chamorro Warriors and Godmothers Meet Uncle Sam: Gender, Loyalty and Resistance to US Military Occupation in Postwar Guam." In *Gender, Power, and Military Occupations: Asia Pacific and the Middle East Since 1945*, edited by Christine De Matos and Rowena Ward, 98–117. New York: Routledge, 2012.

Teaiwa, Teresia. "Bikinis and Other S/Pacific N/Oceans." In *Voyaging Through the Contemporary Pacific*, edited by David Hanlon and Geoffrey White, 91–112. Lanham, Md.: Rowman & Littlefield, 2000.

Teaiwa, Teresia. "What Remains to Be Seen: Reclaiming the Visual Roots of Pacific Literature." *PMLA* 125, no. 3 (2010): 730–36.

Tedlock, Dennis. *Finding the Center: Narrative Poetry of the Zuni Indians; From Performances in the Zuni by Andrew Peynetsa and Walter Sanchez*. New York: The Dial Press, 1972.

Tedlock, Dennis. "On the Translation of Style in Oral Narratives." *JAFL* 84 (1971): 114–37.

Te Punga Somerville, Alice. *Once Were Pacific: Māori Connections to Oceania*. Minneapolis: University of Minnesota Press, 2012.

Thaman, Konai Helu. "Of Daffodils and Heilala: Understanding (Cultural) Context in Pacific Literature." In *Navigating Islands and Continents: Conversations and Contestations in and Around the Pacific*, edited by Cynthia Franklin, Ruth Hsu, and Suzanne Kosanke, 40–50. Honolulu: University of Hawai'i Press, 2000.

Thompson, Laura. "The Function of Latte in the Marianas." *Journal of the Polynesian Society* 49, no. 3 (1940): 447–65.

Thompson, Laura. *Guam and Its People: A Study of Culture Change and Colonial Education*. 1947. Reprint, New York: Greenwood Press, 1969.

Thompson, Nainoa. "Non-Instrument Navigation." *PBS Hawai'i*, n.d. Accessed September 10, 2014. http://www.pbs.org/wayfinders/wayfinding2.html.

Thornberry, P. *Indigenous Peoples and Human Rights*. Manchester: Manchester University Press, 2002.

Tolentino, Dominica. "Ancient Chamorro Kinship and Land Tenure." *Guampedia*. Accessed August 9, 2014. http://www.guampedia.com/ancient-chamorro-kinship-and-land-tenure/.

Tolentino, Dominica. "Social Classes in Traditional CHamoru Society." *Guampedia*. Last modified December 17, 2019. https://www.guampedia.com/social-classes-in-traditional-chamorro-society/.

Tolentino, Dominica, and Faye Varias. "Clotilde 'Ding' Castro Gould." *Guampedia*. Accessed June 28, 2020. https://www.guampedia.com/clotilde-ding-castro-gould/.

Topping, Donald, Pedro M. Ogo, and Bernadita C. Dungca. *Chamorro-English Dictionary*. Honolulu: University of Hawai'i Press, 1975.

Torres, Robert Tenorio. "Colonial and Conquest Lore of the Marianas: A Critical Commentary." *Micronesian Journal of the Humanities and Social Sciences* 2, no. 1–2 (2003): 23–30.

Torres, Robert Tenorio. "Post Colonial and Modern Literature of the Marianas: A Critical Commentary." *Micronesian Journal of the Humanities and Social Sciences* 3, no. 1–2 (2004): 26–44.

Torres, Robert Tenorio. "Pre-Contact Marianas Folklore: A Critical Commentary." *Micronesian Journal of the Humanities and Social Sciences* 2, no. 1–2 (2003): 3–15.

Torres, Robert Tenorio. "Selected Marianas Folklore, Legend, Literature: A Critical Commentary." MA thesis, San Diego State University, 1991.

Torsch, Vicki. "Grandparenting Among the Chamorros of Guam." *Pacific Studies* 30, nos. 3/4 (December 2007): 81–101.

Trask, Haunani-Kay. *From a Native Daughter: Colonialism and Sovereignty in Hawai'i*. Monroe: Common Courage Press, 1993.

Trask, Haunani-Kay. "Writing in Captivity: Poetry in a Time of Decolonization." In Hereniko and Wilson, *Inside Out*, 17–26.

Trask, William R. *The Unwritten Song: Poetry of the Primitive and Traditional Peoples of the World*. New York: Macmillan, 1966.

Underwood, Robert A. "American Education and the Acculturation of the Chamorros of Guam." PhD diss., University of Southern California, 1987.

Underwood, Robert A. "At the Edge of Chamoru and English." *Pacific Daily News*, October 13, 2017. Accessed June 12, 2020. https://www.guampdn.com/story/opinion/columnists/2017/10/13/chamoru-and-english/760395001/.

Underwood, Robert A. "The Consciousness of Guam and the Maladjusted People." In Souder and Underwood, *Chamorro Self-Determination*, 101–7.

Underwood, Robert A. "English and Chamorro on Guam." *World Englishes* 8, no. 1 (1989): 73–82.

Underwood, Robert A. "Excursions into Inauthenticity: The Chamorros of Guam." *Pacific Viewpoint* 26 (1985): 160–84.

Underwood, Robert A. "Hispanicization as a Socio-historical Process on Guam." Unpublished paper, Richard F. Taitano Micronesian Area Research Center, 1979.

Underwood, Robert A. "Language Survival, the Ideology of English and Education in Guam." *Educational Research Quarterly* 20, no. 4 (1984): 72–81.

Underwood, Robert A. "On Being ~~Guamanian Guamese Guamite Guamian~~ Chamorro." *Xanadu II*, Spring 1982, 1–13.

Underwood, Robert A. "The Role of Mass Media in Small Pacific Societies: The Case of Guam." *Pacific Islands Communications Journal* 10, no. 3 (1981): 60–72.

University of Washington. "Brown Tree Snake Could Mean Guam Will Lose More Than Its Birds." *Science Daily*, August 10, 2008. Accessed October 23, 2014. www.sciencedaily.com/releases/2008/08/080808090313.htm.

Va'ai, Sina. *Literary Representations in Western Polynesia: Colonialism and Indigeneity*. Samoa: National University of Samoa, 1999.

Van Peenen, Mavis Werner. *Chamorro Legends on the Island of Guam*. Mangilao, Guam: Micronesian Area Research Center, 1974.

Vidal, John. "As Forests Are Cleared and Species Vanish, There's One Other Loss: A World of Languages." *The Guardian*, June 7, 2014. Accessed on October 14, 2014. http://www.theguardian.com/environment/2014/jun/08/why-we-are-losing-a-world-of-languages.

Viernes, James Perez. "Fanhasso i Taotao Sumay: Displacement, Dispossession, and Survival in Guam." MA thesis, University of Hawai'i, Mānoa, 2008.

Vizenor, Gerald. *Narrative Chance: Postmodern Discourse on Native American Indian Literatures*. Albuquerque: University of New Mexico Press, 1989.

Warrior, Robert. "The Native American Scholar: Toward a New Intellectual Agenda." *Wicazo Sa Review* 14, no. 2 (Fall 1999): 46–54.

Warrior, Robert. *Tribal Secrets: Recovering American Indian Intellectual Traditions*. Minneapolis: University of Minnesota Press, 1995.

Waterson, R. "Houses and the Built Environment in Island South-East Asia: Tracing Some Shared Themes in the Uses of Space." In *Inside Austronesian Houses*, edited by J. Fox, 227–42. Canberra: The ANU E-Press, 1993.

Waterson, R. *The Living House: An Anthropology of Architecture in South-East Asia*. Oxford: Oxford University Press, 1997.

Watts, D. J. "Factors Affecting Marshallese Student Achievement in an Elementary School: A Case Study." PhD diss., University of Arkansas, 2011.

We Are Guåhan. "About." We Are Guåhan (website). Accessed March 20, 2015. http://www.weareguahan.com/about-weareguahan/.

Wendt, Albert. "Inside Us the Dead." In Wendt, *Lali*, 284–87.

Wendt, Albert, ed. *Lali: A Pacific Anthology*. Auckland: Longman Paul, 1980.

Wendt, Albert, ed. *Nuanua: Pacific Writing in English Since 1980*. Auckland: Auckland University Press, 1995.

Wendt, Albert. "Tatauing the Post-colonial Body." *Span* 42–43 (April 1996): 26–27.

Wendt, Albert. "Towards a New Oceania." *Mana Review* 1, no. 1 (January 1976): 49–60.

Wesley-Smith, Terence. "Net Gains? Pacific Studies in Cyberspace." *The Contemporary Pacific* 15, no. 1 (Spring 2003): 117–36.

Wiecko, Cynthia Ross. "Jesuit Missionaries as Agents of Empire: The Spanish-Chamorro War and Ecological Effects of Conversion on Guam, 1668–1769." *World History Connected*, October 2013. Accessed May 28, 2014. http://worldhistoryconnected.press.illinois.edu/10.3/forum_wiecko.html.

Wiget, Andrew. *Native American Literature*. Boston: Twayne Publishers, 1985.

Willens, Howard P. *An Honorable Accord: The Covenant Between the Northern Mariana Islands and the United States*. Honolulu: University of Hawaiʻi Press, 2002.

Williams, Mark. *Post-colonial Literatures in English: Southeast Asia, New Zealand, and the Pacific, 1970–1992*. New York: G. K. Hall, 1996.

Wilson, Norma. *The Nature of Native American Poetry*. Albuquerque: University of New Mexico Press, 2001.

Wilson, Rob. "Oceania as Peril and Promise: Towards Theorizing a Worlded Vision of Trans-Pacific Ecopoetics." Paper presented at the Oceanic Archives and Transnational American Studies Conference, Hong Kong University, June 4–6, 2012.

Wilson, Shawn. *Research Is Ceremony: Indigenous Research Methods*. Nova Scotia: Fernwood Publishing, 2009.

Winduo, Steven Edmund. "Unwriting Oceania: The Repositioning of the Pacific Writer Scholars Within a Folk Narrative Space." *New Literary History* 31, no. 3 (Summer 2000): 599–613.

Womack, Craig S. *Red on Red: Native American Literary Separatism*. Minneapolis: University of Minnesota Press, 1999.

Woodward, Valerie. "'I Guess They Didn't Want Us Asking Too Many Questions': Reading American Empire in Guam." *The Contemporary Pacific* 25, no. 1 (Spring 2013): 67–91.

Yamamoto, Caitlin Yuri. "Emergent Voices of (Neo)colonial Resistance: The Contemporary Literatures, Cultures, and Histories of 'Micronesia.'" PhD diss., University of California, San Diego, 2016.

INDEX

ABOUT THE AUTHOR

Dr. Craig Santos Perez (familian Gollo) is an Indigenous CHamoru (Chamorro) scholar and poet from the Pacific island of Guåhan (Guam). He earned an MFA in creative writing from the University of San Francisco and a PhD in comparative ethnic studies from the University of California, Berkeley. He is the author of five books of poetry and the co-editor of five anthologies. He has received the American Book Award, the PEN Center USA / Poetry Society of America Literary Prize, and the Hawai'i Literary Arts Council Award, as well as fellowships from the Ford Foundation, the Lannan Foundation, the Mellon Foundation, and the American Council of Learned Societies. He is a professor in the English Department, and an affiliate faculty with the Center for Pacific Islands Studies and the Indigenous Politics Program, at the University of Hawai'i, Mānoa.